Reconstructing Metaphorical Metaphysics in Traditional Chinese Philosophy

Reconstructing Metaphorical Metaphysics in Traditional Chinese Philosophy

Meta-One and Harmony

Derong Chen

LEXINGTON BOOKS
Lanham • Boulder • New York • London

Published by Lexington Books
An imprint of The Rowman & Littlefield Publishing Group, Inc.
4501 Forbes Boulevard, Suite 200, Lanham, Maryland 20706
www.rowman.com

86-90 Paul Street, London EC2A 4NE

Copyright © 2024 by The Rowman & Littlefield Publishing Group, Inc.

All rights reserved. No part of this book may be reproduced in any form or by any electronic or mechanical means, including information storage and retrieval systems, without written permission from the publisher, except by a reviewer who may quote passages in a review.

British Library Cataloguing in Publication Information Available

Library of Congress Cataloging-in-Publication Data

Names: Chen, Derong, 1956– author.
Title: Reconstructing metaphorical metaphysics in traditional Chinese philosophy: meta-one and harmony / Derong Chen.
Description: Lanham: Lexington Books, [2024] | Includes bibliographical references and index. | Summary: "This book proposes three new metaphysical categories: Meta-One, Multi-One, and Utter-One. The author argues that this new system of metaphorical metaphysics is rooted in and developed from traditional Chinese philosophy and is the metaphysical foundation of twenty-first century philosophy"—Provided by publisher.
Identifiers: LCCN 2023030185 (print) | LCCN 2023030186 (ebook) | ISBN 9781666922042 (cloth) | ISBN 9781666922059 (ebook)
Subjects: LCSH: Philosophy, Chinese. | Metaphysics. | One (The One in philosophy) | Harmony of the spheres.
Classification: LCC B5232 .C485 2024 (print) | LCC B5232 (ebook) | DDC 181/.11—dc23/eng/20230927
LC record available at https://lccn.loc.gov/2023030185
LC ebook record available at https://lccn.loc.gov/2023030186

∞™ The paper used in this publication meets the minimum requirements of American National Standard for Information Sciences—Permanence of Paper for Printed Library Materials, ANSI/NISO Z39.48-1992.

Contents

Acknowledgments		vii
Introduction		1
1	Metaphorical Metaphysics: Object, Method, and Purpose	5
2	Meta-One, Multi-One, and Utter-One	43
3	Corresponding Harmony in Meta-One	81
4	Methodological Principles of Metaphorical Metaphysics	115
5	Meta-One: Metaphysical Foundation of Chinese Philosophy	149
Conclusion		187
Bibliography		191
Index		195
About the Author		201

Acknowledgments

First, I thank senior acquisitions editor Jana Hodges-Kluck, her assistant Deanna Biondi, and Lexington Books. Jana, as the acquisitions editor of my previous book, *Metaphorical Metaphysics in Chinese Philosophy: Illustrated with Feng You Lan's New Metaphysics*, and this book, provided invaluable help through many emails. She provided me guidance about the proposal, manuscripts, format, the title of the book, and other requirements. I am grateful for her and her team's help. I am also grateful for the anonymous reviewers' stimulative comments and constructive suggestions. With their advice, I have substantially revised the initial manuscripts.

My loved teacher, the late professor Vincent Qing Song Shen, passed away; although I did not consult him for this project, the words he advised me eight years ago are still in my mind and will be in my mind forever. His teaching of "keep thinking of it and make it perfect" (念兹在兹，唯精唯一) is a primary principle for me to conduct academic work. Professor R.W.L. Guisso, who supervised my PhD dissertation together with Professor Shen, always encourages me to continue my research and writing when I visit him each time. His spiritual encouragement drives me to move forward.

Mr. Oday Kaghani, on behalf of the central library of the University of Toronto, provided me with a private and comfortable space inside the library, which helped me to work much more effectively. The librarians, Ms. Vera Cheng and Ms. Lucy Gan, assisted me in searching for some rare books and other materials. My colleague Dr. Hansa Deep, an author of several novels in the Indian language, encourages me whenever we meet at the campus. Especially her delightful hardworking and productivity inspired me to work hard.

Please allow me to thank my family. With my wife Chang Shu's long-term selfless and tireless support, I completed eleven years of studies in two PhD programs and published three books (including this one); she never complained about taking care of all housework alone. Although what I did is limited, more than half should be attributed to my wife's lovely support. My son Yue's family also supported my work in their ways, including my seven-year-old grandson Yike Noah and four-year-old grandson Yile Gabriel: One day, we had a birthday party at my house; the two brothers called me while they came up to the second floor. When they saw I was working, they stood behind me for a long time silently and then went down the stairs quietly . . . but I heard one of them saying, "Grandpa is writing his book." At their ages, their understanding deeply touched me.

Ancient Chinese people said one strand of silk does not make a thread, and one tree does not make a forest. I sincerely appreciate all those who helped me and supported me. It would be impossible for me to complete the projects without their help and support.

Introduction

What is the specialty that makes Chinese philosophy different from other philosophical traditions? Does the question turn to questions about what metaphysics is and its specialties of the metaphysics in Chinese philosophical tradition? We must investigate metaphysics as philosophy's core and fundamental theory to answer this question. In my first book Feng Youlan's *New Doctrine of Li*,[1] I characterized the metaphysics in Chinese philosophy as a metaphorical metaphysics from the method perspective and exemplified by Feng Youlan's metaphysics of *li*. The metaphorical metaphysics determined Chinese philosophy as distinct from any other philosophical traditions.

Metaphorical metaphysics includes the following specialties: it describes and characterizes metaphysical objects analogically, like using the mother to analogize the invisible, permanent, and unutterable *dao* or using the moon to analogize the abstract, general, and fundamental *li*. The arguments in metaphorical metaphysics are primarily comprised of analogical reasoning instead of logical reasoning, like deducing the human *dao* or the principles of human behaviors from the heavenly *dao*—which was endowed with perfect personalized characteristics—but not deducing conclusions from reliable logical premises. The metaphysical metaphysics provides theoretical grounds for the judgments of value, guiding people on what people ought to do, but does not provide theoretical grounds for factual judgments about the truth behind the world. It is because metaphorical metaphysics takes the truth behind the world as a base and applies it to human behaviors to establish principles of human behaviors. These specialties of metaphorical metaphysics shaped a unique philosophical tradition.

Metaphorical metaphysics uses analogies to describe metaphysical objects, uses analogical reasonings to create propositions and make arguments, and follows the metaphorical method to deal with various metaphysical issues partially related to the specialties of the Chinese language. Chinese philosophers could not create an abstract metaphysical concept like 道 *dao* by 道-ness, *li* by 理-ness. No matter how abstract the *dao* or *li* Chinese philosophers wanted to express, they had to use the same characters of 道 and 理 . . . When philosophers dealt with those metaphysical concepts, they could interpret them—saying the *dao* I said was not the *dao* in common sense, or the *li* differed from the physical *li*. There were two ways to solve this problem: either by interpreting or with analogies. The history of Chinese philosophy tells us that ancient Chinese philosophers used both ways effectively because they successfully discussed various deep philosophical and metaphysics issues. However, they did not establish a complete system of metaphysics.

The primary task of this project is to systematize the traditional ideas of metaphorical metaphysics and develop the metaphorical metaphysics into a new system in which Meta-One is the core category. From Meta-One through Multi-One to Utter-One shapes a main shaft associated with various models of harmony and forms a non-closed system. The metaphorical system is open, in which various metaphysical categories, propositions, arguments, and discourses primarily possess analogical features. The analogical features are embodied in describing a metaphysical object, stating a relationship between two objects, or displaying harmony among multiple elements.

In the system of metaphorical metaphysics, the Meta-One as a core is incorporated with the traditional metaphysical *dao* in the Pre-Qin philosophy, the *li* in the Song-Ming philosophy, and Feng Youlan's new *li*. With high admiration of those most influential concepts, I absorbed their spirit and created the new category, "Meta-One." I first used "meta" in my article about epistemology in Zhuangzi in 2005.[2] Epistemology deals with how humans gain knowledge, the criterion of truth, and human knowledge. Human knowledge results in the interaction between epistemological subjects and objects. Still, Zhuangzi's fable of fish raised meta-questions of epistemology by inquiring about the epistemological subjects prior to the epistemological activity happening. I keep using the meta- to shape the category "Meta-One" with meanings of priori, origination, potentiality, and beginning of the beginning. The profound components of the Meta-One will be analyzed in the book since it is the core category, and all other elaborations are developed from this core category.

Another core concept in this book is related to metaphor. In English-American analytical philosophy, metaphors were discussed by contemporary philosophers from time to time. I did not connect metaphors with Chinese philosophy until we chose Richard Rorty's (1931–2007) book *Philosophy and the Mirror of Nature*[3] (published in 1979) as a textbook for our graduate students. I recognized "mirror" was a metaphor, and American philosophers like Rorty used the metaphor in their books. In 1994, Richard Rorty went to Columbia University to deliver a lecture. I was a visiting scholar there. During the lecture, I told him that his book had been chosen as the textbook for graduate students. After a brief introduction, he said, "anyway, it was an old book." He went there to promote his new book. Although I did not quite understand his book, the impression of a mirror—a metaphor—a method of studying philosophy was printed in my mind and provided me an angle to observe Chinese philosophy when I wrote my first Ph.D. dissertation at the University of Toronto. This book is a continuous study of Chinese philosophy from the methodological perspective, particularly focusing on how ancient Chinese philosophers described metaphysical objects, created their metaphysical propositions, and how they conducted their philosophical reasoning and argument.

This book is not limited to a historical examination. Still, it targets reconstructing metaphorical metaphysics in traditional Chinese philosophy by creating a new category, Meta-One, and extending Multi-One and Utter-One.

In the first chapter, the discussions begin with the analyses of metaphysical objects, concepts, and the relationship and distinction between objects and concepts. I will then examine the primary methods of which ancient Chinese philosophers gained knowledge, conducted debates, and offered their arguments. And finally, I will explore the essence of the metaphorical metaphysics. All these discussions aimed to clarify the objects, methods, and purpose of metaphorical metaphysics.

Based on clarifying the objects, methods, and purpose of the metaphysical meta-physics, the second chapter proposes three new categories: Meta-One, Multi-One, and Utter-One. It analyzes the features, components, and functions of each category. What is the relationship between the new categories and traditional metaphorical, metaphysical concepts like *dao* and *li,* the advantages and disadvantages of the traditional concepts? Why do we create the new categories? And what is new about the new categories? These will all be analyzed in the discussions.

After clarifying the new categories' source, components, and functions, the third chapter further analyzes the three categories from a static and dynamic perspective. It explores how the multiple things, parts, or elements coexisted in the Meta-One potentially, in the Multi-One individually, and in the Utter-One with completions and new beginnings. The analyses and explorations support an assumption that the corresponding harmony is the common way for all of those elements to co-exist at different stages from Meta-One through Multi-One to Utter-One, but what are the particular ways of their co-existences? Various models of harmony will be characterized and classified in this chapter.

Clarifying the source, components, and function of the categories of Meta-One, Multi-One, and Utter-One has released the core content of metaphorical metaphysics and laid a foundation to establish the methodological principles of metaphorical metaphysics. The fourth chapter will specifically analyze what methodological principles the Meta-One, Multi-One, and Utter-One can provide to us. Classification of the traditional methods and then and suggests a series of new methodological principles of metaphorical metaphysics are two major tasks of this chapter.

Metaphorical metaphysics is an organic and fundamental part of traditional Chinese philosophy. Metaphorical metaphysics has its objects, purpose, profound components, and methodological principles, but it cannot be isolated from traditional Chinese philosophy because it is just part of that philosophy. When we put it into the system of traditional Chinese philosophy, what does the position, function, and relationships with other branches and parts of that philosophy become a critical issue? Based on the features, components, and functions, we assume that the metaphorical metaphysics, which takes the Meta-One as the core, is the metaphysical foundation for traditional Chines natural, social, political, ethical, and moral philosophy, as well as the metaphysical foundation of traditional Chinese aesthetics. The last chapter of this book argues for this assumption.

The entire project comprises a historical examination and a new reconstruction. The historical examination attempts to inherit the spirit and essence of traditional Chinese philosophy by analyzing the advantages and disadvantages of ancient philosophers in dealing with metaphysical issues. The historical examinations provide a base for reconstruction and intend to affirm the reconstruction is based on tradition. Our new metaphysical categories, propositions, and methodological principles are rooted in tradition and are developed from tradition. The historical examination is part of the reconstruction, and the reconstruction is the continuation and development of the historical examination. Essentially, the two aspects are just one: both services to develop a Chinese philosophy in a limited and specific area—metaphorical metaphysics.

NOTES

1. Derong Chen, *Metaphorical Metaphysics in Chinese Philosophy: Illustrated with Feng Youlan's New Metaphysics.* (Lanham, MD: Lexington Books, 2011).

2. Derong Chen, "Three Meta--Questions in Epistemology: Rethinking Some Metaphors in Zhuangzi." *Journal of Chinese Philosophy* 32:3 (September 2005).

3. Richard Rorty, *Philosophy and the Mirror of Nature* (Princeton: Princeton University Press, 1979).

Chapter One

Metaphorical Metaphysics
Object, Method, and Purpose

At the beginning of this project, this chapter focuses on three issues: clarifying the objects of metaphysics in Chinese philosophical tradition, how ancient Chinese philosophers dealt with metaphysical objects, and why ancient Chinese philosophers actively pursued transcendental knowledge. The three issues could be three massive projects, so I specify and limit my discussions to examine how ancient Chinese philosophers described metaphysical objects. How did ancient Chinese philosophers conduct their arguments about metaphysical issues? What was the goal of ancient Chinese philosophers in pursuing metaphysical knowledge? Instead of simply defining and characterizing what metaphysics is in Chinese philosophical tradition and what specialties it has, my clarifications of the three questions identify metaphysics in Chinese philosophy as metaphorical metaphysics and answer why I characterize them as such. With the clarification of the first issue about metaphysical objects, I would argue and show that the objects of metaphorical metaphysics are all-in-one entities rather than pure abstract concepts or categories (concepts); with the clarification of the second issue; I would assert and illustrate that the method of metaphorical metaphysics is analogical reasoning, which differs from logical inference. By clarifying the third issue, I assume and prove that the end/purpose of metaphorical metaphysics is to pursue human value rather than knowledge and truth only; it is essentially a metaphorical theory of value. I divide this chapter into three sections—metaphysical objects: all-in-one entities; metaphysical method: analogical reasoning; and metaphysical goals: the value of human life.

My study of metaphysics in ancient Chinese philosophy mainly focuses on the methodological perspective and is far from an exhaustive survey of the relevant topics; different scholars may choose different angles to explore, characterize, or typify Chinese metaphysics, as scholars have already done, and will continue in the future. I understand different scholars may characterize metaphysics in Chinese philosophical tradition differently from different perspectives, as one says that John is talented in his abilities, while another says that John is excellent in his personality. Although there are and will be different ways to describe metaphysics in Chinese philosophical tradition, my examinations of the metaphysical objects, methods, and the goals or purpose of metaphorical metaphysics aim to initialize the first step to reconstruct metaphorical metaphysics in ancient Chinese philosophy, not for carrying out a historical survey.

OBJECTS: ALL-IN-ONE ENTITIES

In this section, with the acknowledgment and appreciation of the contemporary Western and Chinese scholars' achievements in corroborating metaphysics in Chinese philosophical tradition, I further ask what metaphysics in Chinese philosophical tradition study. What are the specialties of metaphysics in Chinese tradition? How should we characterize metaphysics in Chinese tradition? Each of these questions could be a massive project, so I limit my exploration to the objects of metaphysics in Chinese tradition. I would focus on one topic: identifying what the objects of metaphysics in Chinese philosophical tradition are and recharacterizing the objects as all-in-one entities instead of pure concepts or empty entities. This section is comprised of two parts: metaphysical concepts versus objects and metaphysical objects as all-in-one entities.

Is there anything we may call "Chinese metaphysics?" Contemporary scholars have achieved significant progress and effectively demonstrated the existence of Chinese metaphysics[1] (in this book, I call it the metaphysics in Chinese philosophy). They conducted detailed research from historical, comparative, and textual analytical perspectives. Their work laid a solid foundation for my further study of different topics about metaphysics in Chinese philosophical tradition.

Metaphysical Concepts vs. Objects

Before examining and recharacterizing the metaphysical objects in Chinese philosophical tradition, we need to clarify what the metaphysical "object" is. What metaphysics studies are metaphysical concepts themselves or something that the concepts represent? This question leads us to distinguish between metaphysical concepts and metaphysical objects, as it is very important for us to understand the objects of metaphorical metaphysics in Chinese philosophical tradition. In this part, I would consult Aristotle (384–322 BC) for the concepts of "object," "substance," and "nature," and take the clarifications of these concepts as a theoretical preparation for exploring the metaphysical objects in Chinese philosophical tradition and further recharacterize the objects as all-in-one entities, which differs from Aristotle's substance and existing interpretations of the objects of metaphysics in ancient Chinese philosophy. This part includes examining Aristotle's ideas about metaphysical objects and distinguishing between metaphysical concepts and objects. The statement explicated the nature, task, and goal of metaphysics. Aristotle took pursuing metaphysical objects as the core task of his metaphysics. He stated, "The present subject of inquiry is whether there is any kind of unchanging actual object over and above the perceptible ones, and, if there is, what it is."[2] His "the present subject" means his *metaphysics*, which is after his *physics*; this brief statement implied profound information: metaphysics targets to investigate if there is something that can be called a metaphysical "object" and identify what it is if there is the "object" of metaphysics. Further, the "object" should possess three features: unchangeability, eternality, and transcendence.

In his *Metaphysics*, Aristotle stressed universal is not substance and explained why universal is not substance. In contrast, the substance is the core category in his metaphysical system, and all other nine metaphysical categories, including quantity, quality, time, place, and relation, rely on the substance. There would be no other nine concepts without the substance. All are concepts of substance, matter, form, being, cause, principle, potentiality, actuality, attribute, element, soul, free will, and so on. What is Aristotle's "substance?" He says, "The term 'substance' is spoken of, if not in more, still in four fundamental senses; for the essence is thought to be the substance of an individual, and the universal, and the genus, and fourthly, the underlying subject."[3] The four senses of substance are not all Aristotle's ideas; based on my limited readings and understanding, I noticed that Aristotle himself did not think the universal is substance because of the following reasons: "the substance of a thing is peculiar to it and does not belong to another thing, but a universal is common; for by 'a universal' we mean that whose nature is such that it may belong to many;"[4] and universal cannot function as a subject like "animal" does, animal as essence is in man and horse. For him, substances refer to things like fire, water, earth, and so forth.[5] He, therefore, clearly asserted that "none of the things that belong universally is a substance" and "no substance is composed of substances which exist in actuality."[6] As for the genus, he explained with the example of a "two-footed animal," saying that "'animal' is the genus and 'two-footed' is the differential."[7] As a genus, it cannot exist apart from its species, but it can when it is a matter or form, which depends on the species and genus, because "a definition is a formula composed of the differential."[8]

With consideration of Aristotle's definition of the metaphysical object and combined with my understanding of his detailed discussions, I would outline his main points as the following: the universal that is not the substance in the sense of nature or essence of a thing is not metaphysical objects, the substances that include various actual things like water, fire, or earth are not metaphysical objects, because they are actual and in form; the nature, essence, matter, form of thing are metaphysical objects because they are the essence or nature of perceptible things, like "animal" as the essence in man and horse are metaphysical objects. In addition, he excluded artificial things that humans made from the substance category because those things have no nature. If humans did not make them, they could not exist; artificial things are not metaphysical objects.

As we know very well, all individual things as physical existences in the world are changeable; living beings or nonliving beings, all are changeable; differences consist only of the pace of change: fast or slow; the time of changing, earlier or later; degrees of changing: visible or invisible . . . and none of those individual things are eternal, and they all are changing: from existing to perish; none of those things as physical existences in the world are above form. No matter how tiny an element is or how short the amount of time a thing exists, they are precipitable theoretically. I would assume that all those individual things as physical existences in the world are not "objects" of metaphysics in Aristotle's sense; they do not meet the criteria of the object Aristotle established.

When we undertake further inquiry into the idea that metaphysics takes the substance, nature, and essence of things as objects, we wonder what metaphysical studies are the concepts of "substance," "nature," "essence," "matter," and "form," and more, or are the things that those concepts represented? We must further distinguish between metaphysical concepts and objects to clarify these questions.

Since Aristotle, we have developed metaphysics as a branch of philosophy for over two thousand years, so the number of metaphysical concepts has significantly increased. In *Metaphysics: The Key Concepts*, Helen Beebee, Nikk Effingham, and Philip Goff examined this.[9] Here, I would ignore the number of metaphysical concepts, but focus on quality aspects and assume that, in the traditional sense, studying metaphysics means studying metaphysical concepts and their relationships. As concepts and relationships, they are nonphysical, invisible, unchanging, transcendental or above form, and logical; the way they exist is conceptual but not physical. All individual things, empirical factors, and physical existence cannot be direct objects of metaphysics because they cannot get into humans' thinking. In studying metaphysics, those metaphysical concepts were treated as metaphysical objects, and metaphysical objects were metaphysical concepts. In this sense, metaphysical concepts equalized metaphysical objects.

What is the object of metaphysics studies? Is the metaphysical concept equalized to metaphysical objects? These questions urge us to distinguish between metaphysical concepts and metaphysical objects.

I would first assume that metaphysics studies concepts. Are metaphysical concepts empty, then? The answer could be yes. It is because that only concepts can be taken into human thinking, and concepts as conceptual existences are apart from individual things, empirical factors, and any physical existences. Concepts are pure and empty, with no physical elements. Metaphysical concepts are metaphysical objects, and metaphysical objects are metaphysical concepts.

However, I would further assume that metaphysical studies are not just concepts, but the things the concepts represent. We know each concept has its connotation and extension. The connotation conveys the concept's meaning, nature, and essence, and the concept's extension indicates information about individual things, empirical factors, or other physical elements. The connotation of the concepts shapes the form of concepts as a sort of conceptual existence. The extension fulfills a concept with images, visions, and so on, and enriches the concept in content. No one concept has no connotation, the same as no concept has no extension. A concept must comprise these two aspects; even a concept of something that does not exist in the physical world must include the two aspects. The concept of "round-square" comprises the round and square as its connotation and round things and square things as its extension, although there is no such thing as a round square. Humans combined the round and square in thinking by imaging. Even a concept like a round square is not empty; all other regular concepts cannot be empty. Thus, metaphysics studies are not empty concepts but concepts with profound information about individual things, empirical factors, or physical elements.

We need to take all assumptions above into count, saying that metaphysical objects must not be individual things, empirical facts, or any other physical existences because they could not get into human thinking. We recognize metaphysical concepts are fulfilled with profound content, not empty. Metaphysical concepts are conceptualized from actual things; particular animals conceptualized the concept of "animal." "Substances" is a concept conceptualized from particular substances like fire, water, and so on, as Aristotle mentioned. As for conceptualizing actual reality, it is epistemology; the discussion here is based on the result of conceptualization and skipping out the epistemological process.

When we conceive the conceptualized existences, we have stepped up another dimension of the metaphysical objects, metaphysical objects themselves.

Metaphysical concepts are conceptualizations of individual things, empirical facts, or other physical existences. Once we conceptualized a physical existence, we endowed the physical existence as another formation, an abstract entity. When we conceptualize individual animals by creating a concept or class name "animals," we endow the real animals in the physical world with a new feature as an abstract entity: abstractness. The real animals in the physical world are unthinkable, while the concept or class name "animals" is thinkable. Metaphysical concepts are the direct objects of metaphysical thinking, but this does not mean that metaphysical concepts exist insolently from the extensions of the concepts covered. As the conceptualization of real animals in the physical world, "animals" are filled with profound components derived from individual animals.

Metaphysical concepts are just intermediaries to conceive physical realities and conceive the world. It is the same with all other metaphysical concepts: they are fulfilled with profound components derived from individual things, empirical facts, or other physical elements. When we conceive a metaphysical concept or category, we conceive the conceptualized individual things, empirical facts, or any other physical existence as complete entities. The process of conceptualization makes our thinking, logical inferences, and all other thinking activities possible. In this sense, physical existences, including all individual things, empirical facts, and other actual things, are the ultimate objects of metaphysics.

We may further distinguish between metaphysical concepts and objects by combining Aristotle's theory of ten categories with our analyses. All substances are perceptible, but only the nature of those things is substance. I use "belong" and "is" to distinguish between Aristotle's "natural substances" and "nature," all the natural substances and their parts "belong" to objects. Still, only the nature of those things "is" the object. In my understanding, Aristotle's substances broadly refer to all kinds of objects, as he listed above; the nature of all things except artificial things—essence, principle, and so forth, is the metaphysical object. Artificial things are things made by humans; they do not have nature. If people did not make them, they would not exist. In Aristotle's metaphysical system, a metaphysical concept is a concept with nature. When we conceive a thing with nature in the metaphysical dimension, we ponder the nature of that thing. We can consider the nature of a thing because nature is invisible and exists in that thing. As we have mentioned, for him, fire, water, animals, and so on are visible physical existence, but their nature is invisible. When we conceive the nature of those things, what we are conceiving is not visible, touchable, or physical fire, water, or animals. In my words, we are conceiving the concept of fire, water, or animals. We can conceive those things because we conceptualized them and mainly used concepts to describe their natures; when we conceive them by analyzing them, we explore their natures to a certain degree. As we know, "animals" is a concept or class name derived from physical animals; it concludes the common characteristics of all kinds of animals and denotes the nature of all animals. Animals themselves differ and are individuals; humans employ their conscience ability to create the concept of "animal" or the class name of "animal." By doing so, humans can conceive different and individual animals as abstract entities.

In sum, we may characterize metaphysical concepts as conceptualized entities involved directly in metaphysical thinking. Eventually, we recognize all kinds of natural things through conceiving the conceptualized entities, namely concepts. In this sense, metaphysical concepts function as the intermediaries through which humans recognize various things. The ultimate metaphysical objects are not metaphysical concepts, but all kinds of real things in the world. Further, metaphysical concepts, categories, and all other conceptualized entities and relationships are intermediaries of metaphysics studies of the world, and the world including all things or physical existences from which concepts, categories, and relationships, like cause and effect, are derived from the ultimate objects of metaphysics.

Metaphysical concepts differ from metaphysical objects, but concepts cannot isolate themselves from objects. Metaphysics conceives nature or the essence of natural things, and concepts function as the intermediaries of metaphysics investigating physical existences or the world, so concepts rely on objects and come from objects; concepts cannot isolate themselves from the myriad things; otherwise, concepts could become rootless. For Aristotle, perceptible things have their form and matter. In the broad sense, the substance is the unification of two aspects: form and matter. Form and matter are inseparable and can only distinguish one from another logically. There is an inner connection and logical coherence between his theory of ten categories and his explanations of substance. Aristotle pioneered the system of metaphysics; the substance as one of the metaphysical objects was a typical example.

The issues that metaphysics is concerned with are still popular points in philosophy. Although traditional metaphysics underwent serious challenges from logical pragmatism and other schools in different eras, if humans' inquisitive minds about totality, abstract entities, and transcendental knowledge are still alive, metaphysics will not banish. Philosophers in other philosophical traditions will continue exploring various issues of metaphysics, and bearing this point in mind, as the continuation of partial metaphysical studies, my work limit is to explore the metaphysics of ancient Chinese philosophy.

When we consider only the objects that metaphysics considers, there is no substantial distinction between Western, Eastern, or Chinese traditions. In Chinese philosophical tradition, ancient thinkers also distinguished between the actual things in the form and the transcendental entities above the form. In the *Commentary on the Appended Phrases* (*Xici Zhuan*《系辞传》about *The Classic of Changes* (*Yi Jing*《易经》), ancient thinkers used *dao* and *qi* to distinguish between the above form and in form, saying that "what is prior to physical form pertains to the Dao, and what is after physical form pertains to concrete objects [the phenomenal world].[10] Essentially, it is the same as, at least very similar to, Aristotle's criteria of "above form" and "in form." For ancient Chinese philosophers, *dao* is a conceptualized entity using my terms. It is above form. As it is said, "the reciprocal process of *yin* and *yang* is called the *Dao* [*Yiyin yiyang zhi wei dao*一阴一阳之谓道]. What is this *Dao*? It is a name for non-being [*wu*]; it is that which pervades everything, and it is that from which everything derives. As an equivalent, we call it *Dao*."[11] Since *Dao* is a name, a name must be a conceptual existence and cannot be a physical reality, which is another expression of things. In this sense, metaphysics in Chinese tradition also took transcendental entities or those above physical things as objects.

Since metaphysics in Western philosophy and metaphysics in Chinese philosophical tradition are all concerned with the same or similar objects, such as substance, matter, form, causality, *yin*, *yang*, or *dao*—although philosophers in different traditions used different concepts, categories, or names to express the objects of metaphysics—as the objects of metaphysics, they are transcendental, unchanging, and eternal. With the development of philosophical traditions, Western and Chinese philosophers' broad communications and cultural exchanges have influenced each other. Western metaphysical studies implied Chinese elements, like M. Heidegger (1889–1976), and Chinese metaphysical studies included Western aspects of metaphysics, for instance, Feng Youlan (1895–1990). When we further consider the languages different philosophers used, the habits of thinking they customized, the methods they employed, and the goal or purpose they pursued, we may find that when all these factors merged into metaphysical studies, they caused considerable differences directly or indirectly. We should acknowledge that it is appropriate to classify metaphysics into metaphysics in the Western tradition, metaphysics in the Chinese tradition, and others.

Metaphysical Object: All-in-One Entities

As we have seen in In the *Commentary on the Appended Phrases* about *The Classic of Changes*, the *dao* that implied *yin* and *yang* "pervades everything." Since *dao* is a name (although *dao* is nameless, Laozi reluctantly called it *dao*, so *dao* is a name) and a conceptualized entity, if we inquire further, how is it possible for *dao* to pervade everything? In this context, everything must be particular or individual things. Similarly, Laozi's (sixth-century BC) *dao* is an entity above form (not commonly *dao*), unchanging, and eternal; *dao* is a name and a conceptualized existence; how is it possible for the *dao* to give birth to all things? With the same questions for Zhu Xi's (1130–1200) *li* and Feng Youlan's new *li*, we need to further explore these concepts' features. When necessary, we may need to recharacterize these concepts from the perspective of metaphysical objects. In this part, I analyze Laozi's *dao*, Zhu Xi's *li*, and Feng Youlan's new *li* to exemplify the characteristics and specialties of the objects of metaphysics in Chinese philosophical tradition. Based on examining those metaphysical concepts as metaphysical objects, I would recharacterize them by endowing my understanding of them in terms of necessity.

Since metaphysics in Chinese philosophical tradition studies are typical metaphysical objects, we can naturally further specify the metaphysical objects. To concentrate on the theme of this project, I would first examine the scholarship about metaphysics in ancient Chinese philosophy in this section. Mainly, I would briefly examine *yin* and *yang* in *The Classics of Changes*, then focus on Laozi's *dao*, and take Laozi's *dao* as a typical example to exemplify how ancient philosophers conceptualized metaphysical objects metaphorically. Regretfully, I must leave out other influential philosophers' relevant ideas and theories because of the limited space. Here, I treat *yin*, *yang*, and *dao* as metaphysical objects rather than concepts; I critically analyze the advantages and disadvantages of them as metaphysical concepts in the next chapter.

Before Laozi's *dao*, as we know, the earlier concepts that were related to metaphysical objects may trace back to *yin* and *yang* in *The Classic of Changes* (《易经》 [12] and *The Ten Commentaries Yi-Zhuan* 《易传》. As the primary symbols of the 8/64 hexagrams, *yin* and *yang* referred respectively to two kinds of objects with the features of negativity and positivity or femaleness and maleness. However, if we strictly limit our research to *The Classics of Changes*, which includes only the classical texts of the hexagram (*gua ci* 卦辞) and the classical texts of the six lines (*yao ci* 爻辞)[13] and exclude the *Ten Wings* (*Shi Yi* 《十翼》 or *Yi Zhuan* 《易传》 from our examinations, we find that both the classical texts of the hexagram and the classical texts of the six lines did not use the concepts *yin* and *yang*, nor can we see any definitions of the *yin* and *yang*. We may classify the symbols or signs *yin* "— —" and *yang* "—" into the class of ideographical signs (symbols) or pictorial signs,[14] but the difference in the classification does not affect us to examine the metaphysical objects that the two symbols or signs represented and denoted.

When Confucius and later Confucian scholars commented on and explained *The Classics of Changes*, they developed their explanations of *yin* and *yang* from the perspective of Confucianism. Their commentaries and illustrations contain profound ideas about *yin* and *yang*, including the metaphysical objects that *yin* and *yang* represented and denoted. We have seen that the commentators of *The Classic of Changes* as ancient thinkers have recognized the difference between what is above form, as *yin*, and *yang*, and entitled them as *dao*, and what is in form as physical existences. For the theme of this project, it is efficient evidence for us to clarify what were metaphysical objects in Chinese philosophical tradition. As for more detail about the objects of metaphysics, I selectively examine Laozi's *dao* instead of referring to the commentaries of *The Classic of Changes*. There are no terms "yin," "yang," and "dao" in the classical texts of the hexagram and the six lines. With this concern, when I specify the metaphysical objects in the metaphysics of ancient Chinese philosophy, I focus on Laozi's *dao*, particularly on how Laozi conceptualized metaphysical objects metaphorically by analyzing his most influential *dao*.

Laozi analogized *dao* with Mother, but we usually aside "mother," go around the word "mother," or avoid the word "mother" to interpret its metaphysical features, including the abstractness, generality, and originality of Laozi's *dao*. I would stress that Laozi applied the method of analogical description to describe the *dao* by the word "mother," and the word "mother" is a keyword that we should not avoid in understanding, explaining, and interpreting Laozi's *dao*. As a metaphysical object, Laozi repeatedly used "Mother" to analogize *dao*. Still, we always tried to avoid the meanings of motherhood when we explained or translated it into English or other languages. I am afraid our kindness might lead us to run away from Laozi's idea, mainly ignoring the specialties of his analogical method. I suggest returning to Laozi instead of going around Laozi when we interpret or translate his *dao*.

We have recognized that Laozi distinguished between the *dao* in common sense and the eternal/permanent *dao* as the object of metaphysics. Still, we should have paid more efficient attention to his analogies. He repeatedly said that "non-being (wu) is the beginning of the world, being is the mother of the myriad things" (无，名天地之始；有，名万物之母);[15] "there was something undefined and complete, coming into existence before Heaven and Earth. It was still and formless, standing alone and undergoing no change, reaching everywhere and in no danger (of being exhausted)! It may be regarded as the Mother of all things."[16] Laozi used "gives birth," raises, grows, educates, and protects to analogize *dao*'s selfless contributions to the myriad things; he analogized the relationship between *dao* and all things with the relationship between mother and son; he analogized *dao* with the "ancestor" of the myriad things, and the ancestor of Emperor;[17] analogized the relationship between *dao* and all things with ocean and rivers.[18] In addition, Laozi analogized the utmost good with water, governing a large country, like cooking a small fish, using grass and wood to analogize the characteristics of weak and vital human beings, and so forth. Among analogies, Laozi's favorite analogy is that *dao* is like a mother.

Since Laozi analogized *dao* with mother, when we read his following discourses, we don't need to hesitate to interpret the critical term 生 (*Sheng*) as "giving birth." *Dao* gives birth to one, one gives birth to two, two gives birth to three, and three gives birth to all things.[19] When he said that all things under heaven were born from being, and the being was born from nonbeing (天下万物生于有，有生于无). The word 生 *sheng* indeed means that *dao* is like a mother who gives birth to her children. This is what Laozi wanted to express via his analogies. Scholars thoughtfully translated or interpreted the word sheng as generate, initiative, or produce to make Laozi's expression look more philosophical, academic, or neutral. Still, we unconsciously deviated from Laozi's original meanings and ignored his analogical method, which he used widely in his *Daodejing*.

In *Daodejing*, Laozi used the analogical method to talk about the metaphysical object *dao* instead of describing *dao* directly; the eternal dao is unspeakable, invisible, and undescribed. He said,

> Looked at, but not seen—its name is "invisible." Listened to, but not heard—its name is "inaudible." Reached for, but not held—its name is "intangible." These three cannot be discerned—so I will blend them into one.[20]

Since it is hard to describe the above form, eternal *dao*, the analogical description of *dao* becomes a necessary choice for Laozi. Further, Laozi unconsciously recognized the difficulty of defining *dao*, so he was "forced to give it a name" *dao*, because *dao* is the most extensive, ultimate large, and vastest.[21] If using Aristotle's terminology or today's term, it is hard to define *dao* logically. In Aristotle's metaphysics, a systematic and complete theory about the definition is discussed in Book E and Book Z of his *Metaphysics*.[22] According to Aristotle, "a definition is a formula of essence,"[23] "a definition is a formula composed of the differential,"[24] and "composed of the genus and the differentiae." For instance, according to Aristotle, we may say that man is a two-footed animal, but we cannot find a genus above *dao*. We cannot say *dao* is xx, then Laozi said *dao* likes xx—mother. I have no evidence to assert that Laozi was consciously aware of how to make definitions in the sense of logic. Still, I believe that since *dao* possesses the highest generality and abstractness, nothing is more general and abstract than *dao*. It is hard to say that *dao* is like saying man and horse are animals because the concept of animal is more general than human beings in terms of its extension. I believe it is a safe way to assert that Laozi unconsciously recognized that it is almost impossible to define the metaphysical object *dao*, so he grudgingly called it *dao* and used analogies to describe it; mother is the most important and his favorite one. Aristotle also met the same issue: he pointed out that "it is impossible to define individuals among eternal things, especially if each of them is unique, such as the Sun or the Moon."[25] For today's people, the Sun is a star in the solar system, and the Moon is too. The star can be a genus of the sun and the moon. In Laozi's philosophy, *dao* is individual and unique, and we still do not know what a genus of *dao* could be. It is still an effective channel to understand Laozi's *dao* through his analogy of the mother.

It is just a typical example that Laozi used "mother" to analogize the metaphysical object *dao*, with which we exemplify leading philosophers like Laozi employed the analogical method to describe a metaphysical object in Chinese philosophical tradition. According to the inductive reasoning principle, we have achieved a probabilistic conclusion. If we continue searching, we find that not just Laozi but also many other Chinese philosophers employed widely analogical methods to describe metaphysical objects like analogizing heaven and earth with father and mother, *yin* and *yang* with female and male, virtue with Polaris, heaven-earth with a finger, myriad things with a horse, nature with water, and *li* which was advocated by two Cheng brothers, Zhu Xi, and Feng Youlan crossed several centuries with the moon, and *li* referred to the veins on marble and then analogized to a metaphysical concept referring to a metaphysical abstract object or entity metaphorically.

Laozi's *dao* is just an individual case; because of the limited space, regretfully, I cannot present conclusive evidence to support the claim that all Chinese philosophers addressed metaphysical objects by analogical descriptions instead of making logical definitions. However, from the methodological perspective, there is a significant similarity among different metaphysical objects; those objects comprise at least two dimensions: objects of empirical knowledge and metaphysics. Heaven as a metaphysical *object* differs from the sky but is imitated from the sky; *li* as the metaphysical entity *d*iffers from the grain of marble and is be*yond* the hardness of marble. Metaphysical *dao* differs from the road but relates to the road. *Laozi* extended to a permanent *dao* based on the visible road and analogized *dao* with the visible road. That most philosophers described metaphysical objects by analogical descriptions instead of logical definitions is an important characteristic and specialty of metaphysics in ancient Chinese philosophy, with which Chinese metaphysics differs from Western metaphysics in defining metaphysical objects, and this is the first evidence to characterize Chinese metaphysics as metaphorical metaphysics from the perspective of metaphysical objects.

As a typical example of the metaphysical objects in Chinese philosophical tradition, Laozi's *dao* is not just above form, unchanging, and eternal; it is also an entity fulfilled with profound connotations. We can think of *dao* because of its feature of abstractness, we can understand *dao* because of its connotation or component, and we can analogize it with others in terms of the resemblance to other things, like a mother. *Dao*, as a concept, is the same as all other concepts. When we treat it as a name (although it is an alternative name), we can think of it the same as we can think of animals, but we cannot think of an actual horse. We can understand *dao* as someone talking about a unique African animal.

However, the listener has never seen the animal that the speaker referred to in his talk because the listener understands him in terms of his understanding of the connotation or component of the concept of animal, with which he knows what the speaker is talking about. What helps the listener understand is the concept of "animal" and the empirical elements like the images of various animals he has seen and inputted into the animal. This is the foundation of communication and understanding each other among people verbally and in writing. If a speaker tells a listener a strange name or concept that the listener has never heard before, the listener cannot understand the speaker; if a speaker tells a listener that he saw extraordinary things in Africa or any other place where most people rarely visited, but he does not know the name of that thing, he cannot get listeners to understand him; but if he analogizes that thing with something that the listener might be familiar, either a similar name or similar characteristics like color, shape, size, and so forth, this can allow the listener understand him, not because of the pure name or concept, but because of the component that name or concept implied, with which the listener, based on similar features, images, and characteristics, enriches the name or concept, and then he may understand the speaker. If the speaker never gives a name, concept, or a name of similar things but describes the unique thing he saw with analogical descriptions, the listener can understand him. People who communicate and understand each other cannot solely rely on pure concepts, but on the names or concepts that are fulfilled with profound components. A concept, including a metaphysical concept, cannot be isolated from its component or connotation. From the perspective of metaphysical objects, metaphysics studies are not pure abstract concepts or categories, but concepts that fulfilled profound components.

Further, a concept, including metaphysical concepts, cannot isolate from its connotation or component, but also cannot isolate from its extension. For a concept, its connotation and extension are inseparable.

When we conceive the abstract entity, the entity is abstract but not empty. The same as we conceptualized the entity, we also conceptualized all the individual things, parts, or elements that the entity implied. When we conceive *wu*/thing, we conceive *wu* thing as an entity. We cannot imagine the *wu* as empty. When we conceive *yin*, *yang*, *dao*, and *li*, we conceive them as concepts or categories but also entities fulfilled with profound components and wide extensions. When we conceive *yin* and *yang*, for instance, we are conceiving the *yin* and *yang* that contain all kinds of individual things that possess the features of *yin* and *yang*—the same as *dao*, *li*, and other traditional metaphysical concepts or categories. We may logically separate *yin* and *yang* from all the things that possess *yin* and *yang* features, but we cannot separate them into the practical activity of thinking. Whenever we conceive *yin* and *yang*, we naturally conceive the individual things that possess *yin* and *yang* through the concepts of *yin* and *yang*. When we physically touch any items that possess *yin* and *yang* features, we understand the concepts of *yin* and *yang* through the individual things that possess the essence of *yin* and *yang*. When we speak out the word "man" and "woman," or "male" and "female," we more or less, or directly or indirectly, consciously or unconsciously, self-recognized or not, refer to the characteristics, images, or shapes of man, woman, male and female in talking and thinking; otherwise, we may not know what we are talking about.

We don't separate the information of individual things from the concept that covers them. When we physically ride a horse, the concept of "horse" is involved in riding the horse simultaneously because we know we are riding a horse, not a cow. Even if we are touching an animal that we have never seen, we relate that animal to a similar one, or at least we know we are touching an "animal" but not a stone. If we do not know at all what thing we are touching, for instance, eating something that we had never eaten, then the concept that covers all those kinds of things is unclear to us; we put that food in a class that is close to the one we have already known. We cannot isolate our physical activities from our thinking; we can neither act without thinking nor conceive of a concept without components. We cannot isolate concepts from the contents conceptualized from individual things, empirical facts, or physical elements. As metaphysical objects, when we conceive them in the metaphysical dimension, we regard them as abstract entities; we believe all individual things, empirical facts, or physical elements are entities through conceiving the concepts or categories. We conceptualize all individual things, empirical facts, or their features while we generate a concept. In our system, I characterize all metaphysical objects as all-in-one entities. When we take God as a metaphysical object, God is a three-in-one entity, not an abstract concept or empty; when we conceive *yin* and *yang* in a metaphysical dimension, we do not regard them as pure metaphysical concepts, but as all-in-one entities in which the information of all the individual things that possessed the features of *yin* and *yang*. *Yin* and *yang* are not purely abstract concepts, but all-in-one entities that fulfilled profound components. *Dao* is not a purely abstract concept; it is an all-in-one entity in which the characteristics of a mother and the features of motherhood are included. In addition, the relationships between all individual things under heaven and the idea of *dao* are like those between a mother and her children.

As the object of metaphysics, the *dao* that the concept "*dao*" represents is fulfilled with all individual things, just like the mother surrounded by all her children. The *dao* gave birth to the one, two, three, and all things but never held them back for the *dao* itself, which is like a mother contributes and sacrifices everything for her children but never ask for rewards from her children. Similarly, *li* is not an empty or pure abstract concept. As a concept, *li* as a metaphysical object is an all-in-one entity fulfilled with all individual things that share the *li*. As Zhu Xi analogized, the moon (*li*) is reflected in all rivers. If no rivers reflect the moon, the moon would be isolated; if we regarded li as a pure concept, it would have lost its components, becoming an empty shell.

We have discussed the distinction between metaphysical concepts and objects and claimed that metaphysical concepts are not equalized to metaphysical objects. Metaphysical concepts are derived from metaphysical objects and are the conceptualization of metaphysical objects. Metaphysical concepts are intermediaries through which metaphysics deals with metaphysical objects, but the ultimate objects of metaphysical studies are realities of the world. In Chinese philosophical tradition, the most influential metaphysical concepts, *yin*, *yang*, *dao*, *li*, and so forth are concepts and conceptualizations of the realities in the world. The conceptualization of reality, including individual things, empirical factors, or physical elements, constituted the profound connotations or components of those concepts like *yin*, *yang*, *dao*, *li*, and so forth are not purely abstract concepts but are fulfilled with conceptualized characteristics and features of the things that possess *yin*, and *yang*, derived from *dao* and shared the *li*. These analyses lead us to recharacterize metaphysical objects as all-in-one entities, which differs from the popular understanding and interpretation of metaphysical objects in Chinese philosophical tradition.

METHOD: ANALOGICAL REASONING

For metaphysics, it is just an initial step to clarify the metaphysical objects, no matter describing them by making definitions or analogizing one with another. The following step is mainly to conduct arguments, arguing for or against the ideas about various metaphysical topics. In this section, I selectively, not conclusively, explore how the leading philosophers or the founders of philosophical schools in the Pre-Qin, the Han Dynasty, and the Song-Ming Dynasties handled metaphysical issues, based on which I would characterize their primary method as an analogical method of reasoning. This is not a historical project, so I use keywords to substitute the dynasties in the headings. However, my brief examinations cover the Pre-Qin, Han, and Song-Ming dynasties and examine Feng Youlan's employment of analogical reasoning in his New Metaphysics. I skip over many influential philosophers, even though they used many methods of analogical reasoning in their arguments.

In a strict sense, the analogical method differs from the metaphorical method. The analogical method is a method to describe a metaphysical object and release its components through another similar thing and its members; the metaphorical method is a method to define a metaphysical object and release its details with meanings and features beyond its originals. The two methods have three common features: to say something by saying something else, what one wants to say is beyond what one is saying, and both are based on certain similarities or sameness. Considering the common features, I interchangeably use these two phrases and attribute the analogical method to the metaphorical method. I am saying a metaphysical *dao* with an empirical *dao*, expressing the components of a metaphysical dao by the implications beyond the meanings of an empirical *dao*, like road or path.

Dao of Heaven vs. *Dao* of Humans

In Chinese philosophical tradition, we know very well that Pre-Qin was a brilliant period in philosophy. When we trace back to ancient philosophers' arguments, we may find that most philosophers granted heaven with the metaphysical foundation for social, political, ethical, and moral theories. The principles that heaven created and followed were regarded as those humans should follow. For convenience, I use the *dao* of heaven to represent all kinds of heavenly principles and the *dao* of humans to refer to all principles derived from heaven that humans should follow. The particular topics that philosophers argued for or against may be different, but analogizing the *dao* of heaven with the *dao* of humans was widespread. In this section, I respectively examine the arguments about human nature by analogical reasoning in *The Classic of Changes*, Confucius (551–449 BC), Mengzi (372–289 BC), Xunzi (third-century BC), Mozi (470–391 BC), and Han Fei Zi (280–233 BC) in the Pre-Qin and Dong Zhongshu (179–104 BC) in the Han Dynasty. I take Zhu Xi as a representative to explore the philosophers in the Song-Ming dynasties and finally examine if Feng Youlan employed the metaphorical method in his *New Metaphysics*, since my goal of this project is to continue speaking after Feng Youlan. Based on these examinations, I intend to characterize metaphysics in the Chinese philosophical tradition from a methodological perspective.

In the commentary about *The Classic of Changes,* the hexagram *Xu* (*Xu Gua* 《序卦传》), philosophers explained the hexagram *zhun* 屯, saying, "when there were heaven and earth, then afterward all things were produced. What fills up (the space) between heaven and earth are (those) all things."[26] Once the myriad things were born after heaven and earth, human society, social classes, social justice, and ethical relationships among humans appeared one after another. I just picked up the keywords from a long discourse, "all (material) things have existence. Afterward, there came males and females," then came "husband and wife," then came "father and son," then came the "ruler and minister," and then came "high and low," and "when (the distinction of) high and low had existence, afterward came the arrangements of propriety and righteousness."[27] In these discourses, the authors neither explain what heaven is nor what earth is, not analyzing the inner connections between different things but directly offering a series of statements drawing a picture of the natural world and human society. If we analyze this discourse in the dimension of metaphysics, this is a unique way to describe the originations of heaven, earth, humans, human society, and social affairs. Heavenly ranks, orders, and relationships between first versus later, high versus low, and respective versus inferior analogically described the ranks, orders, and relationships in human society. The existence of the myriad things existed after heaven and earth, male and female after countless individual things, the existence of husband and wife after males and females, existence of father and son after husband and wife, existence of ruler and minister after father and son, the existence of superior and inferior after ruler and minister, and the existence of rituals and righteousness (justice) after superior and inferior. This chain is coherent with that of Laozi's *dao* gave birth to one, to two, to three, and then to the myriad things, but provided a complete picture and filled with more details. From the methodological perspective, we have seen how the commentators analogically draw the picture of humans' social and ethical ranks and relationships from that of heaven.

Besides commentaries of *The Classic of Changes*, there are uncountable arguments and discourses conducted by analogical reasoning in Chinese classics, I would say, too much to count, so I narrow my examinations to a specific topic: how ancient Chinese philosophers employed analogical method to deal with the issues about human nature, with which to exemplify the essence and features of analogical reasoning.

In *Analects*, Confucius analogizes loyal ministers with filial sons, from which withdraws a famous conclusion that if a man is an obedient son, then he must be a faithful minister in royal court;[28] and analogizes respecting parents with feeding dogs and horses, then understands the difference that humans' filial piety toward their parents with respectfulness differs from feeding animals;[29] Confucius analogizes faithfulness of humans with the connectors between hours and carriage and withdraws an essential conclusion from the analogical reasoning that if a man has no faith, he must not be able to establish himself in society, the same as the carriage cannot move without the connectors. In Confucius' words, "if someone is untrustworthy despite being a man, I do not know what he will do. If carriages have no means of yoking horses to them, how are they even made to go?"[30] In the *Documents of Mean*, the author himself explained *dao* and believed that *dao* was approachable for humans. Still, to strengthen his arguments, he quotes the analogy of hewing an ax from the *Book of Odes* (*Book of Poetry*), quoted that "hew an axe handle, hew an axe handle; the model is near at hand."[31] Here, "the model is near at hand" meant metaphorically that *dao* is near to man; if it did, it would not be *dao*. In the *Great Learning*, the author used family animals to analogize profit; the fowls, pigs, ox, and sheep metaphorically refer to profit, wealth, or interest, opposite to decency and justice.[32] Confucius mostly answered his disciples' questions directly. If we detect the entire Analects from the methodological perspective, we find that the primary method of argument is analogical reasoning, not logical or other. Still, when he conducted arguments, including explaining his ideas positively, like the North Star, to analogize virtue in governance or criticizing someone, he analogized a nonpromising person with rotten wood.

In *Mencius*, the arguments about human nature also rely on analogical reasoning. When Mengzi debated with other philosophers, he and other philosophers always used analogies to express their ideas metaphorically. To give some examples, "the philosopher Gao said, 'Man's nature is like the *qi*-willow, and righteousness is like a cup or a bowl. The fashioning benevolence and righteousness out of man's nature is like the making cups and bowls from the *qi*-willow.'"[33] Here, Gao Zi (420–350 BC) used a tree to analogize man's nature and the wood cup and bowl to analogize righteousness; he metaphorically argued that men's nature is inborn, but humans established righteousness postnatally and artificially. Mengzi's arguments also employed analogical reasoning; he pointed out that you cannot make cups and bowls if you follow the nature of the willow; if you want to make cups and bowls, you must cut or do "injury" to the willow. Mengzi argued, "if you must do violence and injury to the willow to make cups and bowls with it, on your principles, you must, in the same way, do violence and injury to humanity to fashion from its benevolence and righteousness!"[34] Mengzi (372–289 BC) and Gaozi continued their arguments by analogizing human nature with water, comparing human nature with dogs, ox, and so forth.[35] The limited space does not allow us to list all the analogical reasonings in their arguments about human nature and does not mention the arguments about other topics. The abovementioned examples exemplify that Mengzi, one of the most influential philosophers, used much analogical reasoning to argue for his ideas and criticize others' claims.

Once we open Xunzi's book, the first paragraph on the first page shows that Xunzi used green, blue, ice, water, wheel, and wood to argue that if we keep learning and never ceasing, rethinking ourselves from time to time, we could get wisdom and make no mistakes in behaviors; like the green color comes from blue but better than blue, the ice comes from water but is much colder than water.[36] About human nature, Xunzi analogized the inborn nature of human beings to original materials like wood and postnatal efforts to beautify them to make them great. If there were no material (human nature), there would be no place to make postnatal efforts; if there were no postnatal efforts, the material (human nature) could not beautify itself.[37] Xunzi claimed ordinary people could become sages if they accumulated enough goodness, like collecting water from rivers and getting mud-shaped mountains. He metaphorically argued that sage is sage not because of its inborn nature but depends on people's postnatal efforts.

Further, Xunzi analogized propriety and righteousness with the brilliance of the sun, moon, fire, and water depth and width, metaphorically showing the importance of propriety and righteousness to a country. Just pick an example. Xunzi said, "Among the features of Heaven, none are more dazzling than the sun and moon. Among the features of Earth, none are more dazzling than water and fire. Among things, none are more dazzling than pearls and jade. Among human beings, nothing is more dazzling than ritual and *Yi*.[38] The line of thinking in Xunzi's discourse typically represented ancient philosophers' thinking; they always conducted their reasoning from heaven to humans. Heaven and behaviors of heaven, principles of heaven, the *dao* of heaven, or heavenly *dao* functioned as the premise of logical inference in the Western tradition.

Mozi used dyeing silk to argue metaphorically that external factors influence a country and people, as the silk changes its color with distinct colors. *On Dyeing*, Master Mo Zi told us how: when he saw someone dyeing silk, he sighed and said, when you dye something with blue color, that thing becomes blue; when you dye it in yellow color, it becomes yellow.[39] Mozi discussed precisely "dyeing silk," but this is not what he wanted to say. Mozi withdrew a critical issue from the analogy of dyeing silk and said, "this applies not only to silk dyeing. States also have 'dyeing.'" He listed Shun, Yu, Tang, and King Wu who praised their ministers and "dyed" them positively; therefore, they received excellent reputations and made outstanding achievements in governing their countries, while the King Jie (桀) of Xia (seventeenth king of the Xia Dynasty), the King Zhou of Yin 殷纣王 (Kingship 1075–1046 BC), King Li (周厉王BC890-BC828), and King You (周幽王 approximately ?–771 BC) of the Zhou were "dyed" by their ministers negatively as well as improperly; they dyed with shamefulness, and they destroyed their kingdoms. Mozi (486?–376 BC) extended his arguments from states to individual humans, saying, "not only states but also individuals are subject to influences."[40]

From the perspective of human nature, Mozi claimed that man is not good or evil at birth but depends on influences from external factors and environments, like dyeing silk.

Further, Mozi showed the weakness in human nature metaphorically. He used tools like "awls," "blades," "well," "trees," "tortoises," and "serpent snakes" to analogize the advantages and disadvantages of human beings. He told people that the sharpest awl must be the one that was first broken, the keenest blade must be the one that was first dulled, the sweetest well must be the one that was first used up, and the tallest tree must be the one that was first cut down, and so on. Then, he extended to humans analogically, saying that the bravest historical figures died of their braveness, outstanding abilities, or beauty. He used all these analogies to argue a general principle, which is "'the more egregious, the more difficult to endure.'"[41]

His arguments had no logical premise, but his ideas were fulfilled with strong logical power; his conclusion did not rely on any correct connection between logical premise and conclusion, but the conclusion was reliable and convincing. For most people, being supreme, vigorous, outstanding, or successful are good things and goals to pursue for a lifetime. People indeed made significant efforts to achieve those goals, but Mozi warned that over supreme, vigorous, outstanding, and successful could be dangerous. However, people rarely recognize the disadvantages derived from their advantages. Mozi metaphorically described the weakness of human nature via analogies. He analyzed the advantages and disadvantages of nonliving beings like tools, living beings like snakes, totals, and trees, then human beings, and finally made a reliable conclusion. This is a process in which analogical reasoning was effectively employed.

Han Fei Zi discussed the weaknesses of humans, and he analogized royalists with mirrors, saying that "men of antiquity, because their eyes stopped short of self-seeing, used mirrors to look at their faces; because their wisdom stopped short of self-knowing, they took Tao [*dao*] to rectify their characters."[42] Han Fei Zi started with a real mirror that could reflect people's faces but ended with a *dao* that could rectify people's behaviors. The mirror is visible, while the *dao* is invisible. Han Fei Zi analogizes the mirror with the *dao* in terms of the similarity between the mirror and the *dao*. Similarity or resemblance is the key to analogizing one thing with another, the same as many other philosophers; Han Fei Zi used analogical reasoning to argue for his idea.

When we continue reading his analogies, we will find the logical power in his nonlogical reasoning; I mean analogical reasoning. Han Fei Zi argued, "the mirror had no guilt of making scares seen; Tao [*dao*] had no demerit of making faults clear. Without the mirror, the eyes could not rectify the whiskers and eyebrows; without Tao [dao], the person had no other way to know infatuation and bewilderment."⁴³ This is another powerful analogy; although the conclusion is not referenced from a logical premise, the conclusion is reliable, verifiable, and trustable. We can gain a correct conclusion by deductive reasoning if the premise is correct and the middle term is distributed; we can gain a reliable problematical judgment if we properly use inductive reasoning; I would assert that based on an appropriate comparison and similarity or resemblance, we can gain trustable conclusion by analogical reasoning. Here is an example, based on the examples of some historical figures who functioned as the "mirrors" of lords; Han Fei Zi concluded that "therefore, the ruler who supplies scarcity with abundance and supplements shortness with length is called 'an intelligent sovereign.'"⁴⁴ The "mirrors" made the ruler an intelligent sovereign, and the royalists were good mirrors of rulers; when rulers recognized their improper behaviors from their royalists (mirrors), they corrected themselves in terms of *dao*. *Dao*—Han Fei Zi called it the origination of the myriad things and is the discipline of right or wrong.⁴⁵ In addition, Han Fei Zi analogizes law with mirror and balance,⁴⁶ analogizes *dao* with mother, humans with the tree, virtue with tree roots,⁴⁷ and more. Han Fei Zi's many analogies effectively show that analogical reasoning is one of the metaphysical methods; it differs from any other reasoning methods but has the same or similar effectivity and reliability. Analogical reasoning differs from logical reasoning; it has logical, solid power in conducting metaphysical arguments.

After the Pre-Qin philosophers, I chose Dong Zhongshu (179–104 BC) as a representative of the Han Dynasty to exemplify how philosophers in that era discussed human nature metaphorically. In *Chun Qiu Fan Lu*《春秋繁露》, Dong Zhongshu argued that human nature was initially good, but he disagreed with the point of view that human nature was already good. He used various analogies to argue for his ideas. For example, he said, "now people said that human nature was good; does not this mean it is unnecessary to educate people and let them as they were?"⁴⁸ As a Confucian scholar, Dong Zhongshu did not deny humans possess goodness, but he did not think that human nature was always good enough. He argued against the idea that human nature was good inborn and did not need self-cultivation. He analogized goodness with rice to argue for his idea, "Goodness is like rice; nature is like rice seedlings. Although rice seedlings produce rice, the rice seedlings cannot be called rice. Although nature came from goodness, nature cannot be called goodness."⁴⁹ This analogy corresponds to his raised question, from which we can read the meanings between the lines: human nature is not already good; education makes it suitable, like the seedlings, they are not yet rice; sunshine, water, and nutrition make them able to produce rice.

In Dong's analogies, we may find that he believed that nature was derived from heaven. Heaven-determined seedlings are seedlings, rice is rice, and humans are humans. Heaven determined what things they were, but whether they were good was beyond heaven's duty. A man is a man because of heaven; if the man grows up good or evil, it is not heaven's duty. Based on this assumption, he then distinguished between nature and goodness, claiming that goodness is not nature, as the rice is not the rice seedlings.

As other ancient philosophers did, Dong Zhongshu took heaven as the primary supposition of his arguments. For instance, he said, "Sages continue heaven's work to make gunny as cloth, make silkworm cocoons as silk, make rice as food, and make human nature good. Sages made all in continuation of what Heaven has made, the natural temperaments cannot achieve, so cannot be called nature."[50] We can see from his discourse that there is a heaven above, and there are sages under heaven; sages followed heaven to serve humans. One of the essential things that sages did for humans was to "make human nature good," as forgoing mentioned. Dong repeatedly stressed that humans could achieve goodness through education and training but could not achieve it by uncultivated nature and feelings. Therefore, we cannot call goodness nature. How did Dong argue for this point? He always used the methods of analogical reasoning with a series of analogies.

Besides his arguments about human nature, Dong Zhongshu used analogies to discuss different issues. He said, "After over twenty days of incubation, eggs transformed into poults, underwent boiling and de-flossing. The silkworm could become silk; after educating and training, human nature could become good."[51] Education and training make people good at analogizing the processes of the eggs to poults and from silkworm to silk. In his arguments, Dong clarified the relationships between human nature and goodness with the relationships between millet and rice, uncurved gem, and jade, arguing that rice comes from millet, but millet cannot be called rice; jade comes from uncurved rock, but the uncurved gem cannot be called jade, and goodness comes from human nature, but human nature cannot be called goodness.[52] In this way, Dong Zhongshu metaphorically argued against the idea that human nature was good inborn. He pleaded for his claim that goodness was the outcome of education and training and that human nature cannot be called goodness.

The examinations showed that philosophers' interpretations of human nature were various in the Pre-Qin (the period before 221 BC) and the Han Dynasty (202 BC–220 AD), either claiming that human nature was originally good, saying that human nature was initially evil, or believing that human nature was neither good nor bad. Still, there is a common characteristic: most of them employed analogical reasoning to argue for their claims and against others' claims if we observe their debates from the methodological perspective. The examinations above are the second reason to support my claim that metaphysics in ancient Chinese philosophy can be characterized as metaphorical metaphysics from the methodological perspective.

Human Nature vs. Water and *Li* vs. Moon

As the successor of the two Cheng brothers, Zhu Xi used a lot of analogies in his arguments about different metaphysical issues, including the origination of the universe (the era when heaven and earth were undivided), *li*, the relationship between *li* and *qi*, the characteristics of heaven, and the nature of humans, and so on. I just take his theory about human nature as an example to exemplify how Zhu Xi conducted his arguments; it is not the purpose of this project to study Zhu Xi systematically.

Zhu Xi analogized human nature with water. He claimed human nature is good, as water is pure. If you pour water into a white bowl, it will appear as one color. If you pour it into a black bowl, another color will appear. It will appear yet another color if you pour it into a green bowl.[53] Water is one of Zhu Xi's favorite analogies. He further clarifies nature by the analogy of water, "nature is like water; it was originally clear. When storing the water in a clean container, the water is clear; storing the water in an unclear container. The water stinks, storing the water in a dirty container. The water becomes sordid. Although the original clean is still there, once it becomes stinky and sordid, it is hard to be clear again."[54] In today's terminology, human nature was originally good, but external factors like the environment, educational background, bad social atmosphere, and living habits affected human characteristics.

Zhu Xi analogically distinguished between human beings and other things. He claimed that everything under heaven has its nature; there is no such thing without nature and no such nature without a thing.[55] Humans and other things possessed nature but were endowed with *qi*. *Qi* is an old concept. Ancient philosophers combined with *yin* and *yang* and formed concepts of *yinqi* and *yangqi*. Zhu Xi accepted the concepts of *yinqi* and *yang qi*, and further distinguished between the quality of *qi*, like clear *qi* and turbid *qi*. The literal meanings of the word *qi* include air, gas, and breath. Essentially, it referred to physical existence. According to Zhu Xi, when humans had their nature, they appeared as humans; when given in other things, others become other things. He used sunlight to analogize nature and distinguished between human nature and the nature of other things. He said, "the nature is like sunlight and the difference between humankind and things in their nature is like the difference between the amount of light penetrating through a big crack and that through a small crack."[56] It is also the same as drawing water from a river—people might get more, and others might get less.[57] In his arguments, there is no logical reasoning, but analogies.

Zhu Xi further analogically explained the differences among humans. Since humans received their nature from heaven, "why," as someone asked, "does nature differ one from another?" Zhu Xi answered this question in different places and with different analogies. For instance, in his commentaries on the *Documents of Mean* and *Analects*, he argued that human nature is good without evil, all people are the same, and the differences comprising of dark, brilliant, weak, or firm are not inborn, but dependant on individual abilities. If a person does too many evil things, he cannot restore good nature, like a person submerged in water too deep to get back. Those who tried to restore the original nature, which was good, just like making something that is not beauty into beauty, need to spend time on their efforts. Just like birds practice flying repeatedly, it requires doubled effort. Zhu Xi expressed his deep thinking on human nature through many analogies; he did not rely on logical reasoning, but his conclusions were logical. It is the similarity that laid a solid foundation for his analogies.

Another reason people's natures are different is that people inherited their natures from heaven differently. Zhu Xi agreed with Cheng Yi (程颐 1033–1107), believing that nature is *li* (*Xing Ji li* 性即理); humans and all other things have *Li*.[58] He analogizes nature with water, saying that nature is the same as a river. If you take water from the river with a spoon, you receive a ladle of water; if you use a bowl, you get a bowl of water; with a jar or barrel, you receive a barrel of water. Everyone differs from another with different container quantities, so everyone's *li* (nature) is other.[59] When Zhu Xi discussed the differences between human nature *(li)* and the nature of natural things, he analogized the differences with grass, tree, animal, bird, boats, carriages, four seasons, day, and night to support his arguments metaphorically.

Zhu Xi entirely agreed with Cheng Hao's (1032–1085) idea that nature and vital force are inseparable[60] and claimed that "nature is just *li* (*Xing zhi shi li* 性只是理)."[61] Here, we must combine Zhu Xi's words with Cheng Hao's idea about *qi*. According to Cheng Hao, *qi* is the container of nature, and nature relies on *qi* to store it like water needs a container to be stored. Cheng discussed the relationship between nature and *qi*, while Zhu Xi extended the relationship between destiny and temperament. Comparatively, Cheng's argument is more accurate; Zhu Xi equalizes the nature of character with Cheng Yi's *qi*. The difference is that what Zhu Xi considered is all about nature: the nature of destiny and temperament, but Cheng talks about nature and *qi*. Zhu Xi analogized the nature of destiny with water, and the nature of the character as the container of water is inaccurate because, according to Zhu Xi, one kind of nature relies on another type of water; in Cheng Hao, nature relies on *qi* just like water depends on the container. Of course, if we interpret Zhu Xi's "temperamentality" as Cheng Hao's *qi*, his analogies perfectly correspond to

Cheng's argument. It is not my task to comment on their arguments; I take this chance to stress that whether analogical reasoning is reasonable and adequate depends on whether the analogy is based on actual resemblance or similarities.

Zhu Xi consistently insisted that human nature from heaven (nature of destiny) was originally good; some peoples' behaviors are good, and others' behaviors are evil because of the difference in humans' nature of temperamentality. His analogies of water vividly clarified the differences between people in temperamentality. He used the same analogy to explain the difference between humans and animals: "Those with clear and positive temperamentality get nature to become human beings; those with dirty and slating temperamentality get nature to become dark and animals."[62] We might ask why some people are good while others are bad since all human beings are born with the same nature. The social reality from ancient times to now urged us to raise this question.

The nature of human beings is invisible; we can see just the behavior determined by nature. It is easy to tell whether a behavior is good or evil regarding a particular moral or ethical criterion. Still, it is hard to know that nature is beyond behavior. Primarily, it is hard to discover the inner connection between nature and behavior. People have reasons to doubt if nature can determine a behavior or an action, or even question if there is something that we can call human nature. Human beings are human beings; they do whatever they want and whatever they can do. Where does human nature exist? In mind, heart, body, or the brain? It is hard to point out the existence and functions of the connection between nature and behaviors. Zhu Xi's ideas about human nature are not a scientific conclusion, which differs from scientific research like the studies of genes of criminology that make efforts to find the connection between genes and crime. From the scientific research perspective, we may set aside Zhu Xi's conclusions about human nature, but it is still worth investigating what made humans are humans, as what made horses eat grass instead of other edible food without ever needing to be educated. In the discussions above, we are concerned with the metaphysical method displayed in his arguments.

The core of his methods in conducting arguments is the similarity between two or more things. Zhu Xi's analogies were based on the similarity between personalized heaven and humans. He analogized the mind with the lord based on the similar functions of the mind and lord. Both mind and lord functioned as the core of governing systems; the former controlled human behaviors, and the latter ruled a kingdom. This example tells us that Zhu Xi, the most influential philosopher in the Song Dynasty, the same as many other ancient philosophers, used analogical reasoning to argue for his claim about human nature.

Feng Youlan is a successor of Cheng-Zhu's doctrine of *li*, but a Westernized philosopher. In his *New Doctrine of Li*, Feng defined destiny (*ming* 命), nature, and *li*. He said, "In the sense that the individual things (members) in a class must correspond to the *li* of that class, which is called destiny; in the sense that the individuals are to be attributed into that class because they corresponded to the *li*, which is called nature."⁶³ Feng defined the states that individual things "must correspond to" the *li* as destiny, and the individual things becoming that thing because of corresponding to the *li* of that class as nature. Feng Youlan also applied analogies to argue for his ideas. He said, "for instance, an airplane must correspond to the *li* of the airplane and then become an airplane."⁶⁴ As we know, the airplane is essentially different from human beings, and the *li* of the aircraft is also different from the *li* (nature) of human beings. Still, based on the similarity and common features between airplanes and humans, Feng asserted that both must correspond to the *li* and become what they are. By using analogical reasoning, Feng made his ideas of human nature as *li* understandable for him. *Li* is a particular class of things.

Feng further analogically argued that "the *li* of human beings (*renli* 人理) is something that human beings are human beings; the *li* of a horse is something that horse is a horse. The nature of a class of individual things, namely that class of things, corresponds to a certain *li*, based on which becomes that class of things. For instance, the nature of human beings is what human beings correspond to, with which human beings become human beings. The nature of a horse is something that a horse corresponds to, with which horse becomes a horse."⁶⁵ Human nature is like horses in that both must correspond to the *li*. What is nature? *Li*. What is *li*, then? Feng did not explain or define it directly, but we can reasonably say that his *li* is just a class name. This understanding is because he repeatedly used the *li* of an airplane and other analogies to analogize the *li* of human beings and other things like the *li* of square and the *li* of round, and so on.

I said that Feng's *li* in those discourses is a class name because, according to him, horses are horses because those animals correspond to the class name of horse; human beings are human beings because they correspond to the name of human beings. It is not just for horses and humans, it is also the same for all other things. Feng's *li* is also a generation of the common nature, which can be expressed with another concept of essence. A horse is a horse because it possesses the essence of a horse; the *li* of human beings is the essence of human beings, and those who have the essence are human beings. However, according to Feng, the essence or *li* seems to be outside of individual things or saying that there is a *li* or essence to be corresponded by individual things, as we take individual things to compare with a criterion and see if that thing meets the criterion. The nature of a thing must be in that thing; the nature of an airplane must be inside the aircraft. If there is no airplane, there will be no essence (*li*) of the plane. For Feng, on the contrary, there must be a *li* of aircraft and a thing which corresponds or, according to (*Yizhao* 依照), the *li* of the airplane, then it becomes an airplane. Is Feng's *li* just a name? Is Feng's *li* a logical concept?

Whatever we talk about the *li* itself, we go beyond Feng Youlan's analogical arguments because we cannot find further explanations for the *li* itself. A question arises: does analogical reasoning, or in a broader sense, analogical method, result in any new knowledge? It does not; why do we need the analogical way? Again, these questions relate to the goal and functions of analogical reasoning or the purpose of the metaphorical method. I discuss this in the next section of this chapter.

We have seen that most philosophers in Chinese tradition employed analogical reasoning to support their arguments. However, we only examined some influential philosophers because of the limited space, which did not mean they did not use the methods. Further, although we did not mention Western philosophers in the discussions, which does not mean that analogical reasoning is proprietary to Chinese philosophy, it will be a vast project to study the analogies used in Western philosophy or conduct a comparative study. Again, the theme of this project requires us to conceive of metaphysics in Chinese philosophical tradition within the Chinese context; the examinations above provided the evidence to characterize Chinese metaphysics as metaphorical metaphysics from the methodological perspective.

ESSENCE: META-THEORY OF MORALITY

After we examined metaphysical objects and primary methods, we need further explore the essence of metaphysics in Chinese philosophical tradition. This part discusses two questions: what are the goals or purposes of metaphysics, and what is the essence of metaphysics in Chinese philosophical tradition? The analyses of the first question led us to think of the essence of metaphysics because the goal determined the objects—studies what; methods—how to achieve the goal; and ultimate reason—why study that in that way? All forgoing factors determined the essence of metaphysics in Chinese tradition. Based on the analyses of the goal, I would assume that the primary purpose or goal was to pursue the value of human life or to perfect human life and assert that metaphysics in Chinese philosophical tradition essentially is a theory of value. In the second part of this section, I further explore the components of the theory of value by analyzing a series of propositions that achieved the abovementioned goal, and I specify the theory of value as a metaphorical meta-theory of morality in terms of the feature that the principles essentially are metaphysical propositions related to human behaviors and the feature that most principles were expressed metaphorically. In short, this section comprises two parts, goal: perfecting human life, and essence: meta-theory of morality.

Goal: Perfecting Human Life

What did metaphysics in Chinese philosophical tradition pursue—knowledge, truth, or the value of human life? Philosophy and metaphysics differ from science, which does not result in verifiable knowledge and truth. We know scientific research aims to gain factual truth; therefore, laboratories must verify conclusions via strict procedures. What is the significance or function of metaphysics, then? This is a question about the goals or purpose of metaphysics, not just in Chinese philosophy but also in other philosophies and metaphysics. Because of the limited space, I concentrate only on the goals of metaphysics in Chinese tradition.

What is the goal or purpose of metaphysics in Chinese tradition? In a broad sense, all of them, but in a narrow sense, none of them, because all these goals aimed to answer one question: what are the things in the world—factual truth, conceptual truth, or metaphysical knowledge about substance, reality, or things in the world. If we analogize heaven, earth, and humans to identify their different physical attributes, biological features, and their common feature, our goal is to reach factual truth; if we analogize them as concepts and identify the various meanings, components, and functions, or logical incoherence of those concepts, what we do is to explore conceptual truth; if we analogize them one with another at metaphysical dimension, our goal is to receive transcendental knowledge. The utmost goal of metaphysics in Chinese tradition was to perfect human life by achieving complete moral and ethical relationships and behaviors.

In Chinese philosophical tradition, the doctrine about heaven, earth, and all things was finally concerned with humans, and the goal was to seek harmony among heaven, earth, and humans. Laozi's *dao* is metaphysical, but we rarely recognize that Laozi's theory of *dao* was just a preparation for his theory of virtue or morality. We know his book was entitled *daodejing*, including the classic of *dao* (chapters 1–37) and the classic of *de* (virtue) (chapters 38–81), we usually pay efficient attention to his theory of *dao* but inefficiently paid attention to his contribution to the theories of morality or virtue, even to a certain degree ignored the importance of his theory of virtue. His classic of *dao* was the theoretical foundation of his classic of *de*. In his book, Laozi begins with *dao* but completes with *de*, and his utmost goal was to talk about *de*, not *dao*. Notably, according to Laozi, to behave like a *dao* means to act like a mother. The *dao*, mother, or heaven gives birth to everything but never requests rewards from them; they made profound contributions to them but never held them for repayment. The *dao* or mother acts, behaves, and lives in a way that follows nature and never violates it; *dao*, treats all people equally—like shooting an arrow, if too high, press the arrow down; too low, raise it; too left, adjust it right . . . in one word, Laozi told us, humans should follow *dao* the same as behaving like their mothers, do everything selflessly, ceaselessly, and equally, take nothing back from their children. This is what Laozi wants to tell people metaphorically about his analogies. Studying Laozi's metaphysical *dao* isolated from his *de*, the study is incomplete because ignoring Laozi's goal; looking at Laozi's virtue (*de* 德) isolated from his *dao*, the study is groundless because ignoring the theoretical foundation of his doctrine of *de*.

Zhu developed Confucian and early Song philosophers' ideas. Zhu Xi analogized human nature with water, as examined above; his analyses of water and human nature aimed to argue that human nature was good inborn because human inherited their nature from heaven. Since the water was clear, human nature was originally good, so humans should keep the original good, like keeping water clean. Zhu thinks that those who take the clear water in a small container receive less clear water, which means to inherit less of the original good than others. Those people should make a significant effort, in his words, "hundred times of effort" (*Baibei qigong* 百倍其功) to keep the water clean or to make dark brilliant. Eventually, Zhu stresses making human nature good or better. All his previous arguments serve one goal: to keep human nature good by self-cultivation.

In Zhu Xi's analogies, the two series are explicit: water originally was clear, water could turn to turbidity, dirty, and stink because of containers, the aqueduct, and more; human nature was supposed to be good initially, but some people are not good, some people misbehave, and some others' behaviors can be called evil. The two series are parallel and have no interaction; when Zhu used water to analogize human nature, the analogy did not provide new knowledge about water and human nature. The function of the metaphor comprises expressing the invisible human nature, making the abstract existence concrete, and finally making the unthinkable existence understandable in terms of the features of the water because water is visible, touchable, and changeable. Thus, analogical reasoning does not function to result in new knowledge but pursues the value of human life.

What ought human beings do? Heaven covers everything, and nothing is not under its cover—open, broad, and gentle; the earth carries everything, and nothing is out of its carries—kind, strong, and tolerant . . . what ought we to do? Follow the ways of heaven and earth, behavior like heaven and earth. In Zhu Xi's case, since water originally was clear—our nature was originally good, what should we do if we misbehave? We should clean our containers to make containers clean—make efforts to improve our behaviors toward the original good. With these points in mind, we should not separate his doctrine of *li* from his theory of *dao*—morality—to understand Zhu Xi.

Instead, we should understand his doctrine of *li* and the doctrine of *dao* as an organic unit. His doctrine of *li* lays a foundation for his doctrine of *dao*, and his doctrine of *dao* is what he devoted himself to promoting. In this sense, we may characterize his entire doctrine of *li* and *dao* as the doctrine of morality and ethics (doctrine of *daoxue* 道学), not the doctrine of *li* (*lixue* 理学). His doctrine of *li* is the ground from which his doctrine of *dao* developed. If we understand Zhu Xi's *li* but are isolated from his doctrine of *dao*, our understanding will be incomplete because it is short of his purpose; if we know his *dao* separated from his doctrine of *li*, our knowledge would be rootless because his doctrine of *dao* rooted in his doctrine of *li*. I withdraw this assumption from his analogical reasoning about *li* and human nature. Even if we disagree with this assumption, we must treat his doctrines of *li* and nature as one organic system in which the *li* of destiny (*tianli* 天理) and human desires are inseparable. In short, like Laozi, he talks about *dao* but aims to speak about humans, setting models for human behaviors.

Feng Youlan devoted himself to constructing a purely logical, metaphysical system. Still, in his *New Doctrine of Li* 《新理学》, he spends about two-thirds of the book discussing all kinds of *li* of human beings and human affairs, and only one-third for pure logical *li*. In Feng, the *dao* or *li* of human beings and the *li* of human society are organic parts of his new system of metaphysics. He said, "what we called heaven (*tian* 天) refers to the wondrous totality (*daquan* 大全) and refers to the universe. The universe, or the wondrous totality, implied all *li*, and the universe, or wondrous totality, implied all the *dao* of humans (*rendao* 人道)."[66] This is the complete picture of Feng Youlan's new metaphysical system in which *li* exists throughout the universe, including the natural world, human society, social organization, and individuals. *Li*—the *dao* of heaven, the nature of humans, the *li* of humans' minds, moral issues, history, righteousness, fine arts, ghost, divinity, and sage all have their *li*. *Li* functions as a theoretical ground of all theories about all issues, but *li* is not the final goal humans aim to achieve. What are the goals of metaphysics in Feng's new system of metaphysics?

Feng thinks that, on the one hand, the studies of the realm of truth-ness do not care about reality, so it is useless. Just like the squareness of a square table, the squareness is futile; only the square table is helpful. Thus, philosophy is vain.[67] However, Feng argues that if we observe the realm of truth-ness with a restful heart, we will comprehend the realm of truth-ness intellectually. He says, "the intellectual comprehension of the realm of truth-ness is the ground we talk about the *dao* of human beings."[68] Here, "philosophy" refers to his new metaphysics because it discusses the realm of truth-ness. The core point of his argument is that intellectually understanding *li* is the ground for understanding *dao*. Feng also takes the doctrine of human *dao* as the goal. The debates about the uselessness and usefulness of metaphysics tell people the importance of theoretical foundation and the utmost goal of metaphysics. His arguments also clarified the relationship between the theory of *li* or truthness as the outcome of the idea of *li* and the theory of the *dao* as the principles of human beings. The former functions as a ground for the latter, and the latter is the goal and result of the former. Although Feng Youlan disagreed with previous philosophers' basic views of metaphysics, on the point that the studies of heaven, *dao*, or *li* are not the final goals, the final goals of philosophy and metaphysics attributed to humans and human society, Feng's points of view about the goals of metaphysics are in line with ancient Chinese philosophers.

Further, after he comments on Mengzi's ideas about human nature, he distinguishes himself from Zhu Xi in knowing heaven and serving heaven. Feng summarized his views, saying that "the doctrine of sages begins with philosophical activities and ends in moral behaviors."[69] As one of the essential philosophical activities, the goal of "investigating into things is to attain knowledge" (*Gewu zhizhi* 格物致知) is not just for acquiring knowledge but for improving our moral behaviors. The knowledge gained from investigating things should merge into our ethical behaviors.[70] I would assert that, although Feng devoted himself to building up a purely logical system of metaphysics, this is an effort to Westernize Chinese philosophy. Still, Feng's whole academic work's spirit keeps traditional Chinese philosophy: to know heaven, serve heaven, and eventually serve humans.

The examination above shows us that the goal of Chinese metaphorical metaphysics is not just to reach factual, conceptual, "fundamental truth," which differs from Western philosophy, "aiming to discover fundamental truths about the world and its structure using a priori reasoning" as Amie L. Thomasson stated—knowledge or language games. The utmost goal of Chinese metaphysics is to withdraw principles of human behaviors from heaven, earth, sun, moon, star, *dao*, *li*, and the myriad things. The approach to achieving this goal is just analogical reasoning; all conclusions withdrawn from analogical reasoning answer the general question: what should humans do? The decision about "ought to" falls into the category "judgment about value" or value judgment, which is based on, but different, from the factual conclusions about the fact. The knowledge about facts answers another general question: what is it (the world), or what are they (the myriad things)? I agree with Feng Youlan that knowledge about the world and all things should merge into one, and end with the one about what we ought to do; this is the goal/purpose of metaphysics in Chinese philosophical tradition.

Essence: Meta-Theory of Morality

In the previous part, we showed that the goal of metaphysics in Chinese philosophical tradition was to perfect human life; once the goal was set up, the theoretical principles of behaviors can be developed to target to achieve the goal. The theory of value is not empty. It comprises countless principles of behavior, and most were derived from heaven and extended to humans. In addition, most of them were expressed with metaphysical propositions metaphorically. As stated in *The Classic of Changes* commentaries, "heaven moves powerfully, and gentlemen should be self-strong never cease"[71]; that humans should take heaven as an example and act as heaven is doing. Laozi said it is the *dao* of heaven to get away from the outstanding achievements you made.[72] In Laozi's eyes, heaven produced the myriad things but never occupied what it made, so humans should act like heaven. Confucius educated people to behave like heaven, earth, and the four seasons, doing their work but never speaking out.[73] In the Doctrine of Mean, we may read, "sincerity is the *dao* of heaven, and to carry out the *dao* of heaven is the *dao* of humans."[74] Mengzi warned people, "those who are obedient to Heaven are preserved; those who go against Heaven are annihilated."[75] Like many other principles, this is also primary: never try to go against heaven. How to obey heaven? There is no detail in this proposition. Xunzi educated people that "the destiny of people is determined by heaven, and the destiny of the state depends on virtual."[76] Like all other propositions, an abstract and general principle stresses the importance of *li* for a state. Han Fei Zi advised people to fulfill their duty and wait for their destiny from heaven on a practical level, but not in a metaphysical dimension. Dong Zhongshu assumed, "The *dao* of heaven is dedicated to enriching its spirit, and sages are dedicated to recruiting talents."[77] He advised Emperor Han Wu should recruit talented people like heaven enriches its spirit. How? This proposition does not denote. Just some examples here; each of the philosophers issued many similar propositions.

We have partially noted from my short comments about the selected quotations that what those propositions expressed are principles of human behavior and were extended from the goal targeting to achieve success in human life from load to ordinary people (I call these propositions in terms of the expression and principles in terms of the content). However, those propositions cannot directly help people perfect human life in social reality because those propositions were established between heaven-earth and humans and are yet to be practicable principles of behavior. Those propositions did not tell people how, where, in what things, in which way, and to whom to carry out the principles derived from heaven.

These propositions have three features: abstractness—they express abstract ideas but not practical principles; generality—they widely apply but do not specify; eternality—the general ideas implied in those propositions will not lose their value with the changes of era and time, because people can always combine with their current reality to get advice and general guidance. The three features shaped those propositions as typical metaphysical propositions. Those propositions were withdrawn from heaven and expressed analogically with the principles (for convenience, in one word, the *dao* of heaven or heavenly *dao*), so I call those propositions metaphorical, metaphysical propositions. Since those propositions expressed were metaphysical principles of behavior and were metaphorically expressed, and the theory of value was made up with those principles, I further specify the theory of value as the meta-theory of morality. I mean by "meta-" that all practicable principles of behavior were derived from those propositions; I entitle all those propositions and call it "theory" because, although those propositions were not systematically organized in a strict sense, Chinese philosophical tradition is a system in a broad sense; and I use the term "morality" in terms of the shared nature or essence of those propositions—almost all those propositions are related to human ethical principles and moral behaviors. These essential specialties of the metaphysical propositions in Chinese philosophical tradition differ from other traditions.

The goal and practicable principles of behavior were extended and developed from the principles in the meta-theory of morality but resulted in the relationships among humans. For instance, the idea of the superiority of males and the inferiority of females was developed from that of heaven and earth in *The Classic of Changes*. As a proposition in the meta-theory of morality, it tells people that male is superior to female, just like heaven is superior to earth. According to the *Records of Rituals XiaoDai Liji* 《小戴礼记》, during the Qing Dynasty (1636–1912), Chinese people were taught that men were in charge of women. It was believed that if a woman married, she should obey her husband; if her husband passed away, she should obey her son. Even if the son is her son, since a son is a man, the mother must obey him because he is a male. These principles are practicable and specify how a man is superior to a woman. Confucius' most influential principle, "let the ruler be a ruler, the minister a minister, the father a father, and the son a son,"[78] mainly requires different people to do what they should do. Because of the limited space, just one more example from Confucius exemplifies the practicable principle's features. He advised people, "if contrary to ritual, do not look; if contrary to ritual, do not listen; if contrary to ritual, do not speak; if contrary to ritual, do not act."[79] These principles are particular, practicable, and timeless. With the development of society, the components of "ritual" are changeable, accordingly whether one ought to look, listen, speak, and act or not, depending on the criteria of specific historical eras.

We have seen many examples in previous discussions about the metaphysical method. From the perspective of the way of expressing practicable principles, I pick up Dong Zhongshu's three ethical principles and five constant virtues (*Sangang wuchang* 三纲五常), which particularly regularize the relationships between lord versus minsters, husband versus wife, father versus son, and five practicable virtues as an example to clarify its analogical features. In addition, most of these kinds of practicable principles were analogically expressed. Dong analogized lord, husband, and father with the headrope of a fishing net. Since a husband is the headrope of a wife, people further developed Dong's idea analogically, saying, "if married a rooster, stay with the rooster; if married a dog, stay with the dog." Here, rooster and dog do not refer to rooster and dog but mean whatever kind of husband; once you marry him, stay with him. This is a vulgar and metaphorical expression of Dong's principle about the relationship between husband and wife.

In comparison, the practicable principles of behavior are much more than the above-mentioned metaphysical principles in Chinese philosophical tradition. This principle has three features: particularity, practicability, and timeliness. I call all the practicable principles of behavior in the Chinese philosophical tradition "practical theory of morality." I claim that the meta-theory of morality is the metaphysical foundation of the practical theory of morality, and the practical theory of morality is the particular application of the meta-theory of morality.

Humans can achieve the same goals from different approaches and others from the same approach, determined by various objects, methods, and purposes. The goals or purposes of metaphysics in Chinese philosophical tradition originated, were argued, and expressed metaphorically. This is the third piece of evidence for me to characterize metaphysics in Chinese philosophical tradition as metaphorical metaphysics.

We have selectively examined how the leading philosophers in the history of Chinese philosophy described metaphysical objects, employing metaphorical methods and achieving the goals or purpose via metaphysical knowledge by analyzing the specialties of the metaphorical metaphysics of ancient Chinese tradition. Notably, we have clarified that Chinese philosophers described the objects of metaphysics by analogical descriptions rather than making definitions. Chinese philosophers argued for or against their claims by analogical reasoning rather than logical inferences; they aimed to withdraw the principles of human behaviors in terms of analogical reasoning rather than acquiring factual, conceptual, fundamental, and metaphysical or transcendental knowledge or language games. These unique characteristics and specialties shaped the metaphysics in ancient Chinese philosophy as metaphorical metaphysics.

In sum, we characterize metaphysics in Chinese philosophy as metaphorical metaphysics from the methodological perspective in terms of three aspects: First, the ways ancient philosophers conceptualized various metaphysical objects and based on the analyses of those objects, we defined the objects of metaphysics as conceptualized all-in-one entities and claimed that ancient philosophers conceived different metaphysical entities via concepts as intermediaries. Second, with regard to the methods ancient Chinese philosophers used to develop their arguments, based on the examinations of various arguments about human nature, we characterized their primary method as analogical reasoning. Third, based on the analyses of the goal of metaphysics and the essence derived from the goal, we asserted that metaphysics in Chinese philosophical tradition is a meta-theory of morality. Since the object, method, and goal were expressed analogically, we characterized the metaphysics in Chinese tradition as metaphorical metaphysics.

NOTES

1. *Chinese Metaphysics and Its Problems*, edited by Chenyang Li and Franklin Perlins (Cambridge: Cambridge University Press, 2016).

2. Aristotle, *Aristotle's Metaphysics: Books M and N*, translated with introduction and notes by Julia Annes (Oxford: Clarendon Press, 1976), 91 (1076*a* 10).

3. Aristotle, *Aristotle's Metaphysics*, translated and with commentaries and glossary by Hippocrates G. Apostle (Grinnell: The Peripatetic Press/Indiana University Press, 1966), 110 (1028*b* 35).

4. Ibid., 129 (1038*b* 10).

5. Ibid., 109 (1028*b* 10).

6. Ibid., 130 (1039a 5).

7. Ibid., 128 (1038*a*).

8. Ibid., 128 (1038*a* 5, 30).

9. For metaphysical concepts that refer to metaphysical objects, see Helen Beebee, Nikk Effingham, and Philip Goff, *Metaphysics: The Key Concepts* (London and New York: Routledge, 2011).

10. *The Classic of Changes*, translated by Richard John Lynn (New York: Columbia University Press, 1994), 67.

11. Ibid., 53.

12. Ibid., 6.

13. *Yao*爻: lines. Ibid., 1.

14. Bo Mou, for instance, characterized the symbols *yin* and *yang* as ideographical signs in his article "Becoming-Being Complementarity: An Account of the Yin-Yang Metaphysical Vision of the Yi-Jing," in *Comparative Approaches to Chinese Philosophy*, edited by Bo Mou (Aldershot: Routledge, 2003), 88. If we believe that the symbol ⚋ (*yin*) was derived from the image of the virgin female, and the ⚊ (*yang*) as the root of male (*Nan gen nü yin*男根女阴), then the symbols ⚋ and ⚊ can be characterized as pictorial signs or symbols.

15. Laozi, "The nameless is the origin of heaven and earth. The named is the mother of all things." Laozi, *Daodejing: A Literal-Critical Translation*, translated by Joseph Hsu (Lanham, MD: University Press of America, 2008), 3.

16. Ibid., 41.

17. "The world has a beginning, which is the mother of all things. Knowing their mother, you will know her children. Knowing her children, and holding on to their mother, you will incur no danger all your life." Ibid., 84.

18. "譬道之在天下，犹川谷之在江海也。" *Tao Te Ching*, translated by D.C. Lau (Hong Kong: The Chinese University Press, 2001), 7.

19. "*Dao* is to the world, what rivers and seas are, metaphorically, to small valleys." Laozi, *Daodejing: A Literal-Critical Translation*, 54. Here, the Chinese text that Hsu's translation was based on is different from the version of Laozi's *Daodejing* that Wang Pi's commentaries were based on. Hus referred to the Jiang Xi Chang's commentaries, the version of Ma Wang Dui and the baboo versions of Guodian "譬道之在天下，犹川谷之于江海。" Rudolf G. Wagner, *A Chinese Reading of Daodejing: Wang Bi's Commentary on the Laozi with Critical Text and Translation* (Albany: State University of New York Press, 2003), 224. In my understanding, there is no essential difference between the two pieces of Chinese texts, both analogized the existence of *dao* in the myriad things with the existence of streams and rivers in seas and oceans.

20. Laozi, *Daodejing: A Literal-Critical Translation*, 23.

21. Ibid., 41

22. *Aristotle's Metaphysics*, 102–36 (1025*b*–1040*b*).

23. Ibid., 114 (1030*b* 10).

24. Ibid., 128 (1038*a* 30).

25. Ibid., 133 (1040*a* 30).

26. Huang Kan (黄侃), *Shoupi Baiwen Shisanjing* 《黄侃手批白文十三经》 *Thirteen Classics: Huang Kan Manually apostilled punctuations* (Shanghai: Shanghai Ancient Books Publishing House, 1983), 53.

27. Ibid., 53.

28. Confucius, *Analects*, translated with an introduction and notes by Raymond Dawson (Oxford: Oxford University Press, 1993), 3.

29. Ibid., 6.

30. Ibid., 8.

31. *Maintaining Perfect Balance* (*Zhong Yong*). *The Four Books*, translated by Daniel K. Gardner (Indianapolis: Hackett Publishing Company, 1990), 116.

32. *The Four Books*, translated by James Legge (Hong Kang: Wei Tung Book Co., 1969), 20–21.

33. Mengzi, *Mencius*, translated by Irene Bloom; edited and with an introduction by Philip J. Ivanhoe (New York: Columbia University Press, 2009), 121.

34. Ibid.

35. Ibid.

36. Xunzi, *Xunzi: The Complete Text*, edited and translated by Eric L. Hutton (Princeton, NJ: Princeton University Press, 2014), 1.

37. Ibid., 207.

38. Ibid., 17.

39. While Mozi saw someone dyeing silk he sighed and said, "When something is dyed by blue [dye], it becomes blue. When it is dyed by yellow [dye], it becomes

yellow. What [the dye] enters changes in that its color changes. Five entries [of dye] create five [different] colors. Therefore, dyeing must be given careful attention." Mozi, *The Mozi: A Complete Translation*, translated by Ian Johnston (New York: Columbia University Press, 2010), 15.

40. Ibid., 15–17.
41. Ibid., 7.
42. Han Fei Zi, *The Complete Works of Han Fei Tzu*, translated with introduction and notes by W.K. Liao (London: Percy Lund, Humphries & Co., vol. 1, 1959), 258–59.
43. Ibid.
44. Ibid.
45. Ibid., 30–31.
46. Ibid., 164.
47. Ibid., 183.
48. Dong Zhongshu, *Chun Qiu Fan Lu* (*Luxuriant Dew of the Spring and Autumn Annals*), vol. 10, chapter 36, edited by Wang Yun Wu (Tai Bei: Wen Yuan Ge, 1975), 8. I use Mou Bo's English translation of the title. See *Chinese Philosophy A–Z* (Edinburgh: Edinburgh University Press 2022), 182–92. Dong Zhongshu said, 今谓性 "已善，不几于无教而如其自然！" 《春秋繁露》王云五主编，台北：文渊阁 1975 年，卷十《实性》第三十六第8页。
49. Dong Zhongshu said, "善如米，性如禾。禾虽出米，而禾未可谓米也。性虽出善，而性未可谓善也。" Dong Zhongshu, *Chun Qiu Fan Lu*, 8.
50. Dong Zhongshu said, "天之所为，止于茧麻与禾。以麻为布，以茧为丝，以米为饭，以性为善，此皆圣人所继天而进也，非情性质朴之能至也，故不可谓性。" Ibid., 8–9.
51. Dong Zhongshu said, "卵待覆二十日而后能为雏，茧待缲以涫汤而后能为丝，性待渐于教训而后能为善。" Ibid., 9.
52. Ibid.
53. Zhu Xi, *Zhu Xi: Selected Writings*, edited by Philip J. Ivanhoe, translated by Ivanhoe (Oxford: Oxford University Press, 2019), 17.
54. Ibid., 72–73.
55. *Getting to Know Master Zhu Xi: English Translations of Selections from Zhu Zi Yu Lei*, translated by Wang Xiaonong and Zhao Zengtao (Beijing: China Social Science Press, 2018), 17.
56. Ibid., 24.
57. In Zhu Xi's words, "The principle is like the water in a river. When you take it by a ladle, you get only a ladle of it, and when you take it by a bowl, you get only a bowl of it. In the same vein, when you take it by a barrel or even a vat, you a get much more." Ibid., 25.
58. Zhu Xi, *Chu His: Learning to Be a Sage: Selected from the Conversations of Master Chu, Arranged Topically*, translated by Daniel K. Gardner (Berkeley: University of California Press, 1990), 90.
59. *Getting to Know Master Zhu Xi*, 26–27.
60. Ibid., 52.
61. Ibid., 53.
62. Ibid., 73

63. Feng Youlan, *San Song Tang Quanji* (《三松堂全集》 *Complete Works of Feng Youlan*, 二点。 Cai Zhongde, vol. 4 (Zheng Zhou: Henan Remin Chubanshe, 2000), 80. Hereafter, *Complete Works*. Feng Youlan said, "某一类中之事物所必依照于其理者，自其必依照而不可逃言，谓之命。自其因依照某理而得以成为某一类事物言，则谓之性。" 冯友兰，《三松堂全集》第4卷第80页。Feng Youlan, *Complete Works*, vol. 4, 40.

64. Feng Youlan said, "例如飞机必依照飞机之理， 方可成为飞机。" Ibid., 80.

65. Feng Youlan said, "例如人理即人之所以为人者；马理即马之所以为马者。" Ibid., 80–81.

66. Fen Youlan explained, "我们所谓天，是指大全， 指宇宙。一切理皆包含于宇宙或大全中， 人道亦包于宇宙或大全中"。Ibid., 106.

67. Ibid., 13.
68. Ibid.
69. Ibid., 188.
70. Ibid.

71. Xiang Zhuan《象传》 "天行健，君子以自强不息." Alfred Huang, *The Complete I Ching, The Definitive Translation by the Taoist Master Alfred Huang* (Rochester: Inner Traditions International. 2007), 24.

72. Laozi, *Daodejing: A Literal-Critical Translation*, 16.

73. The Master said, "Does Heaven speak? The four seasons pursue their courses, and all things are continually being produced, but does Heaven say anything?" Gardner, ed., *The Four Books*, 46.

74. 《中庸》：22："诚者天之道，诚之者人之道。" I use my own translation. Other translations are available; for example, "To be true is the Way of heaven. To make oneself true is the Way of man." Gardner, ed., *The Four Books*, 121.

75. *Mencius*, translated with an introduction by D.D. Lau (London: Penguin Books, 1970), 120.

76. Xunzi, 《荀子》《强国》， "人之命在天，国之命在礼。"《荀子集解》下 （北京：中华书局，1997），291. Xun Zi said, "the fate of a person rests in Heaven, and the fate of a state rests in ritual." *Xun Zi: The Compete Text*, translated and with introduction by Eric L. Hutton (Princeton, NJ: Princeton University Press, 2014), 163.

77. Dong Zhongshu: *Chun Qiu Fan Lu* (Luxuriant Dew of the Spring and Autumn Annals," vol. 6, chapter 19, edited by Wang Yun Wu (Tai Bei: Wen Yuan Ge: 1975), 9. 董仲舒《春秋繁露》《立元神》卷六第十九章第9页："故天道务盛其精，圣人务众其贤。"

78. Gardner, ed., *The Four Books*, 36.

79. Ibid., 35.

Chapter Two

Meta-One, Multi-One, and Utter-One

As the first step to reconstruct metaphysics in Chinese philosophical tradition, we have characterized the metaphysical objects as conceptualized all-in-one entities, the primary method as analogical reasoning, and the essence as the meta-theory of morality. In this chapter, based on critical analyses of some of the most influential concepts, I will propose three metaphysical categories, Meta-One, Multi-One, and Utter-One, and concentrate on three aspects: Meta-One and its components, Multi-One and its members, and Utter-One and its components, and argue for the three categories from a static angle.

For each category, I trace back to the source, explore its components, and analyze its metaphorical functions. By tracing back to the origins of each category, I argue that the three categories are rooted in the abundant soil of the Chinese philosophical tradition. By exploring the components of each category, I further display the particular content of the three categories, and by analyzing the functions of each category, I aim to clarify the roles of each category in metaphysics in Chinese tradition.

META-ONE: SOURCE, COMPONENTS, AND FUNCTIONS

When I distinguished between metaphysical concepts and objects, I treated heaven, *yin-yang*, *dao*, *li*, and so forth as metaphysical objects instead of concepts and stressed that metaphysical concepts are not equal to metaphysical objects. Now, I regard heaven, *yin-yang*, *dao*, *li*, and so forth as metaphysical concepts instead of objects to analyze and follow with a new metaphysical category, Meta-One (*yuanyi* 元一), which incorporates the terms *yuan* 元 (meta) and *yi* 一 (One) and existed separately in *The Classic of Changes*, discourses of Laozi, Zhuangzi, Dong Zhongshu, and Feng Youlan.

Meta and One: Trace to Source

In ancient philosophy, *dao* comprised *yin* and *yang*; Laozi's *dao* gave birth to one, two, three, and myriad things. For Zhou Dunyi (1017–1073), there is no nonultimate outside the great ultimate, which means the great ultimate is one; and nothing is outside Feng Youlan's great entirety (*daquan* 大全), Feng's great entirety is one. Although there is no existing category called Meta-One (元一*yuanyi*) in the history of Chinese philosophy, ancient Chinese philosophers widely used *yuan* and *yi* separately. The discourses about these concepts allow us to propose the new category Meta-One.

According to the book *Explain the Graphs and Unravel the Written Words* (*Shuwen Jiezi* 《说文解字》) in the Han Dynasty, the character *yuan* means beginning (始也). Xu Shen wrote that *The Yi of the Nine Schools* (*Jiujia yi* 《九家易》) explained the word *yuan* as the beginning of *qi*.[1] *Yuan* (元) is a metaphysical concept because the *yuan* is the beginning of *qi* but not the beginning of *yin qi* (negative *qi*) and *yang qi* (positive *qi*). The *qi* is a state in which *yin* and *yang* are divided, and the division of *yin* and *yang* was potentially not yet realistic. *Yuan* is the beginning of *qi* and is essentially the beginning of the beginning, like the beginning mentioned in the earliest Chinese dictionary, *Erya* 《尔雅》. This beginning is still a metaphysical concept expressed by the character *yi* 一(one).

In the category Meta-One, the word 元 (*yuan*) implies the meaning of the beginning, as explained in *Er Ya* and the book *The Yi of the Nine Schools* Xu Shen indicated. Besides the meaning of beginning, *yi* also implied the meaning of *zu* 祖, ancestor. Humans, animals like horses, birds, and many other living beings have their first ancestors. The phrase *shizu* 始祖, which Chinese people widely used as a combination of the two words, meant "beginning" and "ancestor." As a fixed term made up of the two words, *shizu* is not yet a metaphysical concept; it means the first ancestor and emphasizes the originations of humans, animals, and other living beings. The category Meta-One absorbed the basic meaning of beginning and further defined it as a metaphysical category using the English prefix meta- to change the word One. I use "*yuan*" (元) to strengthen the meaning of the beginning of the beginning and the authority as the first beginning; I use One to denote the meanings of unification, a unified entity, and entirety in which all parts or items are unified. We may call it *yuanyi* 元一in in the Chinese language.

The explanation of One from the perspective of Daoism shows the metaphysical features; *dao* was based on One and is One; it initialized heaven and earth and gave birth to myriad things. The character *yi* 一 (One), according to Xu Shen, established the Great Ultimate in One just in the beginning, divided into heaven and earth, and then transformed into myriad things. We can see from this explanation that 一(*yi*) also included the meaning of beginning but emphasized One itself. When we combined the word One with the word *yuan* to create the category Meta-One, we kept the metaphysical feature of the concept of One and stressed that One does not refer to any physical things in the world.

Ancient Chinese philosophers widely used the character *yuan* 元 and inputted various meanings to the word. In *The Classic of Changes*, the concept *yuan* (元) was used in the comments about the diagram *Qian*; the *Qian* represents what is great, originating, penetrating, advantageous, correct, and firm.[2] The word *yuan* (元) means "originating." In the *Commentaries of Tuan* (彖传 *Tuanzhuan*), it is said about Qian, "how great is the fundamental nature of Qian! The myriad things are provided their beginnings by it, and, as such, it controls Heaven."[3] Further, "Qian manifests its fundamentality in providing for the origin of things and granting them prevalence."[4] Furthermore, "[Qian] is strong, dynamic, central, correct, and it is absolutely pure in its unadulteratedness and unsulliedbess."[5]

Based on these elaborations, we say that originating and beginning are the basic meanings of the word *yuan*/元. *The Classic of Changes* used *yuan* (元) to explain the diagram. *Yuan* includes the meaning of greatness, originating, and beginning in the word. The two commentaries stressed the meanings of great and originating of *yuan*; *Wenyan Zhuan* explained the word *yuan* from the perspective of Confucianism, saying that *yuan* means "the great and originating is (in man) the first and chief quality of goodness." The category Meta-One imbibes the meanings of the beginning and originating of the word *yuan* (元) but further endows the term with potential. Meta-One partially incorporates the implications of *yuan* (元) used in *The Classic of Changes*.

One is another essential core concept in *The Classic of Changes*. Philosophers endowed the term One (*yi* 一) with different meanings in the dimension of metaphysics. Laozi said, "One *yin* and one *yang* were entitled *dao*." As the core metaphysical category, Dao implies two essential elements, *yin* and *yang*. *Yin* versus *yang* corresponds to each other, and *yin*'s decrease follows *yang*'s increase and vice-versa. The correspondence, increase, and reduction of *yin* and *yang* constructed a dynamic progression, but dao limits to *yin-yang* two elements.

Laozi condenses *dao* into *one*. As we have seen in the previous chapter, Laozi blended the attributes of invisibility, inaudibility, and intangibility of *dao* into one. He further pointed out that one is the "code of *dao*" (*daoji* 道纪)."[6] According to Laozi, one is "ceaseless," "we can not name it," and it possesses all attributes of *dao*. From the philosophical language perspective, Laozi's one is a typical metaphysical concept. The category Meta-One is associated with the metaphysical features of Laozi's one, including formlessness, invisibility, inaudibility, and beginning, as mentioned. Laozi's one is a typical metaphysical concept.

46   Chapter Two

The category Meta-One is not just a simple combination of the words "meta" and "One" (*yuan* and *yi*), it is rooted in profound traditional Chinese philosophy, and its rich components are derived from the tradition.

Meta-One and Its Components

A seed is a physical existence, while Meta-One is a metaphysical category. Meta-One comprises the components of Laozi's One but further strengthens One's abstractness, originality, and potentiality by adding "Meta" to One. Meta-One, as a metaphysical category, implies all potential parts, items, elements, or aspects, depending on what the Meta-One analogically refers to; Meta-One is not empty. Meta-One is like an apple seed in which all parts—for instance, the potential branches, leaves, flowers, and fruits—all exited into the apple seed potentially. Still, the leaves, flowers, and fruits were not yet shaped and do not appear as anything we can see from an apple seed apart from the apple seed itself, but all branches of the tree, leaves, flowers, and fruits originated and developed from the seed. The analogy of seed metaphorically shows the potentiality originality we are discussing in the category Meta-One; unavoidably, we need to follow a metaphorical approach to analogize Meta-One: Meta-One is just a metaphysical "seed."

However, as a metaphysical category, Meta-One does not specify any actual things' originality and potentiality. The analogy of apple seed only partially expressed the meanings the Meta-One implied. Meta-One implied the meaning of the beginning of the beginning; the first "beginning" in the expression is kept open and not yet specified. The first beginning leaves for the future. As a philosophical hypothesis, we leave it unspecified because scientific research, techniques in exploring the universe, and philosophical thinking of the world are ongoing, and our knowledge is still limited. There is still unlimited room for humans to study further. For instance, we may already know how the universe developed today, so we may know something about its beginning, but we still do not know what the beginning of the beginning is. Even though people say there is no beginning of the universe, no beginning is still another way of beginning. Theoretically, there must be a beginning, and a beginning of a beginning. Humans' knowledge today is far from announcing that we have already known everything, including the beginning of the beginning. We must be humble to confess the limitation of our knowledge. The category Meta-One implies the general originalities and potentialities of all things, and nothing's originality and potentiality are not implied in it, which is the beginning of the beginning and an essential component of the category.

The category Meta-One is rooted in Chinese philosophical tradition and imbibes the components of the concepts of *yuan* (元) and the idea of *yi* (一).

Still, it is neither a simple repetition nor a simple addition of Meta to One. As an organic combination of the Meta and One, Meta-One is a highly abstract metaphysical category; it eliminated the nonmetaphysical elements implied in Laozi's *dao*, including path, road, and the way to deal with actual things. From the perspective of a metaphysical object, Meta-One differs from Laozi's *dao*. It is a conceptualized all-in-one entity in which all particular elements are implied as the formats of images, impressions, or ideas. Meta-One is not an empty concept; it was fulfilled with profound components. People understand Meta-One, just like comprehending metaphysical *dao* through its members, not dependent solely on the idea. People can understand a metaphysical *dao* by metaphorically conserving the images, impressions, shapes of paths, roads, ways, motherhood, etc. Meta-One is like *dao*, a metaphysical category with the feature of abstractness and a conceptualized all-in-one entity.

We regard *dao* as a metaphysical category in terms of its metaphorical meaning, not the literal meaning of *dao* itself. *Dao* is not an idealist concept for metaphysics, as Laozi acknowledged he did not know how to name it and just grudgingly called it *dao*. Therefore, I am proposing the category Meta-One instead of reinterpreting the word *dao* or endowing the *dao* with other meanings. In comparison, the Meta-One category, besides Meta, does not refer to any individual physical existence. One is a highly abstract term and does not refer to material things like paths or roads as the *dao* does. When we claim dao is metaphysical *dao*, we must distinguish it from the dao in daily life, saying that the *dao* that can be spoken of is not the eternal *dao*, as Laozi did. One is already a conceptualization of all individuals; it does not refer to particular things like *dao* dose-referring to path, road, or way in terms of its literal meanings. One is one; it is not any specific individual thing, but can refer to anything whose number is one. One is qualified to be a metaphysical concept because of its higher abstractness than *dao*.

When we combined the two words "meta" and "one" to create the category Meta-One, the result was 1+1>2. Meta-One has more components than those two separated words as a fixed term. Meta-One includes the meanings of the head, origination, beginning, first, authorization, oneness, unification, whole, sole, and entirety. As a metaphysical category, Meta-One has profound components. It does not refer to any particular individual, as we said, but it can refer to anything conceptually and concretely; Meta-One has the features that all metaphysical concepts possess, including abstractness, generality, and eternality. As a metaphysical object, it is a conceptualized all-in-one entity, the images, impressions, or ideas of universal, cosmic, heaven, earth, sun, moon, stars, living beings, and nonliving beings, and their parts or elements to all individual things like an apple seed, are its components.

Let's explore the universe's origination in a metaphysical dimension, not scientific research. When we deal with metaphysical issues, the Meta-One component entirely depends on particular topics. The beginning of the beginning of the universal, the image of the universal, and the information about all things in the universe are components of meta-One. The universal is not empty, and Meta-One is also not empty; it is fulfilled with profound information about the universal. Philosophers conceive the universal through the components derived from the universal and all things in the universe, not through an abstract concept of the universal.

In short, Meta-One as a metaphysical category is fulfilled with profound components, and as an object of metaphysics, it is a conceptualized all-in-one entity.

Metaphorical Functions of Meta-One

Meta-One does not function as a premise of logical inference, but it rolls as the ground of analogical reasoning in arguments. I entitle this function a metaphorical function; with this function, Meta-One can metaphorically analogize to *dao*, *li* (principle), ultimate-great, heaven, the son of heaven, emperors on the earth, and all others with similar features of origin, action, beginning, oneness, and authorities in origination.

Meta-One has multiple metaphorical functions; I just briefly exemplify its metaphorical functions as the following: Meta-One implies the meaning of the beginning of beginning beyond any actual things and is the generalization of all real beginnings at a metaphysical dimension. Any subject has its metatheory, a theory beyond the topic itself; changing the word "One" with the prefix "Meta" means that this One is beyond all actual ones. When we combine the Meta with One, we mean One is not anything's number; it is the generalization of all kinds of individual ones. It is one of all ones. Meta-One is abstract, general, and beyond all empirical ones. Oneness is the core that makes Meta-One a metaphysical category. As the generalization of all ones, no one is not implied in One. When we take Meta-One as a ground of analogy, we may use *dao* to exemplify the Meta-One, saying *dao* belongs to Meta-One, is Meta-One, and *dao* is a metaphorical reference to the Meta-One. We may use *dao* to interpret Meta-One metaphorically, but saying *dao* is Meta-One does not mean that *dao* is equal to Meta-One, because, strictly speaking, *dao* is between the metaphysical realm the realm of reality, as we analyzed. In contrast, Meta-One is a typical metaphysical category that can analogically express all single and complex entities that comprise various individuals, parts, or elements.

Meta-one is the first of first and the beginning of the beginning in logic; what do I mean by saying the first of first and the beginning of beginning?

These are also metaphorical expressions. In the physical world, all things are countable, and everything has a beginning, while, as a highly abstract category, it is uncountable and cannot see its beginning. Both the concepts "first" and "beginning" are understandable in the physical world, while the first "first" and the first "beginning" mean what? In the expressions of the first of first, the first "first" is uncountable, and it is Meta-One; it is nonbeing (*wu*无); and in the expression of "the beginning of the beginning," the first "beginning" is invisible, and it is Meta-One. The terms "first" and "beginning" are just metaphorical expressions; these terms are used to exemplify the highly abstract metaphysical category Meta-One; the "first" and "beginning" are metaphorical references of Meta-One in which all elements are implied in the Meta-One but not yet realized themselves. If we regard the realization of an element as a beginning, before the element realizes itself there must be a potential beginning existed in Meta-One. The Meta-One is before all actual elements; meanwhile, the Meta-One and all the elements are not separable; both Meta-One and the potential exist synchronously, the same as the branches, flowers, and fruits exist synchronously in a seed. In the dimension of logic, the Meta-One is also before all potential elements as the first of the first, and the beginning of the beginning, Meta-One, and all features exist synchronously.

Meta-One is One that was fulfilled with full potentialities. The Meta-One is abstract but not empty because it implies all potential possibilities. In the Meta-One, multiple elements potentially correspond in harmony, but the corresponding is potential and invisible. Based on what we know, the existence of various features potentially, how do we know the reality of corresponding in Meta-One? We cannot see and show multiple elements and their corresponding harmony by investigating the one itself. Still, fulfillment possibilities convince us that the various aspects and their corresponding harmonies exist. The potentiality of the branches, the flowers, and the fruit of a tree analogically shows that all these were implied in the tree's seed; they exist potentially in the beginning. All elements existed potentially since there is no diversity yet, no differences and all parts are not yet identified and not yet shaped; all are one and in unity, and it has not happened that one corresponds with another. The potential harmony in a single unity is metaphorically similar to a single seed, in our terminology, in the Meta-One. We may use Meta-One to analogize any invisible, potential, undivided, and unrealized harmonical unity based on Meta-One features.

Meta-One possesses the metaphorical feature of one-ness; it is essentially one in terms of its numerical attribution and is one-ness in terms of its metaphysical quality. The Meta-One, as a numerical one, is the unification of diversity that is not a particular one or an individual one that implies all actual elements, although still not yet realized. All potential aspects or diversities will be discovered when developing into the process of Multi-One, which is discussed in the next section of this part. As the metaphysical feature of Meta-One, the one-ness is the generation or abstractness of all ones. Each potential element possesses the oneness derived from all individuals, as Meta-One was generated from all individuals, and Meta-One potentially implies all individuals. When Meta-One was endowed with these features, it functions to express all single entities and all complex unities in which diversities were imaged and numerically possessed.

Meta-One does not function as a premise of logical inference, but it rolls as the ground of analogical reasoning in arguments. I entitle this function a metaphorical function; with this function, Meta-One can metaphorically analogize to *dao*, *li* (principle), ultimate-great, heaven, the son of heaven, emperors on the earth, and all others with similar features of origin, action, beginning, oneness, and authorities in origination.

MULTI-ONE: SOURCE, COMPONENTS, AND FUNCTIONS

Meta-One is an all-in-one entity in which all elements exist potentially. It is the beginning of the beginning, but nothing yet really begins. Once all potentialities become a reality, each potential element realizes itself and moves into multiple developing stages. For this stage, I propose another category, Multi-One. This part first examines the source of Multi-One—by doing so, we can see how the Multi-One was developed from relevant traditional philosophical concepts—then analyzes the components of Multi-One to explain its content instead of making a simple definition, and finally explores the multiple functions of Multi-One to clarify the roles and significance of the category in the system of metaphorical metaphysics.

Multi and One: Trace to Source

Like Meta-One, Multi-One is also rooted in Chinese philosophical tradition and developed from relevant philosophical concepts, including some metaphysical concepts. Because of the limited space, I mainly trace back to the two key concepts, *shu* (殊) and another *li* (理), to trace back to the source of the Multi-One.

The Stimulation from Shu in Classics

As a great potentiality, Meta-One is dynamic, not rest. The process from Meta-One to Multi-One is a process from One to diversities and from potentiality to reality. The realization of potentiality becomes multiple existences in this process; all potential elements identify themselves, realize themselves, and become various existences. I discuss the dynamic process in the next chapter; here, I mainly focus on the source of the category Multi-One.

The same to Meta-One (*Yuanyi* 元一), both multi (*shu* 殊) and One (一*yi*) were widely used separately in the history of Chinese philosophy. As far as I know, there is no existing Multi-One category today. I propose the category Multi-One based on the profound resource of multi, or diversities, *shu* and One discussed by ancient Chinese philosophers.

In the book *Explore the Meanings by Explaining Words*, the word *shu* "殊" in ancient China meant that if a man were sentenced to death because of his crime, he would be beheaded, which means his head and body would have been separated from each other, which meant *shu* (separated). Literately, the word *shu* was usually combined with another word, *si* 死 (death), and composed a phrase (*shusi* 殊死) that meant "desperate." The word's original meanings were related to, even originated from, ancient peoples' real lives. However, the word *shu* had different meanings in philosophical texts, including the implications of difference, varieties, separation, and diversities. If we further explore the meanings of the word *shu* in philosophers' writings, we may find that different philosophers endowed it with different meanings.

In the "Great Treaties" of "*The Classic of Rites*" *Records of Rites* 《礼记》,[7] the concept *shu* (殊) functions as a verb, which means to differ or distinguish between one from another; as a noun, *shu* implies difference. According to the *Great Treaties*, 殊 *shu* means to specify an emblem of one house or family to distinguish between one house's logo and another. *Shu* also represents the moral principles of loving parents, respecting respectful people, and obeying old brothers, the male and female ranks unchanged. Besides these meanings, all others, like musical instruments, dresses, and the colors of the dress, and so on are all changeable and could be various.

No such category is Multi-One in *Daodejing*, but Laozi discussed the relationship between One and diversities. He stated *dao* gave birth to one, two, three, and the myriad things. In my understanding, when the one, two, three, and all things were derived from the one, one has the feature of what we call Multi-One, because multi elements like two, three, four, and the myriad things were potentially implied in *dao*, while *dao* is one. After those multiple things were born, the two, three, and all things, multi-elements, or diversities, became existence. However, they still belong to the one: multiple items were unified in One before they were given "birth." As we analyzed, Laozi's *dao* is a concept between metaphysical and physical realms. When he defined his *dao* as an eternal *dao*, he endowed the *dao* with metaphysical features; when he claimed the *dao* gave birth to myriad things, the *dao* analogically referred to an invisible and eternal *dao* by using visible actual and expressible existence like "mother." In addition, *dao* precisely refers to road, path, and way. Therefore, Laozi was devoted to distinguishing his eternal *dao* from the *dao* in common sense. In this way, he endowed the *dao* with metaphysical features; when he analogically said that the *dao* gave birth to one, two, three, and myriad things, the *dao* could not be a purely abstract concept. It is neither logical nor reasonable to analogize an abstract, empty, and unchangeable concept with an alive mother. Laozi neither described *dao* as a pure concept nor said that a concept of *dao* gives birth to all things. Instead, Laozi personalized *dao* with excellent moral characteristics shaped an alive *dao*. In Laozi's system, *dao* possessed both abstractness and actuality or concreteness.

Laozi's idea about one, two, three, and all things came from *dao* stimulated me to propose the category Multi-One. *Dao* is one, but all things came from *dao*, which means all things potentially existed in *dao*. Why do we not keep the word *dao,* but create another one?

Meta-One is incorporated with Laozi's *dao* but is beyond his *dao*. The metaphysical features of *dao* primarily relied on interpretations and analogical descriptions. According to Laozi's ideas of *dao* solely, we could shape a category of multi-*dao*, which could mean that all things came from the *dao* and existed potentially in the *dao*. In comparison, one is more powerful in the features of abstractness, generality, and eternality as a metaphysical category than *dao*. When meta changes one and combined with one together, we make it a typical metaphysical category.

In contrast, the metaphysical features of Multi-One were derived from the category itself. It is unnecessary to distinguish the one that can be spoken of from the one that cannot be spoken of, as Laozi did for his *dao*. Saying anything else, like his wisdom of life rather than this is beyond Laozi, would be ignorant or delusional. My critical analysis is limited to the *dao* as a metaphysical concept only.

Like other ancient Chinese philosophers, Mengzi used analogies to express his ideas about *shu* (殊) metaphorically. In his arguments about the relationship between diversities (*shu* 殊) and sameness or similarity (*tong* 同, *xiangsi* 相似). Mengzi analogized human nature with wheat, growing well or not depending on the place, time, and efforts to care for it. Mengzi stated that in a good year, young men performed well, and in poor, bad. "it is not because heaven conferred on them different natures (*Jiangcai ershu* 降材尔殊); it was because other circumstances changed their minds."[8] His argument is long, so I summarized his main points here. In other analogies, Mengzi also talked about *shu*. For instance, he said all shoes have the same shape because we have the same feet, we all like music because we have the same ears, and we like beauty because we have the same eyes, and we enjoy good tastes because we have the same mouths, we admire justice and *li* because we have the same minds.⁹ He thinks the only difference (*shu* 殊) comes in things like humans and animals.

Zhu Xi's explanations and analogies metaphorically expressed the relationship between sameness and diversities (*shu*), but the *shu* (or difference) and sameness are based on actual things. The category Multi-One absorbed Mengzi's ideas of difference and sameness as its components but further emphasized that all diversities (*shu* 殊) are the diversities in the same unity (One). The diversities are not parallel to Multi-One. The multi in the category Multi-One includes the meaning of *shu* (difference) but emphasizes diversity, not just the difference. As a metaphysical category, the multi- (*shu*) does not explicitly refer to any difference, as Mengzi listed. Still, a generation of all differences of distinct things comprises the common features of all distinct things, but does not specify any particular differences.

The Inspiration from Zhu Xi's Li

Confucius did not mention the word *shu* 殊, but he used the word "one" repeatedly; each "one" he references is related to a particular thing. In Confucius' *Analects*, when he responded to his student Zi Gong's (520–446 BC) critical comments about Guan Zhong, Confucius extolled Guan Zhong (管仲 725?–645 BC), said: "Guan Zhong imposed his authority over all the states and set the entire world into order; to this very day, the people still reap the benefits of his initiatives"[10] In this context, Confucius recognized that Guan Zhong used his authority to unify the kingdoms (*Yi kuang tianxia* 一匡天下). As a verb, the one in this context partially implied the meaning of Multi-One because many kingdoms were unified into one. However, the word "one" did not reach the metaphysical dimension; the one (*yi* 一) in this context means that Guan helped Lord Qi unite many kingdoms. Both "one" and "many" referred to particular things.

Zhou Dunyi (1017–1073) claimed that each thing has its *xing* 性 (nature/attribution), but all things exist in One (Great Ultimate). This idea is stimulative for me to characterize the category Multi-One as a One in which all elements or diversities are implied, and the multi-elements are unified elements in One. No individual parts are outside the Multi-One, and there would be no Multi-One without individual parts as its components. Another significant source for the Multi-One category is Zhou Dunyi's (1017–1073) idea of "each thing specifies its nature." "物各一其性" (*wu geyi qixing*). One (*yi* 一), as a verb, means each thing individualizes or specifies its nature. In my understanding, human nature is essentially the same, but each person individualizes his characteristics and distinguishes himself from all others. The process from Meta-One via Multi-One to Utter-One is the process in which each thing specifies itself, which is discussed in the next chapter; here, I indicate that the components of Multi-One can be traced back to the stimulation of Zhou Dunyi's ideas.

Zhu Xi replaced nature with *li* and repeatedly said things specify their characters/attributions by themselves, so his nature is essentially individualized. He claims that nature is the same as *li* (principle), and nature is just *li*. He said, "nature is a principle, and it is humanity, rectitude, propriety, and wisdom, and that's all."[11] None since Confucius and Mencius have ever had this insight. None from ancient times on has ever made such a bold statement.[12] Zhu Xi's idea of "one *li* manifests in multiple things" (*liyi fenshu*理一分殊) developed the two Cheng brothers' idea of *li* and interpreted Zhou Dunyi's Great Ultimate and Nature with *li*. According to Zhou Dunyi, when the Great Ultimate (*taiji*太极) moves to generate *yang*, and when the Great Ultimate rests, it generates *yin* (*Dong er shengyang, jing er shengyin*太极动而生阳，静而生阴). Zhu Xi explained, "the Great Ultimate is just the *li* of Heaven and Earth." What moves to generate *yang* is just a *li*; what creates *yin* is also a *li*.[13] It seems to Zhu Xi that all that Zhang Zai (张载1020–1077) said in *The Western Inscription Xi Ming* is just a *li* (principle): One *li* is shared by multiple things.

Zhou Dunyi believed everything possesses its Great Ultimate (*wuwu yi ta ji*物物一太极); it seems to Zhu Xi that everything has a *li*. In different commentaries, Zhu Xi interpreted Zhou Dunyi's nature as *li*, and said, "Nature is the principle [*li*] of heaven. All things innately receive it. There is not one thing that does not contain principle."[14] The *dao* of heaven is the natural substance of the *li* of heaven; it is just a *li*, as he said, "nature is just a *li*" (*xing, ji li* 性，即理也).[15] Zhu Xi said, "All things have their principle [*li*], for principle is not outside things or affairs."[16] Zhu Xi also analogically explained the relationships between things and *li*, "from the Ultimate of Nonbeing and the Great Ultimate above to a small thing like a blade of grass, a plant, or an insect below, each has its principle [*li*]."[17] It seems to Zhu Xi that not just things like grass have its *li*, but other things are the same: a book has its *li*, an affair has its *li*, and an item has its *li*. If we cannot read the book, do not examine the affair, or do not investigate the things, we will miss their *li*.[18] Zhu Xi's *li* is also one. He clearly said, "principle [*li*] is one. It is called destiny in terms of what Heaven has imparted to the myriad things, and it is called nature in terms of what they have received from Heaven. Actually, the different names express different points of view. That is all."[19]

We have read from the discourses above that Zhou Dunyi claimed each thing has a great ultimate; simultaneously, he said everything has its nature. Zhu Xi interpreted the grand ultimate and nature as *li*, so two names are just one. Zhu Xi's idea of one *li* laid a theoretical foundation for his theory of "one *li* in all things" (*liyi fenshu* 理一分殊).[20]

Zhu Xi said, "the one and the many, each having its correct state of being, means that principle [*li*] is one, but its manifestations are many."[21] *Li* is Zhu's core concept, "One *li* in all things" is his core idea, and "One Moon reflected in ten thousand rivers" (*yueying wanchuan* 月映萬川) is the best interpretation of his core idea, which significantly inspired me when I created the category Multi-One. I keep using the two words *shu* 殊 and *yi* (一) but endowed the category with different meanings and components and further targets to eliminate the core concept *li* from the category Multi-One.

When Zhu Xi interpreted Zhou Dunyi's "nature" with *li* and stressed that "nature is just *li* (性，即理也),"[22] he criticized Cheng Yi's "what is inborn is called nature" as not "entirely satisfactory" because nature is mixed with physical nature, but he praised Cheng as the first person who said nature is identical with *li*.[23] Zhu Xi inherited Cheng's basic ideas about *li*.

What is Zhu Xi's *li*? In his writing and conversations with his disciples, we may find that he used different words to express the idea of *li*. According to him, heavenly *li* or the *li* of heaven is just a *li*, "so-called Heaven, only a *li*."[24] Destiny is also a *li*. When Confucius sighed, "once I understood the *dao* in the early morning, I would be satisfied if I died in the evening," Zhu Xi called Confucius' *dao* as *li*.[25] Mostly, he used one *li* (一理 *yili*) or *li*. It seemed to him, "heaven and people are the same things, and inner and outer are one principle [*li*]."[26] I would characterize the *li* as a general concept referring to general *li*. The same as the Moon with which Zhu Xi metaphorically described *li*: the moon is shared by ten thousand rivers. Another is individual *li*, which is possessed by all things. Although Zhu Xi did not use the terms individual *li* and general *li* when he criticized Zeng Zi, saying Zengzi did not know the ten thousand *li* is in one *li*. Zhu Xi analogized the individual *li* as coins and the general *li* as a wire that was used to string coins together (ancient coins had a hole in the center).[27] The general *li* is the *li* of all *li*(s). Zhu Xi distinguished between individual *li* and general *li* in his way.

I interpret Zhu Xi's keywords *fen shu* 分殊 as a verb meaning "to share." This is essential for understanding the difference between the Multi-One category and Zhu Xi's ideas. One asked Zhu Xi about "One *li* is shared by multiple things," and he answered, "if you do not know each of the myriad things has its *li* but just saying one *li*, you would not know where the one *li* (理一 *liyi*) is."[28] One *li* exists in all things, and each item has a *li*. He also said that although human affairs are various, there is only one *li*. This is called one *li* being shared by multiple things. Zhu Xi said that *fen* 分 does not mean cutting it into parts; *fen* 分 is just like the moon reflected off the surfaces of ten thousand rivers. I would say that his *fen* exactly means to share, and the word *shu* means diversities; the category Multi-One incorporated with Zhu Xi's ideas and even borrowed the word *shu*, but it is contrary to Zhu Xi's one was shared by or existed in all (diversities), Multi-One implies all (diversities) co-existed in one.

Multi-One appreciates Zhu Xi's point of view about the relationship between his *li* and the things that shared the *li*. Zhu Xi said there is the air, and the *li* exists in it; without the air, *li* would have no place to exist; there must be water; the moon can reflect on the surface of the rivers; it will be impossible to reflect the moon without water.[29] In the same analogical approach, Zhu Xi metaphorically exemplified the key political things that have shared the fundamental principle (*li*) and stressed that there is one *li*, but it exists in different things. A house, just one *li*, but there are living rooms and halls. Grass and trees, there is only one *li*, but there are peaches and plums. Zhu Xi did not separate his *li* from the natural things; he also applied the same idea to explain the relationship between *li* and humans. He explained that if you have the same people—John and Peter—Peter cannot be John, and John cannot be Peter. Like *yin* and *yang*, *The Western Inscriptions* talked about the fact that multiple things have shared one *li* in this way. *Li* cannot exist isolated from things—this idea was eliminated by Feng Youlan in his New Doctrine of Li—but I admire the idea in this book. The category Multi-One accepted Zhu Xi's idea.

The examinations above showed that after Zhu Xi replaced Zhou Dunyi's nature with *li*, the *li* is one, whether a general *li* or an individual *li*. As general *li*, it was shared by myriad things; as individual *li*, it was possessed by various individual things. I read a core idea from their arguments: *li* is just one that contains the metaphysical feature of oneness. However, *li* is not a metaphysical idea concept because it cannot directly convey the metaphysical feature of oneness; in addition, to distinguish between a metaphysical *li* from a *li* in common sense, we must do as Laozi did, saying that this *li* is not the veins on marble (in terms of the literal meaning of *li*). We used one to create the category Multi-One, not just avoiding the disadvantages of *li* but to move forward a big step in enriching its components.

Rethinking Feng Youlan's New Li

The Multi-One category significantly benefited from Feng Youlan's effort to construct a highly abstract concept. Still, I did not keep using his new *li* in our system by rethinking its disadvantages.

Feng Youlan inherited Cheng-Zhu's doctrine of *li*; he kept using the concept of *li* but further interpreted Zhu Xi's *li* at a higher level of abstractness. In Zhu Xi, *li* is a tentative expression of Zhou Dunyi's nature; *li* exists in particular things like grass, trees, houses, and rivers; otherwise, we could not know where *li* exists. For Feng Youlan, *li* is just an abstract concept; it does not rely on particular things. The *li* of the square is true but not accurate; a square thing is recognized as a square because it corresponds to the *li* of the square. His new *li* no longer relies on particular things because he located *li* in the realm of truthiness and specific things in the realm of reality. In this way, he solved Zhu Xi's worry that *li* would have no place to exist without particular things.

Based on the abstract metaphysical concept of *li*, Feng alternated the core idea of "One *li* in all" (*liyi fenshu* 理一分殊) in Cheng-Zhu philosophy. He argued that Zhang Zai talked about "one *li* in all" in his *Western Inscriptions* was not a metaphysical concept because what he said was about the relationship between people and the real world. Feng claimed that the *li* he talked about is the *li* of a class, not the *li* of any individual things.[30] He divided "class" (*lei* 类) into different ranges. For instance, "cat" is a class; "animal" is a more extensive class because it includes more members. There are several subclasses between "cat" and "ant," like "vertebrate," and so on. In terms of that, the class "animal" covers the class "cat" and similar small classes. The relationship between "animal" and "cat," "dog," "horse," and other animals can be understood as one *li* was shared by all things because the class "cat" and other subclasses share the *li* of the class "animal." Based on the same reasons, Feng said that real things like this cat, that cat, and other cats share the *li* of a cat; the relationship between "cat" and all actual cats is also called One *li* in all.[31]

When we rethink Feng's arguments about "One *li* in all," we find that his class, such as "animal" and "cat," are essentially class names but were entitled "*li*." Square has the *li* of the square, the round has the *li* of the round, and the cat has the *li* of the cat. Where a square, a round, or a cat is square, round, or cat depends on whether these things are accorded with the *li* of them. Since his *li* is neither Zhou Dungyi's nature nor Zhu Xi's *li*, what is the new *li*? Is the new *li* another name for the class? Or the new *li* is just a class name? We may say that a small animal is a "cat" or can be called a cat because this tiny animal is accorded with the class name "cat." Based on the same logic, we may say that this small animal is a "cat" or can be called a "cat" because it is accorded with the concept "cat" instead of the *li* of a cat. Let's go beyond Feng's different expressions to explore the essence of his new *li*. His new *li* is an alternative name of a class name in logic, a concept in philosophy, or a theoretical criterion to classify particular things. As he expected, Feng shaped his new *li* as a purely logical concept and did not allow himself to confuse it with actual existence. His effort to create a new *li* as a strictly logical concept urges me to seek an ideal metaphysical category with abstractness. Zhu Xi inspirited me to enrich the category with profound components by conceptualizing diversities in reality. Because of the latter, I did not keep Feng's new *li* in our system.

The category Multi-One targets to shape a concept with high abstractness, as Feng Youlan made efforts to achieve, but instead of redefining traditional *li* as a new *li*, I intend to endow the category Multi-One with high abstractness of oneness rather than modifying *li*. Although Feng interpreted his new *li* as a pure logical concept, or even an empty concept, the abstractness of the new *li* relies on interpretation.

We recognize a cat is a cat, whatever name you give it. A cat is a cat itself and will not change with the name changes. We may call it "cat" in English or "*mao*" (猫) in Chinese. "Cat" or "*mao*," no matter what we call it, names, class names, concepts, or *li*, all these are outside of the small animal itself and will not lose all attributions of that animal when you change the names.

When we consider the forging of two aspects, it is essential for the category. After all, Multi-One emphasizes that various elements, multiple things, or the world's myriad things are in one entity. One entity is one in which distinct elements, many things, or all things are included. All those things are not isolated from the entity.

There are essential differences between the category Multi-One and Feng Youlan's fundamental principle; multiple things share a *li*.

Feng Youlan's *li* is an abstract logical concept without confirming tangible things, while the Multi-One category directly refers to all kinds of actual entities. The entity could refer to the entire cosmos, the natural world, the animal world, society, a social organization, and so on. All these are real and exist in the world. Even if we define the category Multi-One as an abstract metaphysical concept, we do not think that the metaphysical concept is isolated from the actual reality. Instead, I assume that the category Multi-One is rooted in virtual entities. If there is no entity, there will be no category; if there were no actual cats in the world, the class name "cat" or the *li* of cat would be rootless. We should not cut apart the metaphysical categories and propositions from physical existence to let them become source-less water and rootless trees; it is also not reasonable to rise metaphysical concepts like *li* up from the physical reality to a criterion with which to make judgments of real things.

The category Multi-One is not a sole one, but a Multi-One, any entity that the category multi- implies various elements, multiple individual things, and even myriad things, depending on in which context you used the category. Feng Youlan's *li* is the sole one, while our Multi-One category means many-in-one, which differs from Cheng-Zhu's and Feng's one *li* in all. In Feng's system, no matter whether it is the *li* of the myriad things or the *li* of a big class like "animal" or the *li* of a small class such as "cat" or "square," the *li* of these classes is all one. Zhu Xi's *li* is one, just like one moon reflected in ten thousand waterways. Feng's *li* is one, and the li of the cat covers all individual cats; the *li* of the animal covers all individual animals, but the *li* of animals is only one. In comparison, using *li* to express the abstractness oneness and using one to denote the abstractness oneness, I chose one and gave up *li*.

Further, the category Multi-One emphasizes One is the One in which various elements, multiple things, or myriad things were included. The relationship between One versus all things in the Multi-One differs from the relationship between Feng's *li* versus particular items in the famous principle of "One *li* in all," which he inherited from Cheng-Zhu's doctrine of *li* and alternated. Feng's *li* is true by itself, even with no such thing. In reality, the *li* is true and meaningful by itself, like the *li* of a round square. In the category Multi-One, one is not an empty one. It is true and meaningful because of its profound components derived from diversities in reality. When we conceive Multi-One, we conceptualize all things with diversities and bring them into thinking; we do not take the category as an empty shell to apprehend. If we remove the components from a concept, no matter do we call the concept a logical concept, *li*, Multi-One, or any other, that concept would be meaningless.

Li is a purely logical concept. It is static, which is accordant with the features of abstractness, unchangeability, and eternality. However, all individual items are developing. The logical concept *li* cannot reflect the changes of all particular things. It is acceptable and reasonable. As a metaphysical concept, *li* will not change with the changes of all individual things. However, it is not enough. If we hold a concept like *li*, which never changes with the changes of things that are accorded with that *li*, and ignore all changes that happened in all things, we hold that concept for what? How can we increase our metaphysical knowledge? While we keep an abstract, unchanging, and eternal metaphysical concept, we also need to reflect on the changes that happened in all individual things by the components of the concept. Since the concept of *li* of the round was created till now, uncountable new round things have been made, the same as the universe, the natural words, human society, and all other things, but we keep the concepts or *li* of those things unchanged, but reflect the changes by the components of those concepts or *li* if we keep using the concept *li*. As a metaphysical category, the category Multi-One implies oneness, which is abstract, unchanging, and eternal, but its components convey information about the changes that happened in multiple things. In this category, oneness and conceptualized diversities coexisted in one entity; the Multi-One and its components comprise an organic entity. The Multi-One would be empty without its components, and the components would be massive diversities apart from the Multi-One.

Multi-One and Its Components

According to the literal meanings of the category, Multi-One means that diversities coexisted in one entity or one entity implied diversities. Depending on the entity, the diversities could be various individual things, parts, aspects, elements, or factors; the entity could be anything that existed as a unity. However, as a metaphysical category, the Multi-One neither refers to actual entities nor particular elements. What it denotes are conceptualized entities and specific elements. For an entity, we may use a concept to represent; for the diversities, when we conceptualize them, we need to rely on their physical characteristics like shapes, sizes, colors, and all other characteristics to shape images, visions, impressions, or subclass names of them. These become the particular components of the category and enrich the category with diversities, and the category concludes all components into one. The Multi-One is related to all entities via the components derived from all particular things. The Multi-One is an organic unity fulfilled with profound components.

When we treat Multi-One as an object of metaphysics, it may refer to any entity in which various things or elements were included, but does not explicitly refer to any entity in terms of its generality; the Multi-One can also refer to any entity in terms of its relativity. The universe is an entity in which all things coexist, and an apple tree is an entity in which all branches, flowers, or fruits coexist. When we treat Multi-One as a metaphysical concept, the conceptualized all things in the conceptualized universe are its components, the same as the apple tree, analogically say.

Multi-One is a complex system because its components were derived from diversities, and it is a single unity because of its high unification. There is no *li* behind, after, or outside particular things themselves, and there is no *li* behind, before, after, or outside the entity. The single thing is that thing itself; an entity is that entity itself, and the myriad things are the things themselves, no such a *li* behind, before or after, inside or outside them. From the perspective of the Multi-One to observe the entire universe as a unity, the universe includes all things in the world, the animals, human societies, and so on; there is no *li* behind, before or after, inside or outside the universe. *Li* is a product of humans conceptualizing the universe and all things in the universe, not an inner feature of the universe and all things in the world. All parts in one entity are distinctive and different from one another, which shaped the diversities, and we use "multi" as a name for them. The animal world differs from human society, human society differs from the natural world, and there is no *li* being shared or possessed by all in each community. There is no *li* to be shared by all members or particular things; instead, we see diversity.

Indeed, there must be something common for all members or particular things in a society or a unity; we may call that common feature "nature" or "essence." Nature or essence is inside all things but exists individually. The common features are nature or essence and are just a name. Nature, or essence as a name or concept, is a product of our thinking in conceptualizing metaphysical objects. If we did not compare one member with another, we would have no grounds to identify their common feature. In comparison, suppose we regard *li* as the name of nature or essence. In that case, *li* is more indirect, external, and irrelative than nature or essence in expressing the common feature of all members or particular things.

Similarly, all kinds of social organizations exist in human society, and each has its value, mission, and specialties. A women's rights organization differs from an animal protection organization. Their values and missions determined their nature or essence as social organizations. No such a *li* existed in these organizations or individual *li* in those respective organizations. As a member of an organization, John or Peter, John is John, and Peter is Peter; they have their biological characteristics, social ranks and roles, and social duties. They became members of a social organization because they admired the value and mission of that organization. As members of the organization, they are distinctive and different from one another, with nothing like *li* behind them, inside, after, or outside them. They shared the same value or mission and joined the same organization. The common features like the value and mission of that organization are *li*? It should be. Otherwise, we may not find something that all members shared. Suppose all members of that organization share a common value and mission. If we analyze the concept of "*li*" at the metaphysical dimension, I would say there is no such a *li*. The value and commission of a social organization determine its nature or essence, not any external features like the size or structure of the organization. The value and commission of a social organization are timelines; its value or commission changes with time and social, political, and environmental factors, and even changes with the changes of leaders. They could flourish at a particular time, but vanish at another time.

In the category Multi-One, there is no *li* before any physical things or human affairs before they specify or realize themselves, nor *li* after they know themselves. They are themselves, and they are individuals as well as are in an entity. For an individual human, for instance, the son of heaven or an emperor and his people, the relationship between them was established. Heaven assigned the emperor authority, and the emperor was granted the title, no *li* before and after. An emperor is an individual human; no matter what we call the son of heaven or a human lord, he differs from others (*shu* 殊). All visual humans differ; the multi-(*shu*) refers to all individuals with diversities in one entity called humankind; this is what the One in the category Multi-One refers to. Each human has his nature and attributions, and each physical thing has its nature and attributions, with which one human and one thing differ from another. Nature is individual, and essence is individual; nature and essence exist in individual things individually. Multi-One, a product of metaphysical thinking, conceptualized reality—all in one and one implied all. The Multi-One, as a metaphysical category, has profound components because the "all" admires the world's diversity; meanwhile, all are individuals, not separated or isolated. They all coexisted in certain unities, in the universe or a tiny unity. Multi-One possesses the features of diversities and oneness.

Metaphorical Functions of Multi-One

In the discussion above, we have partially touched up the metaphorical functions of Multi-One, which deals with the static relationship between One and the multiple things in One and describes the dynamic, ongoing process of various things in a particular entity.

The metaphorical functions of the Multi-One were derived from the features of the category itself. Multi-One possesses metaphysical qualities and physical characteristics. Because of its abstractness, Multi-One can be characterized as a metaphysical category with generality when we treat it as a metaphysical object. Muti-One means One fulfilled with multiple things, but it does not explicitly specify any particular things. Similarly, many things refer to various elements, all things, but again, they do not define any real individuals. In this sense, the prefix "multi" is an abstract term that is no longer an ordinary prefix.

The Multi-One together as a fixed term is a metaphysical category and can refer to any entity that possesses abstractness, generalities, eternity, individuality, diversity, and mutuality. In our system, the Multi-One category refers to all kinds of entities, including vain (*li* in its literal meaning). The various elements, multiple things, and myriad things are individual and authentic so that the Multi-One can be characterized as a concept with the features of individuality and diversity. Because of the generality feature, the category Multi-One can refer to an organic entity like the universe metaphorically and refer to any number of tiny things metaphorically, for instance, a piece of grass, and a single tree, if borrowing Zhu Xi's examples. In short, the multi in the category Multi-One can refer to any entity with the features of individuality, diversity, and multiplicity.

Multi-One is Multi-One, and its literal meanings are limited. How can it refer to any entities as abovementioned? It may not make sense if we used this concept in any other logical system and treated it as logical. Still, we are dealing with this category in the Chinese philosophical tradition in which metaphysical objects were metaphorically described, arguments mainly were conducted by analogical reasonings, and the goals of metaphysics were also metaphorically expressed—the Multi-One functions metaphorically, which is coherent with the tradition. Like Meta-One, Multi-One can analogically refer to any entity in which multiple things were enclosed; also, the similarity is like the logical premise, from which we conduct logical deductions and inference.

Based on the similarity between Multi-One and heaven-earth (*tiandi*天地) in ancient Chinese philosophy, the heaven-earth is a typical Multi-One entity. In ancient Chinese philosophy, heaven was the most popular, also as philosophers' favorite concept. It was much more popular than the concept of *dao* or *li*. Philosophers in almost all philosophical schools talked about heaven and earth. They endowed them with different meanings, like a personal god, a heavenly emperor[32] ruling heaven and the human world, the sky or space above the earth, the cosmos, or the universe. When combined with another word, *xia*, "下" under or below, it is shaped as a fixed term under heaven (*tianxia* 天下),[33] denoting the entire world or all people in the world. Aside from the legendary record about heaven and earth and how heaven and earth originated,[34] I consider its philosophical meanings. The core idea was that heaven covers everything, nothing is not under its cover, and the earth carries everything, and nothing is not carried by it. This idea appeared in *The Classic of Changes*, Laozi's *Daodejing*, Confucius's *Analects*, and many other classic texts with similar expressions. The heaven-earth covers all things, including the heavenly emperors, personalized gods, deities in the heavenly palace, sun, moon, stars, all things between heaven and earth, all natural things, humankind, animals, and all things on the earth. Heaven-earth was a Multi-One entity.

As an all-in-one entity, all the things in it are not just various but also are undergoing realizing themselves. All the abovementioned things were no longer potential existence, but all learned and continue to realize or specify themselves in heaven-earth. For easier understanding, I used the apple seed to analogize the Meta-One; for the Multi-One, the apple seed is no longer an appropriate analogy. Suppose we still need an example to analogize the Multi-One. In that case, applying a tree could be an example, as I mentioned in the previous discussion and mention again when discussing the dynamic process of Meta-One in the next chapter. Here, I stress that an apple tree is a typical Multi-One entity. It analogically conveys the meanings of the Multi-One, but does not equalize to and cannot replace it.

Since heaven-earth was already in the tradition of Chinese philosophy and functioned well when ancient Chinese philosophers talked about the cosmos or the entire world, why do we need the category Multi-One?

When we analyze the concept of heaven-earth from the metaphysical perspective, we find it is not an ideal metaphysical concept because of its disadvantages in its abstractness, generality, and eternality.

In the concept of heaven and earth, it does not matter if heaven refers to a heavenly palace, the physical sky, or space; what it can refer to are actual things. Both "multi" and "one" are abstract terms with abstractness. The heaven and earth are all particular existences, and although they cover everything in terms of its things, parts, members, or elements, the heaven-earth as an entity is individual; it is short of generality. Multi-One can metaphorically denote the heaven-earth and take it as a particular case to illustrate the meanings of Multi-One. Still, Multi-One is not limited to the individual example of heaven-earth. Still, functions analogically refer to any entities—like human society, a country, all people, any person, or even an apple tree—as expressed by the concept "under heaven" (*tianxia* 天下), because of its generality. Heaven-earth was derived from ancient people's empirical observation of the environments they lived in, but the eternal heavenly palace is unverifiable; all other components of the heaven-earth are changing—all things under heaven, between heaven and earth, and on the earth are changing. Multi-One is one, and the heaven-earth is also one. However, Multi-One possesses the feature of eternity in metaphysics because it does not refer to any existence, while the eternity of the heaven-earth is in the sense of physics or science because it refers explicitly to heaven and earth as physical existences.

The disadvantages of the concept of heaven-earth in the features of abstractness, generality, and eternity disqualified it from functions as a metaphysical concept in our system; we cannot deny its essential role as a fundamental ground from which philosophers withdrew invaluable philosophical, political, ethical, and moral principles of human behavior.

Among the functions of the Multi-One category, the essential function is to describe the dynamical process of all kinds of entities, including the dynamical process of the development of the universe, cosmos, natural world, human society, states, social organizations, and many tiny entities. We cannot deduce the dynamical processes from the Multi-One category since it is not a logical concept and cannot be treated as premises of logical reasoning. Still, it can be effectively metaphorically applied to the process in terms of similarities between the Multi-One and all kinds of entities in the system of metaphorical metaphysics. The primary rule is to find reliable similarities between the Multi-One and many entities.

UTTER-ONE: SOURCE, COMPONENT, AND FUNCTIONS

In this section, I trace the source of the category Utter-One, explore its components, and analyze its metaphorical functions. As mentioned, Meta-One refers to an entity where all elements potentially exist; all parts are formless, invisible, undescribed, and all in one without distinctions among elements. In the stage of Utter-One, all aspects realize themselves and become mutual in the same or a new entity, depending on what entity it describes. The category Multi-One signifies the ongoing process of all aspects realizing themselves. The category Utter-One (*quanyi*) denotes a fulfilled entity in which the continuous processes are approaching their ends and achieving potential goals in the stage of Meta-One and growing up in Multi-One.

Utter- and One: Trace to Source

Although Multi-One is neither an existing category nor a historical category in Chinese philosophical tradition, it is rooted in and developed by traditional Chinese philosophy. Ancient Chinese philosophers directly or indirectly used the word "complete" (*quan* 全) or "entirety," which partially implied the meaning of the prefix "Utter." I use the prefix to emphasize the core concept of one and create the category Utter-One. I would prioritize Laozi, Zhuangzi, Zhou Dunyi, Zhu Xi, and Feng Youlan to explore the source of the Utter-One category.

Completeness in One: Laozi and Zhuangzi

According to Zhuangzi, Confucius told his disciple Yan Hui, "I do not know the entirety of the heaven and earth (*wub u zhi tiandi zhi daquan ye*吾不知天地之大全也)."[35] Although we can not find any more discussion about the daquan (great entirety) in the books Zhuangzi and Analects, we can see from this statement that thinking of heaven and earth is in a metaphysical dimension. Feng Youlan used the concept of "great entirety" (*daquan* 大全) in his New Metaphysics of Li. I will discuss Feng's concept of *da quan* 大全 later.

Laozi talked about *quan* 全 (completion), but not in the sense I am concerned with, so I would skip his discourses about *quan*. Instead, I would pick up his discussion about "one" and assume that Laozi indirectly touched upon the implication of completion (*quan*) when he elaborated on one, which is partially related to the category I proposed Utter-One. Laozi said, "Of old, these attained One: Heaven attaining One Became clear. Earth attaining One Became stable. Spirits attaining One Became sacred. Valleys attaining One Became bountiful. Myriad beings attaining One Became fertile. Lords and kings attained One Purified the world."[36] We may read from Laozi's discourse that if heaven and earth achieved one, all things under heaven and on the earth would reach harmony, heaven would be clear, and the world would turn serene. All things under heaven and on earth fulfilled their mission and realized themselves; they found their correct positions, and one corresponds to another. We can imagine that if all things under heaven and the earth conflict, fight with each other, and overcome one another . . . heaven and earth must not yet attain or reach One. In my understanding, the one that heaven and earth, rulers and lords wanted to achieve implies the component of unification or amalgamation, which partially denotes the meaning of completion.

Zhuangzi also did not talk about completion *quan* 全 in the metaphysical dimension directly, but when he discussed one, his one implied the meaning of completion. Zhuangzi said, "Heaven, Earth, and I were produced together, and all things and I are one. Since they are one, can there be a speech about them? But since they are spoken of as one, must there not be room for speech? One and Speech are two; two and one are three."[37] In this context, Zhuangzi's one is one with completeness. Nothing is outside the one; the one cannot be spoken. Once you talk about the one, you create two, one is the one, and another is the speech of one. Since there is a speech outside the one, the one is no longer the one that nothing is outside. The one is no longer complete. In this sense, Zhuangzi's "one" is a metaphysical concept. The oneness and completeness are essential features of Utter-One. If we trace back to its source, I will assert that Utter-One is partially incorporated into Zhuangzi's concept of one.

The category Utter-One incorporates the component of Zhuangzi's one but further emphasizes that Utter-One is an entity fulfilled with mutual and realized elements which were developed from a potential state via a growing/developing stage to the mutilated state. The most important feature of the Utter-One is that it implies the implications of relative completion, fulfillment, mutuality, realization, and specification, and meanwhile, it predicates a new beginning. In the following chapters, I discuss these when we characterize the category Utter-One from a dynamic perspective.

In addition, Zhuangzi talked about *quan* "全" in the sense of morality, not the metaphysical dimension. His quan included virtue, body, and spirit. He said those who embraced *dao* have complete virtue (*dequan* 德全) and have entire bodies and souls.[38] If we regard these people as unique entities, they were fulfilled with virtue and possessed the feature of completion.

If we say that Pre-Qin philosophers indirectly discussed *quan* (completion) or not yet endowed the word *quan* with full metaphysical features, the philosophers in the Song Dynasty made significant progress in shaping the concept.

Concept of Entirety: Zhou Dunyi and Zhu Xi

Before Zhu Xi, Zhou Dunyi directly talked about the *quan* and elaborated on the *quan* in the metaphysical dimension. He said: in thinking of the division of *yin* and *yang*, each thing has its nature, but in the sense of unification of *yin* and *yang*, the myriad things were unified into a great ultimate; since everything has its grand ultimate, and each has its nature, and each has its entirety/complete unity, and all existed in each thing. Nothing existed outside of nature, and nature existed elsewhere. He called it the noumenon of nature (*xing zhi benti* 性之本体).[39] It seems to Zhou the Five Elements/agents (*wuxing* 五行, metal, wood, water, fire, earth) are just a *yin* and *yang*; the *yin-yang* is a great ultimate; the grand ultimate was originally the ultimate of nonbeing. Each of the Five Elements has its nature, and the entire grand ultimate exists in each of all things. In this discourse, Zhou regarded the grand ultimate as a complete entity, but he did not use the word *quan* (全) in this discourse.

Zhou Dunyi used *quan* when he elaborated on the substance or entirety of *dao*. He said, "so-called the completion of the substance of *dao*, all unanimously in one unity; but filigree and coarse, the ins and outs, all radiantly existed in it without tiny errors. This is what sages said; either separated or united, either different or the same. We called this the completion of the substance/entirety of *dao* (*daoti zhiquan* 道体之全)"[40] It seems to me Zhou's completion of the entirety of *dao* implied the following stimulative implications: he described the relationship among all things or multiple elements in the whole of *dao*, the entirety of *dao* is not an empty concept, but an entity made up of all parts or components, and we can read from his description of the whole of *dao* the metaphysical feature completeness. All these implications are important sources for me in proposing the category Utter-One.

Zhou Dunyi's concepts of *quan* and *quanti* are stimulative, but we cannot simply take his concepts into our system. I humbly keep using the term *quan* when creating the category Utter-One, but further characterize it as a metaphysical concept beyond his concepts of *yin yang*, nature, and the great ultimate, which he interpreted as just *yin* and *yang*. When we discuss the components of the Utter-One, I will continue explaining what we endowed into the category.

Based on the valuable work of Zhang Zai, Zhou Dunyi, and the two Cheng brothers, Zhu Xi delivered profound discourses about *quan* (completeness) or *quanti* (entirety), from which the category Utter-One inherited the metaphysical feature of completeness. Because of the limited space, I summarize his detailed discourses and relevant arguments as the following points.

Zhu Xi elaborated on the entirety (wholeness of *dao*, *daozhi quanti* 道之全体) when he talked about the essence of *Dao*. He said, "The essence of Tao is an all-encompassing wholeness which contains everything, and which is contained in everything."[41] In his commentaries on *The Doctrine of Mean*, he interpreted large and small from the perspective of morality, saying that the *dao* of gentlemen/superior men was too profound to be achieved. This entire discourse referred to all moral principles the gentlemen/supermen should follow theoretically but practically even sages can not accomplish ultimately. Ultimately, even sages could not reach the utmost. His entirety of *dao* implied multiple ethical principles, so his entirety is not empty, but an entity fulfilled with profound components. Zhu Xi also discussed the metaphysical feature of the wholeness of the mind from the epistemology perspective. It seemed to him an endless process to gain knowledge by investigating things, but if you insist on working on it and never stop, you could gain all kinds of knowledge about different things.

Zhu Xi claimed that human nature is common and the same for all people and other things. In human nature, the distinctions among people and other things consisted only of the *qi* (vital force, material force, or vital energy). He said, "the nature of human beings and other things fundamentally are the same; they only differ because of their respective endowments of *qi*."[42] In Zhou Dunyi, nature was inborn; for Zhu Xi, nature means *li,* as we mentioned, so the entire nature referred to the nature that the sages inherited from heaven or possessed inborn. I value the point that humans have a common nature because the common nature makes humans an entity different from all others, like other animals.

Zhu Xi described the universal principle (*li*) as a complete wholeness in which four virtues were implied. He stated, "universal principle [*li*] is indeed complete wholeness. However, we call it a principle because it has a completely ordered pattern. Therefore, [the four innate virtues of] humanity, rectitude, propriety, and wisdom within it each have their own principle without disorder or confusion."[43] In this discourse, Zhu Xi distinguished between general *li* and individual *li* and claimed that the general *li* contained individual *li*. When he discussed other topics, like the virtues of heaven, the earth, and the virtue of sage, he issued similar ideas. For instance, when commenting on the *Doctrine of Mean*, he accepted its ideas about the distinction between great and mirror virtues. He believed that sage's virtue is like the *dao* of heaven and earth; heaven covers myriad things, and the earth carries all things; all things between heaven and earth growing synonymously will not harm each other, like the four seasons changing in order, like the sun and moon lighting alternatingly. The great virtue is always sincere; the little virtue runs like rivers restlessly and never conflicts. The great virtue is the root of minor nature, and the mirror natures are the division of the great virtue. In these discourses, the great virtue was regarded as an entity in which profound little virtues were enclosed.

We may find from Zhu Xi's discourses about the totalities of *dao*, mind, nature, and virtue that he kept using the term "*quan* 全" (complete/total) to entitle the distinct entities, which intensively stimulated and encouraged me to choose the concept *quan* (全) when I proposed the category Utter-One, and use utter- to emphasize the substantial meanings of One. Utter-One is not a rootless invention but an alternative continuation of the traditional concept. Although it is understandable to Westernize Chinese philosophical tradition, I believe that inheriting and developing tradition is a primary approach. For reconstructing metaphorical metaphysics in Chinese philosophical tradition, we should not stop at what Zhu Xi has achieved.

Zhu Xi elaborated on the entirety of *dao* in the sense of morality. We deeply benefited from his thinking of the totality, although we did not directly accept those concepts into our system. The whole of nature was related to human attributes, the entire mind dealt with humans' ability to recognize, and the entirety of virtue talked about humans' ethical relationships. All those concepts are Zhu Xi's contribution to philosophy, but these concepts have not yet reached the dimension of metaphysics.

Concept of Great Entirety: Feng Youlan

Based on Cheng-Zhu's doctrine of *li*, with the admiration of the abstractness of metaphysics in Western philosophy, Feng Youlan continued talking about completeness/entirety (*quan*) in his *New Doctrine of Li* and *New Doctrine of Original Dao* (*The Spirit of Chinese Philosophy*). According to Feng, there are fundamental things like this table, that cat . . . all real things belong to what he called the "real realm" (*zhenji* 真际), and the names "table," "cat," or "square" belong to "realm of truthiness." The former is real but not true; the latter is true but not real. He located the concept "completeness/entirety" in the realm or sphere of truthiness, which comprised class names like "cat" and the biggest common name like "matter" in terms of the classification of names, the realm of truthiness comprised *li*, the *li* of class like square, round, and the *li* of the myriad things. The realm of truthiness denotes the entirety (completeness) when thinking of it as a complete entity. Feng's *quan* (whole) and *da quan* (great totality) refer to the cosmos, but the cosmos is not the cosmos in physics or astrology. He stressed that the physical universe is part of the great entirety (*daquan* 大全). In short, the same as *li* and other concepts in his system, the great whole is a formal concept (*xingshi de guannian* 形式底观念) and is empty (*kongde guannian* 空底观念).[44] These concepts existed independently of naturalism, all natural things, and they made judgments by judgments about real things.

Feng Youlan made significant efforts to create pure logical concepts to meet the requirement of abstractness. His work made considerable progress in constructing metaphysics. Although the concept of *da quan* appeared as early as in Zhuangzi, and the concept of *quan* was widely used by ancient philosophers, Feng's elaboration of *da quan* directly stimulated me to propose the category Utter-One. When suggesting the category Utter-One, I kept the word *quan* and took abstractness as a primary feature of the category Utter-One. However, Utter-One differs from Feng Youlan's concept of the great entirety ("*daquan*"). Utter-One is not a purely formal concept *n*or empty. It is fulfilled with profound components, including the implications of completeness, totality, and fulfillment. With high respect for his work, I try to move a small step on this topic by suggesting the category Utter-One.

Utter-One is an abstract metaphysical category, but it is not empty; as a metaphysical category, it is incorporated with the core idea of the *quan* 全 expressed in *The Doctrine of Mean*, *Zhuang Zi*, Zhou Dunyi's writings, Zhu Xi's commentaries, and Feng Youlan's *New Doctrine of Li*. Utter-One signifies an entity in which two attributions are unified; as a metaphysical category, it is fulfilled with the metaphysical features of completeness, totality, entirety, fulfillment, realization, development, specification, and a new beginning; as an object of metaphysics, it can refer to any entities in reality.

For instance, Feng Youlan distinguished between the cosmos in the sense of physics/astrology and the cosmos in the sense of philosophy. In our system, there is only one physical universe. We may think of the physical cosmos from a metaphysical perspective, asserting that it is ultimately large and nothing is outside it. In thinking, we conceptualized the physical cosmos and dealt with it with thought. We do not need to practically measure how large it is. We may observe the physical cosmos from astrological or physical perspectives, practically watching it through an astronomical telescope or describing its size with light years. When we use Utter-One metaphorically, we refer to the physical cosmos in terms of similarities. All things in the cosmos were developed and are still developing, corresponding to Utter-One's concept. All things were realized and are still realizing themselves with one unity, which is the cosmos. There is no separate realm of truthiness and realm of reality. The components of the metaphysical category Utter-One are conceptualizations of all diversities in the cosmos; once we take those conceptualized diversities into thinking, they exist as concepts, images, impressions, and so on. When we observe the physical cosmos from a physical or astrological perspective and use the category Utter-One to refer to it, all physical attributions of the cosmos are real, empirical, and practical. There is only one physical cosmos, but we could have a conceptualized concept of the cosmos and the physical cosmos from which all conceptualized components are derived. Utter-One can signify a conceptualized entity like the abstract entity "cosmos" and can also refer to any physical entities like the physical cosmos metaphysically if there are similarities between Utter-One and the entities. Utter-One can unify the conceptualized cosmos and the physical cosmos or, broadly, unify Feng Youlan's realm of truthiness and the realm of reality; the entire secretary comprises the metaphysical feature "oneness" implied in the category Utter-One. The physical cosmos is one, a conceptualized abstract entity, "cosmos" is also one. Oneness is the highest common divider or common feature.

I am just taking Feng Youlan's "cosmos," which was excluded from the philosophical cosmos in Feng Youlan's system, as an example to explain there are essential differences between Feng's *quan* nitride) or *daquan* 大全 (great entirety) and Utter-One. However, Feng's ideas are crucial sources and significantly stimulated us in shaping the category Utter-One.

Further discussion about this issue leads us to explore the components of the category Utter-One.

Components of Utter-One

Utter-One signifies One in which multiple elements are multiplied and developed. As a category, it possesses profound components, including the completeness or entirety, wholeness or totality, fulfillment or realization, and the beginning of a new beginning.

As a critical component of Utter-One, the completeness or entirety was derived from all completed individual things. The completeness includes two primary implications. First, it means all things continue individualizing themselves and reach their individualization. Second, Utter-One is an entity in which all things are included, and nothing is not excluded. We may say that the physical cosmos includes all individualized things. They have already become what they are, although many other things simultaneously individualize themselves. The cosmos is complete, and nothing is not enclosed in it. In the sense of philosophy, the cosmos implies the component of completeness. Let's agree with Feng Youlan that the physical universe is just part of the cosmos in the sense of philosophy. It is questionable if we say the physical universe is part of the philosophical universe because the universe in philosophy must be a conceptualized entity existing as a concept. In contrast, the physical cosmos objectively exists there. In our system, completeness as the component and metaphysical feature is derived from the individualized things and the complete physical cosmos. The completeness is not *li*, not a common name isolated from all natural things, nor an empty concept as a common class name.

As another essential component, wholeness or totality (use wholeness) differs from completeness. Wholeness denotes that each developed individual thing is a whole unity, and each has its nature; each differs from another, and the entity in which all developed individual things exist is complete. When we observe the entire entity as a physical existence, it is fulfilled with all grown individual things. The entity will individually be the advanced individual things, and all developed individual things have grown complete entity. Strictly speaking, all the developed individuals with oneness have become what they are; individually, there is neither "whole entity" nor wholeness in the physical world. However, all grown individual things coexisted in the whole entity, so they connect and interact with each other positively or negatively. They are not isolated from one another. Because of the coexistence, the "whole entity" has a solid foundation, and "wholeness" has its source. When we conceptualize the complete physical entity and the developed individual things, we think of all these and create concepts like entire entities and single unities in English, which could be any other names in other languages. The concepts like completeness, totality, and wholeness are all products of thinking via conceiving physical existences, like the cosmos. The wholeness as the component and metaphysical feature of the Utter-One category is not empty. It denotes one element of any entity, not just the cosmos, and it is the component of the Utter-One, as the metaphysical category can metaphorically refer to any entity.

Realization or fulfillment as one component of Utter-One emphasizes the feature of the ending stage of the process, which differs from the completeness and wholeness we have discussed. Since we are analyzing the entities that the Utter-One is from a static perspective, we ignore the process but concentrate on the ending stage of the process. Compared with Multi-One, which signifies the multiple things in growing, individualizing, and developing themselves, Utter-One represents individual things that have realized themselves and are approaching the ending stage. As a category, Multi-One focuses on conceptualizing the results of any long process, like the evolution of the cosmos and any tiny entities like an insect growing up and reaching maturity. Utter-One does not examine any practical results, maturity, or ending stages, but its components are derived from those and denote their significance. The category Utter-One conceptualizes the entities that are fulfilled with realized or matured individual things and their fulfilments; Utter-One is not empty because of its profound components.

If we take the physical cosmos as an entity and observe it from a static perspective, when we observe today's cosmos, all things are what they are, coexist together, and all are matured broadly. However, when we investigate the cosmos, we find many things are in the state before they are born. Many things are growing up, changing, and developing and are far from mature. Many things are in their ending stages and have reached maturity . . . if we examine the cosmos in a broader scope, we might find that there is another cosmos, or cosmos existed; we may call them parallel cosmoses. Thus, we face two changes. One is that not all things in the cosmos are mature, and another is that the cosmos may not be single. Then how can the Utter-One deal with the challenges?

Both challenges argue against the critical concept *quan* (utter) in the category Utter-One. When Utter-One signifies an entity like the cosmos, it takes the entire cosmos as a metaphysical object. It conceptualizes it in thinking, so what it denotes is an entity as the whole of the "cosmos." The Utter-One does not detail which thing in the cosmos is still growing and which is already matured. As we repeatedly stress, Utter-One (and the other two categories) can metaphorically refer to any entities in which all things are developed or maturated but do not explicitly refer to any entity. When we apply the category Utter-One to signify the cosmos, we conceive it as a whole entity and characterize it as maturated: it exists, it specified itself, it realized what it is, and fulfilled with developed things, the cosmos becomes a cosmos already. Since Utter-One can metaphorically refer to any entity, can we apply the category Utter-One to an apple seed? Certainly not, because it does not meet the primary requirement for the analogical method, which is similarity. The first challenge urges us to consider the complexity of the components of the category Utter-One, abide by the rules of analogical methods, and apply the category coherently.

The second challenge may change the scientific view of the physical universe but cannot shake philosophers' belief about the *quan* (utter). Even scientists discovered another cosmos; for philosophers, *quan* means completeness, wholeness, or totality. No matter how many cosmoses are found, when philosophers apply the category Utter-One to present the cosmos or cosmoses, all fall into the concept of completeness. In the sense of philosophy, especially in the metaphysical dimension, a conceptualized cosmos has the feature of completeness, which as the component, was derived from the developed things in the cosmos. Once one or more cosmoses are discovered, the discoveries increase the components of the category but do not change the category Utter-One itself. As an empirical term, *quan* means complete, whole, or totals; as a metaphysical concept, *quan* (utter) implies completeness, wholeness, or totality and theoretically means nothing is outside it, nothing is not enclosed it, or nothing is not part of it. According to these definitions, if scientists discovered a parallel cosmos, the two cosmoses are parts of one cosmos; if more is found, more elements are included. The discoveries enriched the concept of "cosmos" components but cannot change the nature of the category Utter-One. It is scientists' task to change the definition of the cosmos in terms of discoveries; philosophers are concerned with completeness, wholeness, or totality. If anything is found outside an entity, then that entity is not complete, and the concept of that entity does not possess the feature of completeness, wholeness, or totality. Utter-One is not a logical concept, but it shows logical, solid power when appropriately dealing with the second challenge.

The components of Utter-One differ from those of Meta-One and Multi-One. The components of Meta-One were derived from potential diversities of all things, the components of Multi-One were derived from developing diversities of all things, and the components of Utter-One were derived from maturated diversities of all things.

Metaphorical Functions of Utter-One

I believe that two aspects affect the functions of Utter-One and the other two categories. Utter-One is a metaphysical category, the same as Meta-One and Multi-One; it is not a logical concept and does not function as a logical premise from which we deduce a reliable conclusion. For logical reasoning, philosophers are concerned with the primary premise and procedure. We are concerned with the similarities and the conclusions for analogical reasoning. We cannot conduct effective reasoning without similarities between the Utter-One and the entities we will analogize.

First, the primary function of analogical reasoning is to interpret existing knowledge, but not to increase new knowledge. Its primary function is to use existing knowledge to explain new ideas or knowledge. Just like logical deductive reasoning, like (p → q); p │ q (If P, then q); p, therefore q), or (p → q); (q → r); │ p →r (If P, then q); (if q, then r), q, therefore r). The function of Utter-One is based on the analogy and signifies an entity metaphorically. The knowledge as the premise of analogy and the knowledge as the result or conclusion is all existing knowledge. They were correct independently before involving analogical reasoning. Philosophers analogized one with another, not aiming to increase new knowledge of them but to interpret one with another.

The second aspect that affected the function of Utter-One is that most results or conclusions were related to human ethical and moral behavior but not about knowledge and truth of the world, and focused on what people should or ought to do in terms of particular ethical and moral principles derived from other things like heaven or earth. Since heaven covers everything and earth carries on all things, humans should act like heaven and earth to be generality and tolerant with open minds and enormous love. The conclusions aimed to educate people to learn from heaven and earth, belonging to value, not truth. The personalized behaviors of heaven and earth were the grounds based on which philosophers withdrew the conclusions metaphorically.

Unlike Western tradition, Chinese people and philosophers draw analogies between things with similar characteristics to reach metaphorical conclusions. Here is an example: A has 1) two legs, 2) can walk, 3) can think, 4) can conduct reasoning; B has1) two legs, 2) can walk, 3) can think, 4) . . . We may get a probable conclusion: B can conduct reasoning. As a plausible conclusion, it may be true or maybe untrue. In daily life, for instance, a computer and a human, based on hardware similarities with the human body, the software is like the human brain in terms of its functions, not shapes, so Chinese people call computer *diannao* 电脑 (electronic brain). In philosophy, Laozi said, *Shangshan ruoshui*上善若水 (the utmost good as like water). Goodness is a personal value that belongs to humans. Laozi drew an analogy between human nature and the characteristics of water. Water benefits myriad things but never takes advantage of all things. Thus, we humans should learn from water. This is not a logical conclusion, just a metaphorical conclusion and a suggestive idea. It is reliable since there is a similarity between water characteristics and human values and human morality. Philosophers from all schools widely used this primary and popular philosophical method.

Utter-One as a metaphysical category. Is it possible to draw analogies between the category and different real things since the former belongs to metaphysics while the others belong to physical existence? We can make analogies with all kinds of things based on their components and functions to refer to things with similar characteristics and features. Those metaphorical functions are rooted in the category, not external interpretations. The Utter-One implied the component and metaphysical features like completeness, wholeness, totality, maturity, and Oneness.

According to the methods from which Chinese philosophers drew analogies mentioned above, we may analogize Utter-One with any entities that possess similar features and are fulfilled with multiple mutilated or developed elements. Let's borrow legs from You Lan's example, "table." In our system, a table is just an example that Utter-One could metaphorically refer to. When a staff is called a table, all parts of that staff are shaped, realized, and all aspects are included in the entity, like legs, the desktop of the table, and so on. Those parts have been realized and developed from the carpenter's potential ideas, images, and designing pictures to a complete physical table. When we put "table" into thinking, we do not need to move the physical table in front of us. We conceptualized it as an entity with profound components derived from its parts, shape, size, color, and materials. This example supported the function of the Utter-One: Utter-One, as a metaphysical category, can metaphorically refer to any entity fulfilled with developed elements, but it does not explicitly refer to any entity.

When we explore the functions of Utter-One from the goals or purpose of the metaphorical metaphysics, we discussed in the previous chapter that the metaphorical conclusions mainly serve for the value of human life and happiness of human life by making distinct suggestions. For example, "Stable as Mountain Tai" (*wenru taishan*稳如泰山) is a metaphorical conclusion and a suggestive idea derived from the analogy between the mountain and humans' characteristics. We found that the Mountain Tai as a whole entity is very stable and never moves or shakes under any conditions of weather, from which we found similar features that humans needed: to be stable and face any challenges or risks, we should learn from the Mountain Tai to be stable no matter what happened around us. The principles of behavior in Chinese philosophical tradition are suggestive ideas, and most were derived from analogies of the characteristics of heaven, earth, water, physical staff like jade, tools, and countless natural things—sincerity, faintness, benevolence, civility, wisdom, loyalty, braveness, and so on. Behind almost every moral principle, we may find another thing from which philosophers drew suggestive ideas or set up mandatory rules. I mean by "suggestive ideas" that those ideas educate what people should do or should be like the analogized things because "should" is the core of suggestive statements. This feature makes Utter-One functions different from pursuing truth in the western philosophical tradition and from mandatory rules of behavior issued by political authorities.

Utter-One comprises the components of mutualization, entirety, generality, and so forth; it can metaphorically refer to all kinds of entities that are fulfilled with multiple realized elements with the features of whole and generality. We do not need to exemplify this one by one. One point needs to be stressed here: Different from Feng Youlan's completeness (*quan* 全) and One (*yi* 一), Utter-One not just functions to refer to abstract entirety and one but also functions to refer to any particular things that possess similar features: a maturated person, an established government, an established social organization, the entire world when we view it as an entity from a static angle, namely at a certain point of time, this year, today, this movement . . . , ignoring it is an ongoing process which will be viewed from a dynamical perspective. When we consider all these entities, we need to conceptualize them with the categories we created; Utter-One is just one of them.

In this chapter, we have traced back to the source of the categories Meta-One, Multi-One, and Utter-One. I claimed traditional philosophical concepts provided profound sources to promote the three metaphysical categories. Still, the traditional concepts have disadvantages and cannot be taken into our system. By doing so, while I examined the historical source, I analyzed the necessity of improving traditional concepts and proposing new categories. I then reviewed the components of the three categories from static perspectives and held dynamic analyses of the three categories for the next chapter. Based on the analyses of the components of the categories, I exemplified some metaphorical functions of the three categories and lightly clarified that the categories Meta-One, Muti-One, and Utter-One are the same as many other traditional concepts; they are targeted to conceptualize particular real things—like an insect, an animal, physical stuff like a tale, more complex things like a social organization, the entire world, the cosmos—to meet new demands of our knowing and thinking of the world. Since ancient Greece, ancient China, and all other traditions, philosophers continuously create new categories. When we discuss the Meta-One, Multi-One, and Utter-One, we treat them as concepts and analyze them from a static perspective, but essentially from Meta-One via Multi-One to Utter-One the same as the ultimate of nonbeing to grand ultimate is a dynamic process which is discussed in the following chapter.

NOTES

1. *Shuowen Jiezi*《説文解字》 *Explain the Graphs and Unravel the Written Words*, noted by Duan Yucai (段玉裁), edited by Xu Shen (许慎), and collated by Xu Weixian (许惟贤) (Nan Jing: Feng Huan Press, 2007), 1.

2. 乾：元, 亨, 利, 貞. *The Classic of Changes* (*Yjing* 《易经》), There are different translations of the four characters. For example, "Origin, penetrate, bounty, and inexhaustible" or "All origins penetrating everywhere, heaven is inexhaustible in bringing forth wild bounty." *I Ching: The Book of Changes*, translated by David Hinton (New York: Farrar, Straus and Giroux, 2015), xvi. I would use Lynn's translation. "Begin with an offering; beneficial to divine." *The I Ching (Book of Changes): A Critical Translation of the Ancient Text*, translated by Geoffrey Redmond (London: Bloomsbury Academic Publishing, 2017), 63.

3. *The Classic of Changes: A New Translation of the I Chinese as Interpreted by Wang Bi*, translated by Richard John Lynn (New York: Columbia University Press, 1994), 129.

4. Ibid., 130.

5. Ibid.

6. Laozi, *Daodejing: A Literal-Critical Translation*, translated by Joseph Hsu (Lanham, MD: University Press of America, 2008), 23. According to Laozi, all the true attributes of One are beyond description, so Laozi negatively describes what One looks like. *Dao* is beyond description, as the code of *Dao*, one accordingly is beyond description. Since the One is the code of *Dao*, comprehending the One is the key to recognizing *Dao*.

7. Sun Xidan (孙希旦), *Liji Jijie* 《礼记集解》 中册 *Collections of Commentaries of the Records of Rituals*, vol. 2 (Beijing: Zhong Hua Shu Ju, 1998), 906–07.

8. *The Four Books*, translated by James Legge (Hong Kong: Hui Tung Book Store, 1969), 260.

9. Mengzi said, "What is common to all hearts? Reason and rightness." Mengzi, *Mencius*. trans. with an introduction by D. C. Lau (London: Penguin Books, 1970), 164.

10. *The Analects*, translated by Simon Leys, edited by Michael Nylan (Berkeley: University of California Press, 2014), 42.

11. Zhu Xi, *Further Reflections on Things at Hand*, translated by Allen Wittenborn (Lanham, MD: University Press of America, 1991), 62.

12. Zhu Xi, *Reflections on Things at Hand: The Neo-Confucian Anthology Compiled by Chu Hsi and Lu Tsu-Chien*, translated with notes by Wing-Tsit Chan (New York: Columbia University Press, 1967), 29.

13. Zhu Xi said, "动而生阳，亦只是理；静而生阴，亦只是理." Zhu Xi (朱熹), *Zhu Zi Yu Lei* 《朱子语类》《太极天地上》, vol. 1, edited by Jingde Li (Jingdu: Chinese Press, 1979), 147.

14. Zhu Xi, *Further Reflections on Things at Hand*, 66.

15. Zhu Xi said, 子贡曰："夫子之文章，可得而闻也；夫子之言性与天道，不可得而闻也。Zhu Xi" 性者，人所受之天理；天道者，天理自然之本体，其实一理也。" Zhu Xi (朱熹), *Zhu Zi Yu Lei*, vol. 1《朱子语类》上卷, edited by Li Jingde Li (Jingdu: Chinese Press, 1979), 437.

16. Zhu Xi, *Reflections on Things at Hand*, 16.

17. Zhu Xi, *Chu His: Learning to Be a Sage: Selected from the Conversations of Master Chu, Arranged Topically*, translated by Daniel K. Gardner (Berkeley: University of California Press, 1990), 15.

18. Ibid.

19. Ibid., 10.

20. *Liyi fenshu*理一分殊。Roger T. Armes translated it as "*Li* is one but its instantiations many." *Returning to Zhu Xi*, edited by David Jones and Jinli He (Albany: State University of New York Press, 2015), 2. Andrew Lambert translated 月影万川 as "The Moon has a thousand reflections in rivers." Zhu Xi, *Chu His: Learning to Be a Sage*, 19.

21. Chan Wing-Tsit, *A Source Book of Chinese Philosophy* (Princeton, NJ: Princeton University Press, 1969), 474.

22. Zhu Xi said, "The nature is simply patter-principle." Zhu Xi, *Selected Writings*, edited by Philip J. Ivanhoe (Oxford: Oxford University Press, 2019), 18.

23. Zhu Xi, *Reflections on Things at Hand*, 19.

24. Zhu Xi said, "What makes Heaven Heaven is nothing other than pattern-Principle [*li*]. If Heaven did not have these pattern-principle, it would not be Heaven. Thus, the blue sky is just this Heaven of pattern-principles." Zhu Xi, *Selected Writings*, 118.

25. *Zhuzi Yulei*《朱子语类》上卷. Citations of Zhu Xi, vol. 1. Edited by Jingde Li. Jingdu: Chinese Press, 1979, p. 411.

26. Zhu Xi, *Further Reflections on Things at Hand*, 59.

27. Zhu Xi, *Zhu Zi Yu Lei*, vol. 1, 1979), 416. 朱熹《朱子语类》上卷（京都：中文出版社，1979 年第 416页。

28. Ibid., 418.

29. Ibid., 714.

30. Feng, Youlan (冯友兰), *San Song Tang Quanji* (《三松堂全集》*Complete Works of Feng Youlan*, edited by Cai Zhongde (蔡仲德)，vol. 4 (Zheng Zhou: Henan Remin Chubanshe, 2000), 40–41.

31. Feng Youlan, *Complete Works*, vol. 4, 38–41.

32. Derong Chen, "Di 帝 and Tian 天in Ancient Chinese Thought: A Critical Analysis of Hegel's Views" (English), *Dao: A Journal of Comparative Philosophy* 8, no.1 (March 2009): 13–27. Springer.

33. This concept has different meanings. I classify the use and implication of the term into three aspects: 1) "Under heaven" referred to society, which comprises all families. Just one example, in the diagram (*Jia Ren*家人) in *Yi Jing*, it said, "When a family is in a proper state, then all under Heaven is in a stable condition." *The Complete I Ching: The Definitive Translation by the Taoist Master Alfred Huang* (Rochester, VT: Inner Traditions International, 1998), 307. When Laozi noted there is a *dao* and no *dao* under heaven, his *Dao* referred to society. 2) "Under heaven" referred to the entire country or entire kingdom. Zhuang Zi's writings, like many other philosophers, used the term "under heaven" a lot; it basically meant the old country, such as *zhi tian xia*治天下, which meant to rule the country. Tian *xia zhi* 天下治 (namely, the country was governed well, and so forth. 3) "Under heaven" referred to all people. Many philosophers used the term *Tian Xia* to refer to all people under heaven but omitted the word *ren* 人 (people). For example, Mozi claimed to love all the people in heaven. 兼爱天下*Jian Ai Tian Xia*. Mozi also said that "王天下," "立为天子" "to be a king of all the people Under Heaven." *The Mozi: A Complete Translation*, translated by Ian Johnston (New York: Columbia University Press, 2010), 14–15. The three uses of the term "under heaven" have a common feature: it refers to a particularity in

which multiple things were included; for instance, a society is an entity in which all kinds of social organizations are included.

34. For example, ancient Chinese believed heaven and earth had the same source and were congealed from *qi*. "According to early philosophers, both heaven and earth are components of the *qi*." Hu Jia Xiang, *Basic Principles of Chinese Philosophy*, vol. 1 (Singapore: Would Scientific Publishing Co., 2019), 93.

35. Zhuangzi, *The Book of Chuang Tzu*, translated by Martin Palmer with Elizabeth Breuilly (London: Penguin Group, 1996), 181.

36. Laozi, *Daodejing: A Literal-Critical Translation*, 65.

37. Zhuangzi, *The Texts of Taoism*, vols. 1 and 2, translated by James Legge (Singapore: Tynron Press & Graham Brash, 1989), 188.

38. Ibid., 321.

39. Zhou Dunyi （周敦颐）, *Zhou Dunyi Ji*《周敦颐集》*The Collections of Zhou Dunyi*, noted by Chen Keming （陈克明） (Beijing: Zhong Hua Shu Ju, 1990), 4–5.

40. Ibid., 8.

41. Zhu Xi, *Further Reflections on Things at Hand*, 59.

42. Zhu Xi, *Zhu Xi: Selected Writings*, 17.

43. Zhu Xi, *Further Reflections on Things at Hand*, 59.

44. Feng Youlan, *The Complete Works*, vol. 5, 125–33.

Chapter Three

Corresponding Harmony in Meta-One

This chapter is comprised of three parts: analyzing the dynamical process, discussing the corresponding dynamic harmony, and following with the principles of multiple corresponding harmonies from a static perspective. When we proposed three metaphorical, metaphysical categories, Meta-One, Multi-One, and Utter-One, we first traced the source from which the three categories were developed and then explored the components and metaphorical functions of the three categories from a static point of view. Now I would analyze the three categories from a dynamic perspective and characterize the corresponding harmony throughout the dynamical process from Meta-One via Multi-One to Utter-One.

META-ONE VIA MULTI-ONE TO UTTER-ONE

When we explore Meta-One from a dynamic perspective, we shape a metaphysical proposition from Meta-One via Multi-One to Utter-One. This proposition conceptualizes the dynamical process from an entity with potentiality via an entity with developing diversities to an entity with completeness. The process from Meta-One via Multi-One to Utter-One makes up a latitude route, and different corresponding harmony makes up a longitude. The process is not empty, but a latitude fulfilled with various corresponding harmony like longitudes. In this part, I analyze the dynamic process from Meta-One to Multi-One first and then from Multi-One to Utter-One.

Meta-One to Multi-One

In the dynamic process, the first stage is from Meta-One to Multi-One. This is also a process of all elements within the entity realizing themselves from potential states. In Chinese philosophical tradition, philosophers talked about this issue differently; the ideas about Meta-One and Multi-One are developed from tradition but enriched with new content. In this section, I examine traditional ideas and explain why we need a unique expression from Meta-One to Multi-One.

Potentials to Individuals: Tradition

Meta-One is a metaphysical category conceptualized in which all individuals, parts, or elements were undivided, unindividualized, unrealized, and coexisted as potentials; Multi-One conceptualizes any entity in which all individuals, parts, or elements individualize, develop, or realize themselves. The process from Meta-One to Multi-One is a process in which all potentials individualize themselves, and all potentials transform into individuals. We have set up the beginning of the beginning as a metaphysical hypothesis and left room for new generations and humankinds, so Meta-One is the beginning of Multi-One, and Multi-One is the development of Meta-One.

There is no existing theory expressed above in the Chinese philosophical tradition. Still, if we interpret the tradition from the perspective we are concerned with, we find that there are profound sources.

First, we can find the idea of potentiality, which is the essential feature of Meta-One from traditional philosophical concepts. Ancient philosophers in many academic schools, like the *yin-yang* school, Daoism, Confucianism, and Mohism, created the most influential concepts. For instance, the "great ultimate" in which *yin* and *yang* were implied but yet divided; non-ultimate (*wuji* 无极) in which great ultimate was implied but yet developed; *wu* 无 (non-being) in which all beings were implied but yet were given birth; and *hundun* 混沌 (chaos) in which all were mixed without distinctions and yet in order.

All these concepts described an entity that was fulfilled with distinct elements potentially. Within these concepts, *yin* and *yang* were two core elements, and the two elements potentially existed in the great ultimate, nongreat ultimate, and *dao* (one *yin* and one *yang* were called *dao*) in a balanced state. How do we know the *yin* and *yang* were in a balanced and harmonious state? Since they were in the entities like non-ultimate, great ultimate, and non-being and were not yet born, we have efficient reasons to assert that in those entities, the interaction, the balance, and the harmony of the *yin* and *yang* were potential but not yet realized. The category Meta-One is incorporated with ancient philosophers' ideas expressed by those concepts.

Second, we can find the idea of a dynamic process in ancient philosophers' propositions. Chinese philosophers talked about changing, moving, transforming, and developing. They developed the abovementioned concepts into propositions, like the great ultimate generated *yin* and *yang* (*taiji sheng yin and yang* 太极生阴阳) in the commentaries of *The Classic of Changes*; Zhou Dun Yi, Zhu Xi, and Feng You Lan respectively elaborated from non-ultimate to great ultimate (*wuji er taiji* 无极而太极). Laozi's all beings were born from non-being (*you sheng yu wu* 有生于无). *Dao* was born before heaven and earth (*xian tiandi zhisheng ersheng* 先天地之生而生). In my understanding, all of those described processes possessed a critical feature, dynamics, which is another essential feature running throughout the process from Meta-One through Multi-One to Utter-One.

While I use the term "dynamic" to conclude what I read from ancient philosophers' propositions about changing, moving, transforming, and developing, I use the concept of harmony to complete the particular components of the dynamic process. Besides, philosophers talk about dynamical interactions between *yin* and *yang* when describing the great ultimate, non-ultimate, and non-being; we may find the ideas of *yin-yang* interaction and harmony in *The Classic of Changes*. In the classic texts about six lings of the sixty-four hexagrams, the interactions of *yin* and *yang* drove all changes. When we think of the spirit through reading various judgments, predictions, and explanations of the sixty-four hexagrams from a metaphysical perspective, we find that in ancient philosophers' eyes, the universe is just an entity fulfilled with all kinds of changes. It is *yin* and *yang* driven and this drives all the changes—corresponding relationships between humans' virtue and heaven and earth. Although we cannot find direct elaborations of the dynamical process of change, the feature of interaction between *yin-yang*, and the corresponding relationships between *yin* and *yang*, we can find initial sources for us to describe the process from Meta-One to Multi-One by comprehending and interpreting ancient philosophers' relevant concepts and propositions.

Third, in Chinese philosophical tradition, harmony is a core idea; we may find a lot of discussions and elaborations in classic writings. Philosophers and scholars provided different explanations of the great ultimate and *yin-yang*. Still, one point is common: it is a dynamic process of great ultimate, *yin-yang*, the heaven, earth, and the four seasons of the myriad things. Not just *yin* and *yang* coexisted and interacted. Heaven, earth, and humans are in harmony. Just pick up one example, *Xi Ci* (系词) directly elaborated on harmony, "the superior person is in harmony: In virtue, with Heaven and Earth; in brightness, with the sun and moon; in the orderly procedure, with the four seasons; in good fortune and bad fortune, with the gods and spirits."[1] The commentator limited who could be in harmony with heaven, earth, sun, moon, and the four seasons to superior men, which showed his discrimination against ordinary people if we judge this idea from a political perspective, but seen from a philosophical perspective, he recognized the harmony between humans with the natural world.

In the commentary, the keyword "harmony" is a translation of the Chinese character *he* 合. According to *Shuowen jiezi*, the word *he* 合 comprised three strokes, 人 (people), 一 (one), and 口 (mouth). *He*, as the combination of the three strokes, means that all people said the same: "if three people said the same, it means *he* (consistent, correspond, or harmonious); if ten people spread the same idea, it means old."[2] *He* 合 has the meaning of harmony.

I use the words "corresponding harmony" to emphasize that at least two or more items have the corresponding relationship and harmony or not harmony could happen. Still, ancient philosophers did not use the word "corresponding" and did not use the concept of a corresponding relationship. In the stage of Meta-One and Multi-One, the corresponding relationship among various individuals, parts, or elements is an essential condition of harmony.

Ancient philosophers' concepts of great ultimate, nongreat ultimate, nonbeing, and so on directly or indirectly elaborated the ideas of potentiality, dynamics, and harmony; their propositions developed from those concepts described a dynamical process of changes drowned by *yin* and *yang* and also directly described the harmony between heaven-earth and humans, they provided valuable sources for us to enrich the components of the category Meta-One and Multi-One and to construct the proposition from Meta-One to Multi-One, describing a dynamical process of things from potentials to individuals.

Diversity in One: Beyond Tradition

In the Chinese philosophical tradition, *yin* and *yang* were one. People called the one "non-ultimate," "great ultimate," "non-being," or "*dao*." We contribute the *yin-yang* opposite, corresponds, and harmony model to multiple corresponding harmonies. In Multi-One, all potentials were implied, not just *yin* and *yang*. This section focuses on two aspects, analyzing the advantages of the *yin-yang* model and the disadvantages, which explains the necessity to go beyond tradition.

On the one hand, we must confess the model of *yin* and *yang* interacting with each other is still persuasive even today. The origination of *yin* and *yang*, strictly speaking, is still a mystery. Besides different legendary stories, scholars held different points of view. Aside from other points of view and any mystical stories about the origination of *yin* and *yang*, I would directly refer to a secular explanation, which I believe is more reliable.

According to the *Lexicon*, the ideas of *yin-yang* were derived from the observations of heaven, earth, our bodies, feathers of birds, furs of animals, and appearances of myriad things.[3] In one word, *yin* and *yang* originated from humans' observation of the world. We can imagine the feathers of male birds, the furs of male animals, and the bodies of male humans differ from that of female birds, animals, and humans. Maleness and femaleness are visible characteristics and common attributions. Ancient people distinguished between male and female to classify all living beings. All living beings with the attribution of femaleness were called *yin,* and all the living beings with the attribution of maleness were called *yang*. I believe that the saying *yin and yang* originated from ancient thinkers' observation of the world and corresponded to common sense and science, unless we find more reasonable explanations. Of course, the origination of *yin* and *yang* is not an issue I am concerned with; I am concerned with the ideality of *yin and yang* as a metaphysical concept since the concepts were already created.

It is understandable to distinguish between living beings attributing maleness and beings with femaleness by *yin* and *yang*; how was it possible to apply the criterion to classify nonliving beings?

In another commentary, *Shuogua Zhuan* said that in the ancient era, sages created *The Book of Change* to correspond to nature and destiny. Thus, they established the *dao* of heaven, called *yin and yang*. Established the *dao* of earth, called soft and strong, and built up the *dao* of humans, called benevolence and justice.[4] According to this explanation, *yin* and *yang* are the *dao* of heaven. Hardness and softness are the *dao* of earth, and benevolence and justice are the *dao* of humans. There are no logical connections between the *dao* of heaven, earth, and humans, but there are similarities among them. *Yin*, soft, and benevolence have similar features, and *yang*, hard, and justice have identical features. The similarity is a necessary term for analogies. With the same approach, the *Shuo Gua* analogized all eight hexagrams with the myriad things in the natural world. Just take the two hexagrams Qian and Kun as examples; *Shuo Gua* said Qian symbolizes heaven, so it was called father's Kun, which symbolizes the earth. It was called mother.[5] Further, it also said Qian stands for heaven, round, lord, father, jade, metal/gold, could be, ice, deep red color, and so forth, and Kun stands for earth, mother, cloth, cooking pot, miserly . . . handle, black color as earth.[6]

We have seen from the examples of the *yin* that it stands for the abovementioned things. The distinction between male and female was extended to distinguish nonliving beings. Although there was no such kind of difference between maleness and femaleness among nonliving beings, they were still identified and classified by *yin* and *yang*, which told us that the concept *yin* and *yang* functioned as metaphorical concepts in terms of some similarities. In doing so, the myriad things in the world were identified as either *yin* or *yang* or the creatures of the interaction between *yin* and *yang*. The concepts *yin* and *yang* were widely accepted not just because they are powerful in explaining the origination of the myriad things in the world but also in classifying various things in the complex world into *yin* and *yang*, including distinguishing between living beings with maleness and femaleness and nonliving beings with negative and positive attributes.

We need to note the disadvantages of the *yin-yang* model. The essential issue is that the generality of the two concepts is not general enough when using *yin* and *yang* to identify, classify, or explain the originations of all nonliving beings. In the universe, not everything can be divided into *yin* and *yang* or originated by the interaction between *yin* and *yang*. Theoretically, there must be something between *yin* and *yang*, which can be called neutral, neither *yin* nor *yang*; and there must be something between *yin* and the neutral, which could be called, for instance, under *yin*, or above neutral, the same as between *yang* and neutral. The model of *yin-yang* interaction cannot fully reflect the complexity of diversities in many entities.

In the sense of classification, much singleness, neutrality, and diversity were ignored; in the sense of originations of things, or in the sense of being given birth/generated, not everything was born by the interaction between *yin* and *yang*, for instance, asexual reproduction, clonal propagation; in the sense of constructions, not all things are made of the elements of *yin* and *yang*, for example, primordial unicellular organism. Even if we exercise the yin and yang metaphorical functions, we still cannot analogize these examples properly.

Philosophers pursue generality and metaphysics as the core and the foundation of philosophy and attempt to construct categories with the highest generality. Because of the limitations of ancient science, technology, and cognitive science, we should not blame ancient philosophers for any disadvantages of their concepts and propositions. Instead, we should appreciate their contributions to philosophy by creating powerful concepts and propositions. What we should do is continue their work and develop their ideas.

This concern encourages me to propose Meta-One, Multi-One, and Utter-One categories. Meta-One conceptualizes any entity in which not just *yin* and *yang*, but all other potentials are implied; Multi-One conceptualizes any entity in which all individuals individualize themselves, including yin and yang elements; and Utter-One conceptualizes any entity in which all individuals realize themselves and reach completion with a new beginning. The Meta-One through Multi-One to Utter-One metaphorically describes the process from potential diversities to individualize diversities to realized diversities. In all links of the dynamical process, *yin* and *yang* were parts of the diversities. The dynamical process from Meta-One via Multi-One to Utter-One inherited ancient philosophers' traditional ideas of the dynamical changes of *yin* and *yang* but did not stick to the tradition.

Meta-One and Multi-One are conceptualizations of one entity, thinking from a dynamical perspective. Multi-One is the individualization of Meta-One, and Utter-One is the completion of Multi-One.

MULTI-ONE TO UTTER-ONE

From individualized diversities to completed diversities is the process of a dynamic process. From individualization to completion of potential diversities is the concept of the Multi-One. The transitional stage between Meta-One and Utter-One implied the realization of individualization and the start approaching completion. The analyses of the two aspects are the content of this section.

Realization of Individualization

Multi-One, as a stage between Meta-One and Utter-One, denotes the realization of individualization of potential diversities and the starting point approaching to completion of developing from Multi-One to Utter-One. This section discusses two aspects, the realization of individualization and the beginning of approaching completion.

Realizing the individualizations of diversities could be extremely long. They could be very short and complex, and simple, depending on the entities the category described.

Suppose Meta-One represents the conceptualized cosmos as an entity. In that case, the process is an almost uncountably long time for the diversities to realize their individualization, the diversities in the cosmos including the various star systems, all kinds of planets, the sun, the moon, and all other physical existences on these stars and planets. We may take the universe described in the leading theory about the origination of the cosmos as an example. According to the Big Bang Theory, the process from potential diversities to the gigantic explosion had been long. We may use Meta-One to describe, metaphorically, neither logically nor scientifically, the single infinitive point before the explosion. Besides scientists' calculations, we can imagine the single infinitive point in which all potential diversities coexisted had undergone an extremely long time to gather energies before the explosion. After the explosion, the process of undivided diversities to individualizations experienced another extremely long time to realize individualization, shaping various star systems, like the Milky Way and all other planets, the sun, the moon, and other stars. We may use Multi-One to describe metaphorically the divided, individualized, and realized diversities because they have become what they are, for instance, the solar system. The diversities in the cosmos, which was metaphorically conceptualized as the entity Multi-One, have realized their individualizations and differed from the states at the beginning of the explosion.

The cosmos, as a complete entity, is highly complex. When we observe the cosmos, although most individuals have realized their individualizations and become what they are, many others may still individualize themselves. Others are still in the stage of Meta-One; the diversities are still undivided and potentially coexisted.

We may use Multi-One to describe the process from Meta-One to Multi-One to describe the process from potential diversities (potential parts of the body) metaphorically in a worm's egg to an imago in which all parts, like head, eyes, and wings, were individualized and became what they are. The process and time from Meta-One to Multi-One can also metaphorically describe tiny entities, for instance, an egg. For small entities like a worm egg, the process from Meta-One to Multi-One is very short and straightforward as the process from a worm egg to an imago.

Whether the process and time are short or long, complex or straightforward, the process falls into the formula from Meta-One to Multi-One, which is also a process from potential diversities to divided individuals. The Multi-One denotes the realization of the individualizations of the diversities.

The realization of individualization is also a starting point for approaching completion. The process from Meta-One via Multi-One to Utter-One is a continuous process; we divide the process into three stages just for our convenience of analyzation and analysis, while the process itself cannot be divided and separated. Multi-One symbolizes the stage at which diversities have realized themselves and become what they are. The realized diversities started moving to a new stage, Utter-One. The same as we climb a mountain, the peak of the mountain is also the starting point going down the mountain.

Scientists may know that the point symbolizes the realization of the individualization of the cosmos and the starting point toward completion, as the heat death theory claimed. Multi-One can metaphorically denote a long process, for instance, the cosmos. The Multi-One could also metaphorically show a temporary stage, such as a rose tree, which grows from seed, to a tree booming with rose flowers, to having all its leaves dried. The stage that yearly booms with rose flowers can be interpreted as the point at which the individualization was realized and a starting point toward its completion; that is, all flowers, leaves, and branches dried.

The analogies of the cosmos and the rose tree were based on the metaphorical functions of Meta-One, Multi-One, and Utter-One discussed in the previous chapter; these examples corresponded to and supported the assumptions of the metaphorical functions of the three categories: they can metaphorically describe any entities in which all potential diversities were implied (Meta-One), all individualized diversities were included (Multi-One). All completed diversities were enclosed (Utter-One).

Ancient Chinese philosophers issued similar ideas. *Tuan Zhuan* explained the Hexagram Qian said, "the *dao* of Qian changes, each fulfilling its nature and destiny" (*qiandao bianhua, gezheng xingming* "乾道变化，各正性命").[7] The *dao* of Qian changes, denoting that *yin*, *yang*, heaven, earth, four seasons, sun, stars, and all things change following a certain law. In my understanding, this proposition described a process from Meta-One to Multi-One. The word *zheng* 正 as a verb could mean correct, rectify, justify, straighten, get, realize, fulfill, and so forth; *xing* denotes nature and *ming* (destiny). The verb *zheng* notes a process in which each being gets its nature and achieves its destiny, but not a single action. To "acquire its nature" means to individualize what they are, from potentiality to reality; "achieve its destiny" means to complete its mission, realize what it should be, or achieve what it should accomplish.

In the Chinese philosophical tradition, many ancient philosophers explained this proposition. Zhu Xi was one of them and offered his disciples many explanations about this proposition. He used different analogies in different places, expressing the same idea, and the *li* is undivided and mixed anywhere. *Li* likes a millet seed, grows up to a seedling, then booms flowers, then generates fruits, becoming millets again and returning to their original form. In my understanding, Zhu Xi's analogy described a process similar to the process from Meta-One to Multi-One. In this process, the millet in which all parts were not divided, all parts like roots, stem, leaves, flowers, and fruits were all potentials; during the growing up phase, all diversities individualize themselves and differ one from another, for instance, leaves differ from flowers, all potential parts gain their nature becoming what they are, and then to the stage of maturity, producing new millets—did what it should do—achieved its destiny.

However, Zhu Xi claimed that each thing possesses its *li*. He analogized his idea with corn, saying that "just like a grain of corn growing as a sprout, the sprout produces flowers, the flowers turn to be corns, and then return to be its original shape. One corn has one hundred grains of corn, and each grain is competed individuality. When planning the one hundred grains, each grain produces one hundred of grain of corn. In this way, producing and producing without cease, but all grains of corn were produced from one." Xi summarized, "Each thing possesses its *li*, eventually, there is just one *li*."[8] For him, nature is just *li*; each thing has its *li*, but eventually, just one *li*, like one millet, produced hundreds of millets. According to Zhu Xi, one *li* in all and one *li* produces all.

Unlike Zhu Xi, Meta-One is an all-in-one entity in which all diversities coexist potentially; Multi-One is also an all-in-one entity in which all individualized diversities coexist, so we observe the millet and growing differently. We may use Meta-One metaphorically to refer to the millet seed and the process from Meta-One to Multi-One to describe the growing growth of a maturated millet. In the entire process of growing, all parts of the millet are always in one entity: a seed, a seedling, and a maturated millet. The essential difference between Zhu Xi's descriptions of the millet growing from potentiality to reality and the process from Meta-One through Multi-One comprises the difference between Zhu's one-in-all and the all-in-one in our system. Still, both described a dynamic process from potentiality to reality from different perspectives, in different ways, and with other expressions.

Completion with the New Beginning

This section discusses the two aspects of the dynamic process's completion and the new beginning. The category Utter-One symbolizes the completion, accomplishment, or termination of the entire process from Meta-One via Multi-One to Utter-One also implied a new beginning of a new process.

Utter-One metaphorically describes the completion of the process from Multi-One to Utter-One. At the stage of Utter-One, all divided, realized, individualized things, parts, or elements have reached their ends, or borrowing ancient philosophers' words, fulfilled their destinies—the entire process from Meta-One via. There are two ways to complete the process: from Multi-One to Utter-One, one is changing, and another is transforming. Most changes are visible processes, and most transformations are invisible. We use two names for the same thing. Changing and transforming essentially is one thing; changing is visible transforming, and transforming is an invisible change, changing and transforming as one process runs throughout the entire process. We recognize transformations through changes and know changes because of transformations.

When we use our categories to describe the origination and evolution of the cosmos in terms of the Big Bang Theory, we could say that from the initial infinitive point to the gigantic explosion; the infinitive point had undergone a long time of transformation or evolution. It is said the universe has undergone fourteen billion years from the inflation stage until today.[9] The gigantic explosion is a visible change if we use a scientific term. Scientists called the enormous explosion a sudden event, but from the perspective of philosophy, we could say it resulted from a long time of transformation and a visible change. A long time after the enormous explosion, the star systems, stars, planets, and all things on some planets shaped and appeared. These are visible changes, but behind the changes, a long-time transformation has been running. One could say that the Big Bang Theory is only a scientific hypothesis and could be denied entirely in the future. I would say that even if that happens someday, it will not affect my argument here because I am using the hypophysis to interpret the change and transformation implied in the process from Meta-One through Multi-One to Utter-One metaphorically. The same is true if a person in front of me in the classroom could listen to me because of the limited space; even if there was no such person, it does not affect my argument or supposition.

Suppose we borrow Zhu Xi's analogy of the millet. In that case, we can imagine that in the stage that Multi-One metaphorically described, the leaves were completely green, and the sizes of leaves grew up as large as they could be. It completely shaped the millets as maturated ones should be . . . all these are visible changes, and a long-term transformation had been running behind them. When the maturated millet seedling continues growing up, after a specific time we would see the leaves, millets, and stem turned yellow, dried, and die; the millets fall on the earth. The millet completed its entire process from Meta-One via Multi-One to Utter-One, visible changes and invisible transformations run throughout the process.

Not just the millet; all living beings, including humans, undergo the same process. We use a mirror to watch ourselves every day and cannot see any transformation, but we are getting older every day. Nonliving beings, like the cosmos and all other things, are changing and transforming from potential to reality or maturated to complement and fulfill their destinies. Nothing is outside of the principle, and differences in the process are longer or shorter, more complex, or more straightforward.

Utter-One implied a new beginning of a new process. Completion is the essential feature of the Utter-One, but the completion is relatively not absolute. The completion of one process implies a beginning of a new process. Therefore, the myriad things in the universe can exist continuously and endlessly. Although we still do not precisely know how the universe began, as I suggested, we may regard the beginning of the beginning as a "black hole" in philosophy and leave it for new generations and future humans to continue exploring. We now face a current existing universe. The beginning implied in the Utter-One is not the beginning of the beginning but the beginning of existing things.

For nonliving beings, the processes could be extremely long and complex, like the completion of the cosmos to a new beginning; they could be short and straightforward, like an egg of an insect, like a wooden table from the idea (design) of a table to a constructed table, and then to a stack of rotten wood. The pile of rotten wood is the end of the table, but it implies a new beginning to be another material existence. All living beings continue growing up from their maturated stages and move toward completion. Let us suppose that the end of a life of a living being is a symbolic point of completion. The turning point symbolizes the new process's completion and a new beginning. Although they cannot return to another living being, they will certainly transform into a nonliving being and continue their existence. The death of a living being is a visible change. Still, behind the visible difference, transforming from an alive, living being to a nonliving being is continuous and never stopped. The new beginning is new in terms of the visible change, but it is the continuation of the invisible transformation. In this sense, the new beginning is not new because it was implied in the completion. It is a continuous process from Meta-One through Multi-One to Utter-One. The Utter-One denotes the completion of a process but also signifies a new beginning.

In Chinese philosophical tradition, there were profound ideas about the dynamic process and endless progress of development. Early ancient people believed heaven and earth heaven repeatedly and never ceased; ancient philosophers regarded the process from nonultimate to great ultimate as endless because of the interaction between *yin* and *yang*; Laozi's *dao* runs independently and never slacks off. Of the sixty-four hexagrams in *The Classic of Changes*, the first two hexagrams, *Qian* and *Kun,* were analogized with heaven and earth, which metaphorically described the potentiality that Meta-One describes; the hexagrams from the third hexagram to the sixty hexagrams which covered what the Multi-One describes; and the last hexagram *weiji* (未既) denoted what Utter-One described. (*Weiji*—*Wei* means not yet; *Ji* means benefit to, accomplish, solution, success, and so on.) This could be a vast project; I outline some points here.

The first two, Qian and Kun, analogized with heaven and earth and represented *yang* and *yin*, the same as *yin-yang* in the great ultimate, heaven-earth, made up a complete entity; the myriad things would have no place to live without earth, and the myriad things would no protection without heaven. As *Tuan Zhuan* said, "The myriad things are provided their beginning by *it* [Qian]."[10] *Xiang Zhuan* said, "After Heaven and Earth have come into existence, myriad things are produced."[11] Both Qian and Kun have the feature of "great and originating [*yuan*]," "penetrating [*heng*]," "advantageous [*li*]," and "correct and firm [*zhen*]."[12] In my understanding, the four features are all abstract but not actual characteristics of physical things. The classic texts of Qian used dragons to explain the meanings of the six lines—all undivided *yang analogically*. In short, Qian and Kun introduced the *dao* of heaven and earth, not yet physical things, and human affairs in a strict sense.

Begun with the third hexagram, *Zhun* 屯, in *The Classic of Changes*, talked about myriad things. Although there are various English translations of the name of the hexagram *Zhun*, philosophers and scholars agree that *Zhun* symbolizes the beginning of myriad things. Alfred Huang explained, "the ideography *Zhun* looks like a tiny blade of newly sprouted grass with a root that deeply penetrates the ground."[13] Hence, he translated the hexagram *Zhun* as "beginning." This has been widely accepted by philosophers and scholars, but he expressed the core idea differently. James Legge's (1815–1897) translation said that *zhun* is a "pictorial and should show us how a plant struggles with difficulty out of the earth, rising gradually above the surface."[14] Richard John Lynn translated the hexagram *Zhun* as "Birth Throes"; according to *Tuan Zhuan* 《彖传》, "Zhun means the difficulty of giving birth when the hard and soft interact."[15] Kong Yingda (孔颖达574–678) and other scholars showed, "the hexagram Zhun means the budding stage of grass and trees, symbolizes the nascent stage of myriad things."[16] As commentators summarized, after heaven and earth, myriad things were produced. "What fills Heaven and Earth is nothing more than the myriad things. Therefore, Qian and Kun are followed by Zhun."[17]

Philosophers' and scholars' explanations and commentaries convinced me that Meta-One concords with the descriptions of the *dao* of heaven and earth in the hexagrams of Qian and Kun, and the Multi-One concords with the third hexagram Zhun to sixty-two hexagrams up to the last two. When we continue reading after the *Zhun*, we may find that all those hexagrams talked about human affairs by analogies with natural things like grass, flowers, and animals. Regarding the names of the last two hexagrams, I assume that *jiji* 既济 and *wejii* 未济 can make up a phrase both complete and incomplete. The classic text of Yao talked about the historical event that the Yin emperor defeated (*kezhi* 克之) the minority leader of the kingdom Gui Fang 鬼方 (a kingdom in the Shang Dynasty) in three years. Based on the victory of the Yin emperor, commentators pointed out that *kezhi* (defeated Gui Fang) means *ji* (济), which means complete.[18] There are different translations of the two hexagrams, "Ferrying Complete" and "Ferrying Incomplete,"[19] or "already fulfilled" and "not yet fulfilled,"[20] or any other translations like "complete" and "before competing," and so on. The differences in translation did not affect to convey the core ideas, completion and incompletion. The two hexagrams both told the story of a little fox. In the judgments of the hexagram *jiji*, the fox wet its head but finally crossed the river; in *weiji*, it wet its tail, and many difficulties were in front of it.[21] The analogies corresponded to the historical event and expressed the same meanings metaphorically.

It has been widely accepted that the first two hexagrams are introductions, and the last two are summaries. I would further specify that Meta-One corresponds to the opening and the processes after Meta-One to Multi-One, up to Utter-One corresponds to the various changes described by the sixty hexagrams, and Utter-One corresponds to the content of the last two hexagrams.

In sum, it is a dynamic process from Meta-One via Multi-One to Utter-One in which both the features of completion and incompletion were implied. The entire process was fulfilled with various changes, and the changes were not chaos but in different harmony.

CORRESPONDING HARMONY: DYNAMIC MODELS

The dynamic process from Meta-One via Multi-One to Utter-One is not empty but is fulfilled with harmonies; when we observe the harmonies happened in the entire process from a longitudinal perspective, we may find that the harmonies are realized in the processes of the beginning, changing, or completing, and may characterize the various harmonies as dynamic models, including opposite versus corresponding harmony, potential versus factual harmony, temporary versus permanent harmony, partial versus full harmony, and dynamic versus static harmony. When we observe the various harmonies from a horizontal perspective, we may classify the various harmonies as a static model, which will be the content of the next part. This part analyzes the dynamic models of harmony.

Before classifying harmony, I would first clarify the two concepts, opposite to harmony and corresponding harmony. The interaction of two opposite agencies may cause two models of harmony: either overcomes another and reaches harmony, or another overcomes this to achieve harmony. Three agencies may interact with each other. The results could be one overcoming or defeating others to reach harmony, a joined group overcoming others to reach harmony, or one group defeating another. It is a dynamic process.

The *yin* and *yang* in the great ultimate, non-being, or *dao*, are opposite agencies. The primary relationship between *yin* and *yang* is that when *yin* increases, *yang* decreases simultaneously; when *yang* increases, *yin* decreases simultaneously. In the interactions between *yin* and *yang*, changes happened. If *yin* overcomes *yang*, move to harmony with *yin*, and vice versa: any two opposite things, parts, or elements. Eventually, move toward balance in the natural world through long or short, complex or straightforward interactions. We can regard the investigation of the causes of earthquakes, volcanic eruptions, and tsunamis as tasks of scientific research; from a philosophical perspective, we may conclude all these negative forces and the earth's or planet's stability are positive forces. The two forces are opposite agencies. The negative and positive forces interact and finally cause those phenomena. When those happened, the harmony of the earth was broken; after those happened, the earth returned to harmony. Just as Laozi said, heaven gained one, it becomes clear, and the earth reaches one, and the earth becomes peaceful. In human society, two kingdoms war against one another. The two kingdoms are two opposite agencies, which is a dynamic process. The two fight each other, and it is dynamic progress. One negates another toward harmony, eventually.

Corresponding harmony differs from opposite harmony, as the agents inside the harmonious entity are not opposite but correspond to each other. We may characterize *yin* and *yang* as opposite to each other. Still, we can also regard them as a corresponding relationship when *yin* was analogized with earth, female, soft, and *yang* with heaven, male, and strong. Heaven and earth, male and female, strong and soft, correspond to each other—similarly, the four seasons, myriad things, including the sun and the moon. As ancient philosophers described, it always follows another alternately. For instance, the sun and moon correspond to each other and function alternatively in the harmonious entity heaven-earth. A corresponding relationship denotes the relationship between different agencies or among diversities that do not overcome, fight, conflict, or defeat each other; they pursue harmony by benefiting each other, cooperating, or supporting each other for common goals or destinies. The harmony is also dynamic, not a static process. They coexist, collaborate, or support each other in the process of development from Meta-One through Multi-One to Utter-One.

The corresponding relationship is a fundamental relationship between two things/elements or among multiple things/elements, and an opposite relationship is only one model of the corresponding relationships. Because there must be a corresponding relationship between two or more elements, the two or more elements may have opposite relationships. For instance, *yin* and *yang* correspond to each other, negative force and positive force correspond to each other, the opposite relationship either potentially existed in the very beginning or happened in the process of their development, or in the stage of completion; it is a unique model of corresponding relationships. The opposite relationship could happen at any stage in the process of Meta-One through Multi-One to Utter-One. If there is no connection between two things/elements, other relationships cannot be established. All opposite relationships belong to the corresponding association, but not all are opposite. The corresponding relationship possesses higher generality and is a higher abstract concept, as all other relationships can be attributed to corresponding relationships.

I mean by the category "harmony" that the diversities, including individual things, parts, or elements with corresponding relationships, coexisted in a particular entity in which the diversities interact, cooperate, or support each other for a certain period. Harmony is also a general category; it shows the entity with balance, stability, peacefulness, completeness, unification, realization, emergence, and so forth. The harmony between two or more elements varies because of the different results of their interactions. We may classify different harmonies into dynamic and static models of harmony. The dynamic model includes potential versus factual harmony, temporary versus eternal harmony, partial versus full harmony, and dynamic versus static harmony. The static models of harmony are discussed in the next part of the chapter.

Potential vs. Factual Harmony

The dynamic process from Meta-One via Multi-One to Utter-One is essentially a process from potentiality via Multiplicity to completeness. The process companies with the harmonies from potential harmonies via the realization of completed factual harmonies.

When two or more elements correspond to each other, there will be multiple possibilities to move into deeper interactions resulting in conflict, contradiction, opposite, fight, or one follows another to cooperate, and various elements work together for a common mission toward harmony. Among all those possibilities, every possibility is potentially not yet realized. The potential harmonies mainly existed from the beginning of the corresponding relationship to the potential harmonies realized; how, when, and who or which made the harmonies happen was unclear because unexpected factors could interpret moving into harmony. The primary direction of development still moves toward harmonies. Although the processes could be long, could be short, could be soon, or could be later, the approach to reaching harmony could be through one overcoming another, cooperating with another, or each other. Potential harmony is a positive force. It drives things to move into a better status; it mostly becomes the destination of things' development.

Factual corresponding harmony is a harmony that has become a fact. Real harmony is the realization of potential harmony. An accurate harmony could stand for long, could be short; could be stable, could be unstable; could be interpreted by inner forces or outer forces; it depends on harmonious unities. A factual harmony is not simply duplicating the potential harmony and is not a predetermined result. The realization of the potential harmony is a dynamic process in which many unexpected changes could happen. An originally major force or element, or a side that drives the development toward harmony, could be replaced by another party or element, therefore changing the ways to reach harmony, delaying the process to achieve harmony, or changing the nature or quality of the harmony. In short, potential harmony presages a direction and necessary result of development. In contrast, the realization of potential harmony is a dynamic process involving all alternatives, so factual harmony is not precisely the duplication of potential harmony. Real harmony is not predetermined at the beginning of the process, from potential harmony to accurate harmony.

We may use different things to exemplify the process, from potential harmonies to factual harmonies. The universe before the big bang happened, the universe after the big bang occurred, and the universe in its future; a seed like Zhu Xi's millet seed, the apple seed, as I mentioned, an egg, and all other things with similar characteristics of multiple potentialities. Human disease and health are opposite and conflicting; the corresponding relationship between illness and health has potentially coexisted in the human body since the disease originated. It is a dynamic process, as the disease appears to damage humans' health, or the human immune system until medicine overcomes it. The general direction is to reach harmony; either the disease entirely or partially damaged human health, or the infection was wholly or partially healed to achieve a relatively harmonious state. A war between two countries could have a potential long-term period, then happen, and finally reach harmony via one defeating another or through peaceful talks. It is a dynamic process from a potential war between two countries to the fight happening, and then to ending the war. In the entire process, before the war, the two countries were in a potentially harmonious stage, and a potential war was warming up. When the war happened, the two counties individualized themselves as two fighting sides, and the potential harmony was broken. The potential war turned out to be a fact; a new harmony was reached when the war ended. It is a unique but very popular way to achieve harmony through one overcoming another; all other corresponding harmonies companied with the entire process from Meta-One via Multi-One to Utter-One, the essential difference in the ways to reach harmonies are through cooperating rather than solving conflicts.

It is essential to recognize the process from potential harmony to factual harmony. With this recognition, we need to identify all possibilities in the stage of Meta-One and expect the trends and directions of development, make preplans, and be ready to face any unexpected challenges. With the recognition of the process, we can identify the necessity of the development toward harmonies and any changes in the dynamical process pursuing harmony.

Temporary vs. Permanent Harmony

The temporary harmony reflects the core idea of change. Since it is a dynamic process from Meta-One via Multi-One to Utter-One, changing and transforming are the core features of the dynamic process. If we assume that changing and transforming are absolute and unchanging is just relative, we may say there is no absolute, unchangeable harmony, no matter the harmonies happening in the universe or any tiny existence. Based on this presupposition, I use the word "permanent," which means something that lasts a very long time without marked change or endures for so long as to seem fixed to call all the harmonies to remain relatively long. The difference between a long and a short time is also relative and based on comparing one with another. In short, permanent harmony does not mean that once it is reached, it exists forever, with no changes. Strictly speaking, there is no such kind of harmony.

Most harmonies in human society are temporary, and most harmonies in the natural world are permanent. We have seen in the previous part that ancient thinkers have recognized that sun and moon follow each other, four seasons turning in cycles. We may call these phenomena harmony. The sun and the moon run a cycle shaped by a day. The day is not empty but a harmony in which people work in the daytime and rest in the nighttime; people's minds and energies keep a perfect balance. As to the four seasons, all living beings grow in a sprint, are maturated in the summer, complete their destinies in the autumn, and stored in the winter, running a circle to achieve perfect harmony. For the sun and moon, the four seasons, the harmony caused by their movements is permanent; with their activities, all things on the ear reach perfect dynamical harmony. The permanent harmony is completed if we observe all living beings on the earth in a fixed period. As parts of the permanent harmony, humans and other living beings are temporary; the people in these one hundred years are no longer the same as in the last century. Other living beings are the same. However, the heaven-earth, including the sun and moon as other harmonious parts, is permanent; they remain what they are for a long time without marked changes. What they reached is no longer the same harmony as last year. Based on these analyses, we assert that the harmony of heaven, earth, the sun, the moon, and all other stars and planets is a permanent harmonious system. We say the system is permanent harmony in terms of the assumption that the universe exists permanently. Permanent harmony will no longer exist if the universe vanishes at a particular time.

For human society, most harmonies are temporary. There is a saying in Chinese tradition—the affairs under heaven after long division, unification follows, and after long unification, division follows. In our terms, the division is a situation in that harmony is broken, and unification is harmony. The traditional saying denotes the temporality of harmony in human affairs; a kingdom with another could be friends today and be a hostile kingdom tomorrow; they could unite to reach harmony because of their common interests and fight each other to break down the harmony for their interests. Even today, it is the same; one country with another, or one group of counties with another group, could become allies today and could fight each other because of the changes in common interests. When they united, they reached harmony; when they divided, they broke harmony.

People, especially politicians, need to recognize the temporality of harmony. When they ally with other countries, they should consider the division in the future; when they are in a separation situation or an adversarial situation, they need to think of the union in a specific time in the future, although it is a kind wish for people to pursue a long-term harmony or even permanent harmony. Suppose a politician ignores the temporality of harmony in human affairs and limits their sight to the current situation. In that case, this politician could endanger their country and people. The reason causing the harmony is temporal, not permanent, because human society and affairs are changing. It is a dynamic process, from potential harmony to realizing and breaking down the harmony.

Partial vs. Full Harmony

The model of partial harmony and full harmony includes two aspects: first, it is a process from partial harmony to full harmony; second, a complex, harmonious system usually includes unharmonious parts, and an unharmonious system implies harmonious elements.

On the one hand, it is a dynamic process from potential harmony. It is also a progressive process to realize harmony—to complete or break down harmony. As we said, changing is visible, transforming, and invisibly changing. Changing and transforming are mostly gradually realized and completed, not suddenly happening; from partial harmony to full harmony is one way to realize harmony progressively. The universe's origination, formation, and evolution are incredibly long, so seeing the process from partial to full harmony is hard. As parts of the universe, various star systems, stars, and planets are also undergoing progressive evolution; it is hard for us to identify the processes of their changes and transformations.

If we observe human society, primarily, the realization of harmony or breakdown of harmony happens from partial to full harmonies. I picked up one example from countless historical records to exemplify this harmony model. It was recorded during the Spring and Autumn and the Warring States periods (770–221 BC) that there were "ten thousand kingdoms in the Xia Dynasty, three thousand remained in the Yin Dynasty, one thousand and eight hundred in the early Zhou, and one hundred-forty kingdoms by the period of Spring and Autumn."[22] As we know, there were only seven kingdoms before the Qin unified seven kingdoms into one (221 BC). Although the numbers of kingdoms are not specific statics, during the entire period, the kingdoms gradually decreased from thousands and hundreds to seven kingdoms, which strongly showed the dynamic process from partial harmony to full harmony. The period from 770 BC to 221 BC was filled with endless conflicts, countless fights, and wars. It was unharmonious; from a dynamic perspective, that period was a partial to full harmony process. This corresponds to the stage of Utter-One; the unification symbolized completion but implied a new beginning in the Qin Dynasty. For over ten years, the Han Dynasty replaced the Qin Dynasty.

The dynamic process from partial harmony to full harmony was complex; there were temporary and partial harmonies during the unharmonious period. For instance, Duck Huan of Qi (齐桓公), the ruler of the kingdom of Qi (685–643 BC), allied with kingdoms Lu, Song, Chen, and Zheng in 679 BC against the big kingdom Chu and finally signed an agreement with Chu[23] and reached temporary and partial harmony during the chaotic period of the Zhou Dynasty. Confucius praised Duck Huan (齐桓公 ?–643 BC), "assembled all the princess together, and that not with weapons of war and chariots" (*Jiu he zhu hou, bu yi bing che* 九合诸侯，不以兵车).[24]

Even today, the highly well-organized human society is in harmony as a complete entity. From the first organization, like a kingdom, until today's country, political, economic, ideological, military, cultural, religious, racial, and regional forces functioned positively to drive people to harmony. They acted as negative forces to damage harmony. A history of human society is just a history of the interaction of positive and negative forces. When the positive forces became mainstream, society became harmonious; otherwise, it became unharmonious. Strictly speaking, full harmony in human society is just an idea of humans; mostly, partial harmony is its common status.

Partial and full corresponding harmony are dynamic; the situation of harmony changes with the changes of the positive and negative forces. Partial harmony is complex; partial unharmonious phenomena exist in harmonious eras and areas and are partially harmonious in unharmonious ages and regions. The interaction of the positive and negative forces is endless and rooted in human nature and reality. Humans have not found a solution to realize full harmony. Still, we should devote ourselves to transferring the negative forces to positive forces, approaching a fully harmonious society in the future.

When we extend our sight to the entire universe, the heaven and earth are just parts of the universe; ancient Chinese thinkers described the harmony of heaven, earth, and humankind. Today, we characterize the universe as a harmonious complex entity, the heaven, earth, and humanity as parts are included; we assert that the entire universe is harmony, but there are still many partial unharmonious phenomena—the fall of the planet, one planet hits another, explosion and vanishment of the earth. However, this kind of unharmonious phenomenon can not change the fact that the entire universe is harmonious. The earth, which was defined as "under heaven" (天下 Tian Xia) by ancient Chinese thinkers, is harmony; However, there were many unharmonious phenomena caused by natural disasters like floods and animals, and today partial unharmonious phenomena still exist, including earthquakes, tsunamis, paroxysmal eruptions, tornados, floods, as well as many other disasters caused by humans' abuse of natural sources, like pollution, nuclear disaster, biological weapons, and so forth. The animal world on the earth entity is harmonious; if we investigate the world, we may find many unharmonious aspects. We human beings, as a kind of animal, stand on the top of the food chain; we hunt and feed animals as our food; gigantic animals catch small animals as their food, and small animals eat smaller animals . . . all these behaviors caused partial unharmonious and damage full harmony, and even make full harmony impossible.

Dynamic vs. Static Harmony

The dynamic feature of the process from Meta-One via Multi-One to Utter-One determines that all kinds of corresponding harmony are essentially dynamic; the static feature of harmony is just relative but essentially dynamic. However, theoretically, we still can distinguish between dynamic and static harmonies in consideration of the two aspects: either by the light of whether the harmonious states change with the changes of time or ignoring the time dimension when we observe a harmonious entity. I respectively analyze the two models of static harmonies.

If a harmony state changes with the change of time, that is a dynamic harmony; otherwise, it is a static harmony. A dynamical harmony is an ongoing process in which all individual things, parts, or elements and their relationships change from time to time. Still, the process as a complete entity is harmony. The harmony with profound diversities and changes are the components of the process from Meta-One via Multi-One to Utter-One. The harmonies that happen in the universe, in the natural world, and among all living beings belong to dynamic harmonies. If we observe those harmonies ignoring the time dimension, observing those harmonies at any specific time and specific movements, those harmonies seem to be static, but essentially, they are dynamic.

Is there any static harmony in a strict sense? So-called static harmony means that harmony has been relatively realized. The things, parts, or elements are in a situation of peace and stability and coexist in an entity cooperatively. In the artist world, we may find a lot of static harmonies. A single sculpture statue could be a harmonious entity in which all parts perfectly correspond to each other and the environment around the figure. As an artist's work, the complex aspects of the status could be harmony in the entity and could be harmony with the environment. Once the artist's statue was completed, harmony was reached. If the status exists, harmony exists as well. This kind of harmony can be static harmony. We can also find many static harmonies in paintings, architecture, and calligraphical works. A piece of music comprises various tones, rhythm, melody, timbre, dynamics, texture, and forms; the harmony of all these components produces a piece of music. Harmony is the core of a piece of music, in my understanding.

Not just artist works, all artificially made things belong to static harmonies if they meet the definition of static harmony. We may find static harmonies from new and old buildings, machines, transformation tools, equipment, and facilities for daily life. We may also classify static harmonies into different models, which will be further discussed in chapter 3.

In *The Investigation of Things*, Zhu Xi said the universe is running and never stops. He accepted Cheng Ming Dao's idea that there is only the process of action and response within heaven and earth. Following this line of thinking, Zhu Xi points out, "in the changes and transformations of yin and yang, the growth and maturity of things, the interaction of sincerity and insincerity, and the beginning and end of events, one is the influence and the other, the response, succeeding each other in a cycle. Therefore, they never stop."[25] Zhu Xi interprets Confucius' observation of flowing rivers, commenting, "in the universe's transforming process, the past has just gone, and the future continues to come. They continue without a moment of rest. This is the nature of the Way as it originally was."²⁶

In Zhu Xi's discourses above, three important points need to be stressed here: Zhu Xi asserted everything is growing and never stops, *Dao* governs everything, and growing is a cycle. In addition, Zhu extended the principles to human virtues; the natural world, like grass and the humanities, followed the same principles.

Here, let's focus on Zhu Xi's particular concerns about *Dao*. Like other previous philosophers, Zhu Xi recognized that everything in the universe is an ongoing dynamical process. Zhu interpreted Zhou Dun Yi's ideas about the Great Ultimate and *yin-yang* with *li* (principle). Zhu Xi claimed each thing has a *li*. He said:

> From the Ultimate of Nonbeing and the Great above to a small thing like a blade of grass, a plant, or an insect below, each has its principle [*li*]; we cannot read one book; we shall miss the principle of one book. If we investigate one affair to the utmost, we shall miss the principle of One affair, and if we do not investigate one thing, we shall miss the principle of the thing. We must understand them one by one.²⁷

According to Zhu Xi, all things have their principle, for principle [*li*] is not outside things or affairs (Chu Hsi, Chu Tzu yü-lei, 95:5b-6a). Zhu Xi told us that *li* exists in all things and throughout the dynamic process. If we observe all things from a static perspective, we would say that Zhu's claim is reasonable because everything in the universe has something that determines something is something. A tree is a tree because it has the essence or nature that determines that thing is a tree but nothing else; the "something" that decides that thing is a tree can be called *li*, of course, it can be conceptualized as any other name; this is understandable theoretically. If we observe it from a dynamic perspective, we find that Zhu Xi's claim is questionable. Let's use Zhu Xi's example: a grass has its *li*, namely the *li* of grass; if we say that the *li* of grass exists, throughout growing of the grass, questions accrued: the grass was grown from a seed of grass, according to Zhu Xi's claim, the seed has its *li*, namely the *li* of seed; and further, when the grass reaches its end of life, it terms to be trash; a piece of trash is no longer grass, nor a seed. If the *li* of grass governs or exists throughout the growth of grass, the *li* is static and cannot reflect the changes of the grass from a seed to a grass and then to a piece of trash. The analyses here convince me that Zhu Xi's claim is good for explaining static relationships between *li* and all things but not suitable for describing all things' dynamic process of growth.

In the system of Meta-One, while we absorb previous philosophers' ideas about the dynamical process of things by proposing the formula from Meta-

One via Multi-One to Utter-One, we also stress that Meta-One is the core of the process of development: the Meta-One is the One in which that all potential multiplicities were implied. The Multi-One extends the Meta-One, and the Utter-One is a relatively complete stage. We may borrow Zhu Xi's example about "grass," a seed of grass can be described by the category Meta-One, the mutilated grass with flowers can be explained by Multi-One, and Utter-One represents the stage that the grass is reaching its end of life and is preparing to get into a new process, this is also what the hexagram *Wei Ji* described. In Zhu Xi's system, one *li* in all things, while in our system, all in one: the seed is one; the mutilated grass is one because the leaves, flowers, and all are still in the unity grass; and the trash is still one, further, in the process of development from Meta-One via Multi-One to Utter-One, the corresponding harmony exists throughout the process, which differs from Zhu Xi's One *li* exists throughout the process. In addition, unlike Zhu's cycle, the Utter-One in our system does not mean ultimately end or go back to the origination. Instead, Utter-One implies a new starting point for the process. Indeed, as Zhu Xi said, heaven and earth, the sun and moon, always run in a cycle. Still, the concept of a cycle does not have high abstractness, nor has the generality that metaphysical categories require. Zhu Xi's vision of the cycle cannot apply to explain all things, including things like his "grass." The system of Meta-One reserves the common ideas of the dynamical process but aims to overcome Zhu Xi's disadvantages and carry on their valuable work.

There is a common point among the authors of *Yi Jing*, Laozi, Zhou Dunyi, and Zhu Xi: all of them believed it is a dynamical process from the Great Ultimate to *yin-yang*, from non-being to being, or from non-ultimate to great ultimate, and to the myriad things, they expressed similar ideas in different ways with different terms. Still, all of them did not use the words "dynamical process."

Zhou Dunyi, one of the great philosophers in the Song Dynasty, made significant contributions to philosophy and influenced Two Cheng brothers, Zhu Xi, and later philosophers. In consideration of the theme of this project about the system of Meta-One, our discussion about Zhou Dunyi focuses on the following three aspects: Zhou's development of the dynamical process of *yin-yang* interaction that was initialized in *Yi Jing*, the significance that Zhou selected the hexagram *Wei Ji* as part of his Tai Ji Figure, and the contribution of his doctrine of Five Elements to the theory of harmony.

First, Zhou developed the ideas about the dynamical process of the Great Ultimate, *yin-yang* interaction, by adding Great Non-Being ("Non-Polarity" [*wuji*] ahead to the Great Ultimate ["Supreme Polarity"]). In the system of change, the authors claimed that the Great Ultimate produced the two models, the two models produced four images, and the four images made eight hexagrams; it is a dynamic process from Great Non-Being to *yin-yang* to four images, and to all things, the Great Ultimate was the source from which *yin* and *yang* were produced. Still, how the *yin* and *yang* were produced and where the Great Ultimate was derived from, the system of change did not explain. Zhou Dun Yi developed and enriched the ideas. He attempted to explain further how the *yin* and *yang* were produced and where the Great Ultimate was derived. Zhou accepted the explanation of the commentaries of The Classic of Changes, and claimed that when the Great Ultimate moves, it produces *yang*, and when it moves to its ultimate, it turns to be rest; rest produces *yin*. When the Great ultimate rest on its ultimate, it moves again. The one movement and one rest are rooted in each other, and the two modes were established with the division between *yin* and *yang*. It seems to Zhou that *yin* and *yang* result from the Great Ultimate's movements and rests.

Different scholars have different explanations about Zhou's *Wu ji er tai ji* 无极而太极; I intend to understand it as a description of a dynamic process of how the myriad things were produced. The critical word *er* 而 functions as a proposition and means "to," Zhou stresses by adding Great Non-Being ahead to the Great Ultimate and constructs a proposition describing the process from Great Non-Being to Great Ultimate. He showed that there was no Great Non-Being outside the Great Being, meaning that the Great Non-Being was contained in the Great Being, and the Great Being was developed from the Great Non-Being. The Great Non-Being and the Great Ultimate are not two; they are essentially one. This claim is close to Lao Zi's idea that all things were derived from being, while the Being was derived from non-Being. We do not have proofs to assert that Lao Zi influenced Zhou, but we can see that both Laozi's Being and Zhou's Great Ultimate were derived from non-Being (无 *Wu*). The difference is that Zhou claims that there is no Great Non-Being outside the Great Ultimate; Laozi claims that Being was derived from non-Being but did not claim there was no Non-Being outside the Being. The significance of Zhou Dun Yi's claim from the Great Non-Being to the great ultimate is that he enriched the dynamical process compared to the great ultimate in the system of change and was close to Laozi, who supposed there was a non-being before his Being. Laozi's process of being was derived from non-being, and all things were produced from being. Zhou's claim that from non-being to the great ultimate functions explains the origination of the Great Ultimate. The improvements enriched the content of the *yin-yang* interaction ideas and strengthened the process's dynamic features.

Laozi's Non-Being and Zhou Dun Yi's Great Non-Being produced a primary line of thinking for us to propose new categories and propositions. The essential feature of the Meta-One is its potentiality. We may reasonably interpret the Non-Being and the Great Non-Being as potential beings. Laozi's Non-Being was the source from which the Being was derived, and Zhou's Great Non-Being was the source from which the Great Ultimate was derived;

both were non-being and the origins of the Being and Great Ultimate. I believe both possessed the potential that produces or gives birth to the being and the great ultimate.

CORRESPONDING HARMONY: STATIC MODELS

In Meta-One, the harmony of all individuals, parts, or elements was potential; in Multi-One, the harmony was realized; and in Utter-One, the harmony was completed but implied a new beginning. When we observe the various harmonies from a static perspective and specifically focus on the individual things, parts, or elements for continence—I call those "agents"—we may classify the harmonies into the following five static models in terms of the number of agents in a harmonious entity.

Unitary Corresponding Harmony

Unitary corresponding harmony means that a single thing corresponds with itself to reach harmony. How does a single thing shape a corresponding relationship with itself since it is single? A corresponding relationship needs at least two things, two parts, or two elements; how does a single entity meet the essential requirement? We mainly characterize a single thing as harmonious because we observe it as a unity. If we explore its inside structure or elements, we may find that the single entity is not single but complex. Even a single seed, an egg, or an elementary particle is not absolutely a single but a compound entity. Let's pick up a seed as an example. A seed is a potential compound entity with multiple elements implied; the various parts would individualize themselves to become a seedling with leaves, branches, flowers, and fruits once the conditions are ready, like the soil, sunshine, and water. As a seed, it is a single entity in a self-corresponding stage, and the elements with corresponding potential relationships with each other coexist in the seed.

In the Chinese philosophical tradition, Laozi's being and non-being also belong to the corresponding unitary harmony. His being was derived from non-being (*You sheng yu wu* 有生于无). Before the non-being was produced, the being was a self-corresponding entity because the being was implied in the non-being, potentially but not yet realized. Non-being is one but potentially two, so the harmony between non-being and being is unitary. Once the being is produced, being and non-being form a corresponding relationship and move into a dynamic process similar to Meta-One. Meta-One is a self-corresponding entity in which all potential diversities coexist peacefully, cooperatively, or supportively and reach unitary harmony.

Zhou Dun Yi's non-ultimate (*wu ji*) is a unitary, harmonious entity. For him, great-ultimate (*tai ji*) is not outside the non-ultimate; what he addressed from non-ultimate to great ultimate (*wu ji er tai ji*), in my understanding, is like from Meta-One to Multi-One. The great-ultimate was implied in the non-ultimate potential, and the process from non-ultimate to great-ultimate is a process that the non-ultimate realized itself. It is also the process from potentiality to reality. The non-ultimate and great ultimate essentially are in one since there is no great-ultimate outside of the non-ultimate, the great-ultimate in the non-ultimate shaped a unitary harmony. Just like a human body produced the shadow image of a human body, or a bamboo pole created a shadow image of a bamboo pole, one corresponds to itself, and each corresponds to the other. The essential difference between the analogies of the images of the human body and the bamboo pole is that the non-being is an invisible being. In contrast, the human body and bamboo pole are visible.

Not just the non-ultimate, but also the great-ultimate was also a self-corresponding harmony: when the great ultimate moves, it produces *yang*, and when it rests, it produces *yin*. One movement and one rest-ness built up the two modes. The two modes embody the harmony between the non-ultimate and the great-ultimate. Thus, the great-ultimate was an entity in which the *yin* and *yang* and their corresponding relationship were implied potentially and shaped a unitary harmony.

Following the same principle, I intend to interpret Feng You Lan's *li* and things as a corresponding relationship and characterize the relationship as a unitary harmony. Fen You Lan, who inherited and developed Zhou Dunyi's idea of great-ultimate, Cheng-Zhu's concepts of nature and *li*, claimed a square thing is square because it corresponds to the *li* of the square. Here is a corresponding relationship between the square thing and the *li* of the square, and essentially the square thing corresponds to itself because there is no *li* of the square outside of square things. When a square thing corresponds to the *li* of the square, it essentially is a self-corresponding relationship. If the square thing corresponds to the *li* of the square, they reach a unitary harmony; if it does not correspond to the *li* of the square, they are in an unharmonious relationship.

If we understand the non-being, non-ultimate, great-ultimate, and *li* have conceptualized entities like Meta-One, they belong to the model of unitary harmony. The great-ultimate in *The Classic of Changes*, Laozi's non-being, Zhou Dun Yi's non-ultimate and great-ultimate, the Song-Ming philosophers' and Feng You Lan's *li*, all of those have the feature of the self-corresponding relationship. The corresponding relationship is the foundation for reaching unitary harmony.

Binary Corresponding Harmony

Binary harmony is one of the most popular models of balance and harmony. Harmony is when two agents (things, parts, or elements) correspond to one another and coexist peacefully, cooperatively, or supportively. I call it a corresponding binary harmony. As mentioned, *yin* versus *yang,* heaven versus earth, the sun versus moon, long versus short, beauty versus ugly, and good versus evil all have a corresponding relationship. The corresponding relationship is the primary condition to reach harmony because two isolated agents without interaction or relationship cannot achieve harmony. Two agents are opposite or corresponding to each other to realize harmony or break down harmony. The number of agents could change in realizing harmony or breaking down a harmony, but this is the content of the partial versus full harmony model seen from a dynamic perspective. Here, I limit the agents to two but accept any changes, as two agents changed to two groups, multiple agents changed to two groups, or one divided into two; these belong to the model of binary harmony.

Ancient philosophers observed the phenomena of one corresponding to another and their harmony. Laozi said, "And so being and non-being beget each other; difficult and easy to complement each other; long and short compare each with each other; high and low prop each other; sound and echo harmonize with each other; front and back follow each other."[28]

In Laozi's discourse, existence and nonexistence, difficult and ease, long and short, and high and low correspond to each other. Still, they are not in conflict, harmful to each other, and do not fight or overcome one another because of the differences between each the two; each of them identifies itself and becomes what they are, and based on the corresponding relationships, each of the two has reached perfect harmony.

Zhu Xi observed the phenomena of opposite relationships and explored the inseparable connection of two opposite elements. When someone asked Zhu Xi if *yin* and *yang* coexisted and were not isolated from one another in the very beginning, he answered yes. He also claimed that the opposition between the high and the low, between the large and the small, and between the clear and the turbid existed together. Zhu Xi used these examples to explain his claim about the opposition between *yin* and *yang*. He further stressed that the opposite poles could not be separated or isolated. It is because of *li* (principle) and produced by heaven. Therefore, there cannot be *yin* alone; there must also be *yang*. And there cannot be *yang* alone; there must also be *yin*. There must be opposition. In this opposition, it is not a principle that opposes, but according to principle, there should be opposition like this. This is also a common idea for almost all Chinese philosophers. *Yin* and *yang* always existed together and cannot be isolated from one another.

Zhu Xi's descriptions of opposite relationships fall into the category of corresponding relationships, although he did not mention harmony. If we observe the natural world, human society, and human thinking, corresponding relationships between two things, events, or elements are common. Since the relationships happened between two things, occurrences, or parts, I attribute them to corresponding binary relationships and further interpret the entities with the relationships as binary harmonious entities.

Binary harmony also existed in human society. Common interests between two counties, groups, or people in political, religious, geographical, economic, or military aspects may lead them to ally with one another, build a corresponding relationship, and reach a binary harmony. Conflicts between two countries, groups, or people in political, economic, and other's interests may cause negative interactions, fighting with each other, or even defeating another to break down the established balance and harmony. Eventually, the result of the negative interactions will move to reach a new binary harmony. Harmony is the ultimate destiny, while inharmony is a transitional stage that could be long or short.

In short, corresponding binary harmony widely existed in the cosmos, natural world, human society, architecture and art, fine art, carving art, and daily life. The balance between two things, parts, or elements is a form of corresponding binary harmony.

Ternary Corresponding Harmony

The model of ternary harmony refers to a harmonious entity in which three agents (individual things in a system, parts in a whole unity, or elements in a single entity) correspond to each other, or one corresponds to another, and another corresponds to the third, or correspond to each and another by turn. A ternary harmony implies three factors: there are agents in the harmonious entity; the three agents have a corresponding relationship, either opposite one to another or cooperative with another; and the three agents coexist in the entity peacefully, cooperatively, or supportively. The corresponding relationship among the three agents is the foundation for them to reach harmony. If three items are isolated from one another without connection, the three items cannot achieve corresponding ternary harmony. For instance, there is a piece of a small stone on a sand beach, a sleeper abandoned by a swimmer, and a few tree leaves; since there is no corresponding relationship among them, then they cannot reach corresponding ternary harmony. Unless an artist created a special piece of art with these materials and constructed a relationship of one corresponding to another, the three items could be the agents of a harmonious entity. Not any three individual things, events, or elements that existed together spatially can be counted as the corresponding ternary harmony.

Besides heaven, earth, and humans in Chinese philosophical tradition, we may see a lot of ternary harmonies in the natural world, human society, and daily life. Truth, goodness, and beauty are related to each other. Usually, a behavior with the feature of truth will be recognized with the feature of goodness; a behavior with the feature of goodness would be regarded with the feature of beauty. The three features can benefit, cooperate with, or support each other to establish a corresponding relationship and move toward harmony. A cheating behavior has fakeness; fakeness affects the esthetical judgments of a person's behavior and his behavior is regarded as an ugly performance. His behavior collected fakeness, evil, and ugliness, shaping behavior with negative features. If we regard the person as an entity, the behaviors shaped him as a harmonious entity with negative features.

We can see corresponding ternary harmony in reality, not just individual human behaviors. When three counties are allied with common interests, they establish a corresponding relationship among themselves and can reach corresponding ternary harmony. In a political organization, left-wing, moderate, and right-wing may coexist peacefully, cooperatively, or supportively. However, they may have different claims on many issues; if the three wings are still in the organization, they can form a corresponding ternary harmony. Three buildings or three groups of buildings can shape a ternary harmony in architecture if the designer and builders consciously construct them as a group of buildings in which one corresponds to another in a certain way.

In addition, in a piece of music, treble, mediant, and bass may construct a perfect ternary corresponding harmony because the three tones cooperate and supplement each other in a complete entity. Ternary harmony widely exists in fine arts, like three friends in chilly winter (pine, bamboo, and plum) in many Chinese painters' paintings; in geography, various triangles shape a lot of stable ternary harmony; in people's daily lives, according to the divisions of left, center, and right; above, middle, and below; high, medium, low; large, medium, and small, and so on, people can metaphorically apply these divisions to describe people's social ranks, political attitudes, moral levels, wealth, abilities, knowledge, and educational levels. When people combine each of the three to build a corresponding relationship, they can create various ternary harmonies in terms of distinct division. For instance, in an administration team, old-age, middle-age, and young-age officials occupy an appropriate rate; that team is an ideal structure and forms a ternary harmony.

The trinity as the union of the Father, the Son, and the Holy Spirit in the Christian tradition is a corresponding ternary harmony. Ternary harmony widely existed in the universe, the natural world, human society, and people's social, political, and daily lives. Efficient knowledge, ability, and information is needed to identify whether it is a binary, ternary, or pentabasic entity from multiple countries, groups, or people involved in relevant affairs; one error could cause serious mistakes; we do not discuss this technical issue in this project. Once we identify complex relationships among countries, social organizations, or political groups as a corresponding ternary relation, we should target to explore the three agents and their interactions, grasp the trends of the developments of the three agents, and the whole unit to make the right decisions for our behaviors. Pentabasic corresponding harmony discusses harmony with five agents independently and classifies it as the corresponding pentabasic harmony. In a broad sense, this harmony should be attributed to multiple corresponding harmonies, but the number "five" is extraordinary in Chinese cultural tradition. We may find over two hundred idioms in any Chinese dictionary related to the number five.

Theoretically, each of the five agents could find another that corresponds to it at a particular time based on the assumption that everything has another thing corresponding to that thing. If five things, events, or elements coexist in an entity, they could build up certain corresponding relationships. Once a corresponding relationship is built, a pentabasic harmony is reached or to be achieved in the future because of the interactions among the five agents. The harmony could be a balance among the five agents, a unification of the five agents, an emergence of the five agents, or coexistence peacefully, cooperatively, or supportively in a group.

Ancient Chinese philosophers observed the corresponding relationships and models of harmony among five things; the most popular and classic pentabasic harmony should be the Five Elements theory.[29]

Ancient philosophers believed that melt, wood, water, fire, and earth have corresponding dual relationships of generating and overcoming each other. Too many philosophers have discussed the ideas of the Five Elements to name. I take Dong Zhongshu as an example to exemplify how ancient philosophers extended the views of the Five Elements to many other things. Dong narrated the relationship between the Five Elements: wood generates fire, fire generates earth, melt generates water, and water generates wood.[30] Dong Zhongshu interpreted the Five Elements as five behaviors: Five Elements means five behaviors (*Wu xing zhe, wu xing ye* 五行者，五行也). He then extended the relationships between father and son, lord and ministers. Thus, he said, the earth is the noblest among the Five Elements; the minister's loyalty, the son's filial piety, and justice were generated from the earth.[31] Dong further extended to the five tones (sounds) of music, "the tone of Gong (宮) is the noblest among five sounds, and sweet is the nicest taste among five tastes, yellow is the noblest among the five colors, and filial piety is the most significant of the earth."[32] We can see from Dong Zhongshu's elaborations that not just the Five Elements correspond to each other; the relationships of the Five Elements also correspond to the relationships between heaven and earth, lord and minister, father and son, five sounds, five tastes, and five colors.

Dong Zhongshu did not talk about the relationships of one overcoming another: melt overcomes wood, wood overcomes earth, earth overcomes water, water overcomes fire, and fire overcomes melt. He also did not mention harmony, but his descriptions of the relationship between the Five Elements and human affairs lead to harmony. When we combine Dong's ideas of the interactions between heaven and humans and his advice to the Han-Wu Emperor that heaven warms the son of heaven, emperors, by disasters like flooding if the emperor did wrong things to his people, he wanted his emperor to follow the *dao* of heaven and reach harmony between heaven and humans.

In the universe, five stars: Venus, Jupiter, Mercury, Mars, and Saturn; five directions: east, south, west, north, and center; five colors: green, red, yellow, white, and black; five parts of the body: vessel, muscle, hair and skin, and bone. In the Chinese philosophical tradition, the Five Elements also correspond to many other things; humans' five organs: heart, liver, spleen, stomach, lung, and kidney correspond to humans' five organs: tone-heart, eyes-sliver, nose-lung, mouth-sleep, and ears-kidney. In ethics, there are five permanent virtues: benevolence, justice, rituals, wisdom, and sincerity; five characteristics: intelligence, armed, brave, kind, and sincere; five sounds that create harmonious music, and so forth. All the abovementioned five things make up corresponding relationships and harmonious systems.

The harmony among five things, events, or elements and the harmony between Five Elements and other things, including human affairs, existed widely. The harmony of five items, occurrences, or parts is a particular type of multiple harmonies; because of the specialty of the number five, I characterized it as a pentabasic model harmony.

Multivariate Corresponding Harmony

I define the corresponding multivariate harmony by three factors: the number of agents (individual things, parts, or elements) included in a harmonious entity, the corresponding relationship among various agents, and the ways of the existence of the different agents. If multiple agents coexisted in an entity peacefully, cooperatively, or supportively based on certain corresponding relationships, finally, I call it corresponding multivariate harmony.

Another type of harmony, multivariate harmony, existed widely. The universe is a multivariate harmonious entity in which multiple agents correspond to each other or one with another, interact with each other or one with another, and coexist in an entity peacefully, cooperatively, and supportively. The corresponding relationships are complex and multivariate, including opposite to each other, one overcoming another, or cooperating and support to each other. On the earth, the oceans, lands, mountains, rivers, forests, humans, and other animals all exist on the earth harmoniously, although partial and temporary unharmonious phenomena happen and are happening from time to time. Still, as a complete entity, the myriad things on earth coexisted in harmony.

In human societies, multiple countries, different political groups in a country, and various political, social, and economic claims, interests, and goals coexist simultaneously. I call these "agents." Multiple agents have multiple purposes and goals in a country or an organization; they interact with each other. The differences and disagreements, even fights, affect reaching harmony, but cannot stop the society from moving toward achieving harmony at a particular time. What I say is that the corresponding relationship means that if one political party proposes an agenda, another party or other parties could agree or disagree; if they agree, they build up a corresponding relationship, which is like the one mentioned in the Book of Change, one follows another; if other parties disagree with that agenda, they build up a corresponding relationship, which is what Zhu Xi described, an opposite relationship. In whichever way, once different political groups coexist in a particular society, they build up certain corresponding relationships, which is a starting point from which harmony can finally be reached in a certain way at a specific time. In human societies, not just political groups, economical, military, cultural, religious, and racial groups follow the same principle. The corresponding multivariate harmony either is potential in Meta-One, realized in Multi-One, or completed in Utter-One. The differences, disagreements, conflicts, fights, and wars among multiple agents can only affect the progress to reach harmony but cannot prevent the multiple agents from realizing harmony. Harmony is the general destination of the multiple agents and must be realized in a certain way at a particular time. Harmony is the foundation for all natural things, all kinds of groups in human societies, and the universe's continuous existence.

In sum, the entire process from Meta-One through Multi-One to Utter-One is dynamic. It is a process from potential multivariate to realize multivariate, and the process from Multi-One to Utter-One is a process from realized multivariate to completed multivariate. The entire process was fulfilled with various corresponding harmonies. Seen from a dynamic process, the multiple harmonies are potential in the Meta-One, the different harmonies realized themselves from potential to factual in the Multi-One, the various harmonies from partial to full were fulfilled in the Multi-One to Utter-One, and the realized various harmonies from temporary to permanent were fulfilled in the Utter-One. Seen from a static perspective, the unitary, binary, ternary, pentabasic, and multiple harmonies are all potentials in the Meta-One, the potential harmonies transformed to reality in the Multi-One, and completed in Utter-One. In the stage Utter-One, the completed unitary, binary, ternary, pentabasic, and multiple harmonies possess the feature of incompleteness and implied new beginnings of new harmonies simultaneously.

NOTES

1. *The Complete Yi Jing*, translated by Taoist Alfred Huang (Rochester, VT: Inner Traditions International, 2004), 37. Hereafter, *The Complete Yi Jing*.

2. "人一口也。三口相同是为合，十口相传十为古". See *Shu Wen Jie Zi* 《说文解字》, annotated by Duan Yu Cai and collated by Xu Shen (Shanghai: Shanghai Classics Press, 2007), 394.

3. Kong Yingda et al. (孔颖达), *Mingjia Pizhu Zhouyi*《名家批注周易》 *Famous Scholars' Commentaries of Zhouyi* (Shenyang: *Wanjuan Chuban Gongsi*, 2009), 319. 【唐】孔颖达等注疏，《名家批注周易》李英健编审。沈阳：万卷出版公司，2009年第319页。 In early ancient time, the legendary figure Fu Xi (伏羲) as the king under heaven, he looked up to heaven, and looked below to observe the ways of the earth, observed the feathers of birds and the furs of animals. He drew analogies from all humans' bodies in near and from the myriad things in distance, then he created the eight hexagrams in which *yin* and *yang* were two core elements. to show the virtues, and to classify the states of the myriad things. "古者包牺氏之王天下也 ，仰则观象于天，俯则观法于地，观鸟兽之文，与地之宜，近取诸身，远取诸物，于是始作八卦，以明之德，以类万物之情。"《名家》第319页.

4. Ibid., 330.

5. Ibid., 333.

6. Ibid.

7. Alfred Huang, "The way of the initiating is change and transformation, so that each being obtain its true nature and destiny." *The Complete I Ching*, translated by Alfred Huang (Rochester, VT: Inner Traditions International, 2004), 24. There are different translations of this sentence; some examples: Richard John Lynn, "the change and transformation of the Dao of Qian in each instance keep the nature and destiny of things correct." *The Classic of Changes*, a new translation of the I Ching as interpreted by Wang Bi, translated by Richard John Lynn (New York: Columbia University Press, 1994), 129. James Legge, "The method of Qian is to change and transform, so that everything obtains its correct nature as appointed (by the mind of Heaven)." *The I Ching*, translated by James Legge (first published by the Clarendon Press in 1899; the second edition, New York: Dover, 1963), 57. I use Alfred Huang's translation.

8. Zhuzi Yulei, vol. II., Jingdu, Chinese Press, first edition in 1970, and third edition in 1984), 1089. 朱熹《朱子语类》下（京都：中文出版社，1970年第一版，1984年第三版，第1089页）。

9. Dmitry S. Gorbunov and Valery A Rubakov, *Introduction to the Theory of the Early Universe: Hot Big Bang Theory* (Singapore: World Science Publishing Co., 2011), 20.

10. Wang Bi and Lynn, trans., *The Classic of Changes*, 129.

11. Huang, trans., *The Complete Yi Jing*, 39.

12. Different translations of the four words 元，亨，利，贞：James Legge: great and originating, penetrating, advantageous, and correct and firm *I Ching: The Book of Changes*, trans. by James Legge (New York: Unveristy Press Inc. 1970), 57; Richard John Lynn: fundamentality, prevalence, fitness, and constancy *The Classic of Changes: A New translation of the I Ching., As Interpreted by Wang Bi*. trans. by Richard John Lynn (New York: Columbia University Press, 1994), 129; Alfred Huang: subline and initiative, prosperous and smooth, favorable and beneficial, and

steadfast and upright *The Complete I Ching*, trans. by Alfred Huang (Rochester: Innner Traditional International,2004), 22.

13. Huang, trans., *The Complete Yi Jing*, 56.

14. *The I Ching (Book of Changes): A Critical Translation of the Ancient Text*, translated by Geoffrey Redmond (London: Bloomsbury Academic Publishing, 2017), 63.

15. Wang Bi and Lynn, trans., *The Classic of Changes*, 152.

16. Kong Yingda et al., *Mingjia Pizhu Zhouyi*《名家批注周易》*Famous Scholars' Commentaries of Zhouyi*, 21.

17. Wang Bi and Lynn, trans., *The Classic of Changes*, 153.

18. Kong Yingda et al., *Mingjia Pizhu Zhouyi*《名家批注周易》*Famous Scholars' Commentaries of Zhouyi*, 294–95.

19. Wang Bi and Lynn, trans., *The Classic of Changes*, 538–45.

20. Huang, trans., *The Complete Yi Jing*, 485–93.

21. 《周易》Huang, Kan (黄侃), *Huan Kan Shoushu Baiwen Shisanjing*《黄侃手批白文十三经》*Thirteen Classics: Huang Kan Manually Apostilled Punctuations* (Shanghai: Shanghai Ancient Books Publishing House, 1983), 37–38.

22. *Zhongguo Tongshi*《中国通史》*General History of Chinese*, edited by Lu Simian（吕思勉）(Chang Chun: Jilin Publishing Group, 2013), 33.

23. Ibid., 37.

24. *The Four Books*, translated by James Legge (Hong Kong: Hui Tung Book Store, 1969), 121.

25. Zhu Xi, *Chu His: Learning to Be a Sage: Selected from the Conversations of Master Chu, Arranged Topically*, translated by Daniel K. Gardner (Berkeley: University of California Press, 1990), 27.

26. Ibid., 100.

27. Ibid., 26.

28. Laozi, *Daodejing: A Literal-Critical Translation* by Joseph Hsu (Lanham, MD: University Press of America, 2008), 6.

29. Sun Xidan（孙希旦），*Liji Jijie*《礼记集解》中册*Collections of Commentaries of the Records of Rituals*, vol. 2 (Beijing: Zhong Hua Shu Ju, 1998), 608.

30. Dong Zhongshu (董仲舒), *Chunqiu Fanlu*《春秋繁露》*Luxuriant Dew of the Spring and Autumn Annals*, edited by Wang Yunwu (Tai Bei: Wen Yuan Ge, 1975), 10.

31. Ibid., 10–11.

32. Ibid.

Chapter Four

Methodological Principles of Metaphorical Metaphysics

In the previous chapter, we examined the source, components, and function of the Meta-One, Multi-One, and Utter-One categories. This chapter further discusses the methodological principles of metaphorical metaphysics. I explore what methodological principles we may develop from the Meta-One, Multi-One, and Utter-One. Before doing so, I examine the most influential traditional methods and classify those methods into different types in terms of their ways of dealing with metaphysical objects. Based on the brief historical examination, I suggest a series of methodological principles and analyze the features of each principle. These works establish the methodology of metaphorical metaphysics.

METAPHYSICAL METHODS AND CLASSIFICATION

Before dealing with various methodological principles, I first clarify the concept of the metaphysical method, including examining the essence and features of the metaphysical method. In a broad sense, metaphysical methods differ and are various. The metaphysical approach could be a massive project because there are different supernatural methods in different systems of metaphysics in different philosophical traditions. For philosophers who claimed to deconstruct metaphysics, their methods are metaphysical because they worked in the metaphysical dimension. Deconstructive philosophers can't deconstruct metaphysics by appealing to experience and science, like those who stand on the ground cannot hit on those who stand on a stage. I would address here that metaphysical methods differ and vary; we should not employ a sole criterion for all different metaphysical methods. Each philosophical tradition has its metaphysical systems and metaphysical methods, and each has its specialties, rationalities, and value. I do not appreciate how to take one criterion for all traditions and repudiate others; we need to acknowledge the diversity and complexity of different metaphysical traditions.

The diversity and complexity of metaphysical objects determined the variety and complexity of metaphysical methods. Instead of examining different definitions of the metaphysical method and falling into an endless debate about how to define it, I focus on characterizing metaphysical methods in terms of their essential features. Although different metaphysical objects require employing different methods and approaches, there is one critical feature that different traditional metaphysical methods share commonly: dealing with abstractive concepts, categories, and propositions.

The substance in Aristotle's metaphysical system, or *yin* and *yang* in *The Classic of Changes*, covers countless individual things as their extensions. The substance, *yin*, and *yang* refer to abstract entities and denote abstract ideas and propositions as their connotations. According to the extension of the category of substance, it covers many items, but the countless individual things are not the direct objects that Aristotle's metaphysics deals with; similarly, the various things with negative characteristics or the characteristics of femaleness, and the various things with positive elements or maleness, were covered by the extensions of the categories of *yin* and *yang*. Still, the various things were not direct objects that Chinese traditional metaphysics directly dealt with; the distinctive feature of abstractness located different methods and approaches at the dimension beyond the empirical layer. I call the dimension beyond the empirical layer the "metaphysical dimension."

Direct Methods and Indirect Methods

In the Chinese philosophical tradition, ancient philosophers in different schools dealt with various objects in the metaphysical dimension; they shared a common point of view that all their insights went beyond individual things and empirical facts in the physical world. The common point determined that their work was metaphysical but not scientific, empirical, or technical. As for how philosophers dealt with individual things and empirical facts to reach the metaphysical dimension to deal with different abstract entities, different philosophers had different ways. Some of them went around the individual stuff and empirical facts, like Laozi in the Pe-Qin philosophy; others took particular things into account when they approached the metaphysical dimension, like Zhu Xi in the Song Dynasty; and some others preferred to skip real things and empirical facts to reach the metaphysical dimension of various entities, like Feng Youlan in contemporary China.

Philosophers chose different methods, approaches, and routes to deal with metaphysical entities in the same dimension. As mountain climbers climb to the peak, some rise from the east, others west, south, or north, while others select southeast and northwest sides to approach the peak. The forgoing common point determined the common essence of the work of different philosophers in different traditions, and that "all roads lead to Rome" shaped the variety of metaphysical methods. The diversity provides theoretical support to recognize the multiplicity of metaphysics and metaphysical practices in Chinese philosophical tradition.

We may classify the various metaphysical methods into two types in terms of how philosophers deal with the relationships between the individual things that the extension of the abstract entities like substance, *yin*, and *yang* covered and the connotations of the conceptual entities implied. When philosophers dealt with metaphysical objects like *yin* and *yang*, they followed two routes: one was to aside or move beyond the individual things that extensions of the categories of substance, *yin*, and *yang* covered, and directly took abstract entities like substance, *yin*, and *yang* as metaphysical objects, which is like after stepping on a stage and removing the stepladder, and then concentrating on dancing on a stage. Another route was to deal with abstract entities like substance, *yin*, and *yang* via dealing with similar empirical entities like all things under heaven, females, and males, like dancing on solid ground but imitating dancing in heaven. We may characterize the former as logical methods and the latter as analogical or metaphorical methods.

Metaphysicians could use a single way to deal with different metaphysical topics in their doctrines. They can also use multiple methods and approaches to deal with the same metaphysical issues. Considering how philosophers describe various transcendental objects or abstract entities, the metaphysical methods could be systematic, unsystematic, positive, negative, direct, and indirect. Here, I briefly classify the processes into direct, indirect, positive, negative, and metaphorical methods. This classification of metaphysical methods is based solely on how the metaphysical objects determined the metaphysical methods.

In the ancient Chinese philosophical tradition, metaphysical methods and approaches can be classified into direct and indirect methods regarding how philosophers describe various metaphysical objects.

We may call the methods that philosophers describe metaphysical objects or deal with metaphysical issues directly involving no individual things, physical elements, or empirical elements, from Aristotle dealing with metaphysical categories in his principles of the first philosophy to Heidegger talking about being and non-being, their methods are primarily direct. In the Western tradition, although Socrates, Plato, Aristotle, Hegel, Wittgenstein, and contemporary philosophers like R. Rorty also used indirect methods like analogies to deal with some of the metaphysical issues metaphorically, direct methods are their primary methods.

In Chinese tradition, the first philosopher, Laozi, tried to talk about the metaphysical *dao* directly but failed to do so. He repeatedly said that he did not know its name; it (*dao*) cannot be named or is nameless. For Laozi, the *dao* that people can verbally express is not the eternal *dao*; we are using metaphysical *dao*, and the name that people can name or call verbally is not a metaphysical name. He finally announced that he scarcely called it "*dao*." Confucian philosophers in the Song Dynasty until Feng Youlan in the Modern era tried to use another term, *li*, to describe metaphysical objects or entities directly but faced a big challenge from the language because the character *li* originally meant the veins on marbling; when philosophers used it to describe metaphysical objects, they chose an indirect approach to analogize the *dao* with the mother and the *li* with the moon. For Laozi, the *dao* was like a mother; for Zhu Xi and Feng Youlan, the *li* was like the moon. One moon is reflected in ten thousand rivers, but there is one moon like there is one *li*. Chinese philosophers described metaphysical objects from Laozi's *dao* (road, path, way) to Zhu Xi's and Feng Youlan's *li*. They dealt with metaphysical issues directly by using those empirical terms to explain or express metaphysical entities indirectly, or specifically speaking, metaphorically; this was because of the features of the characters in the Chinese language.

In the Chinese language, as we know, most characters are ideographs, and a few are pictorial images. Using pictorial characters to describe metaphysical objects or express abstract ideas is hard; the ideographical characters include the radicals or character parts to convey specific meanings, but more is needed to express metaphysical ideas. Most ideographs comprise two parts: one tells meanings, and another shows the sound of that character. For instance, in the word 芳, the above part expresses the meanings of these characters, denoting that this character is related to grass; the lower part indicates the sound "fang." We need to clarify that the meanings expressed by the radical character are directly related to individual things or empirical facts, not the ideas widely used in philosophical arguments. Indeed, some ideographs are very close to expressing abstract concepts, for example, *xiang* 想 (to think, to miss). The above part indicates the sound of this character, and the lower part refers to the mind and expresses the meanings of this character: to think, to miss. The implications that the idea-part of the character indicated are humans' conscious activities, which are invisible. Can we assert that Chinese ideographical characters possess the same features as some of the Western languages? We do not have enough proof to say yes. When using the ideographs to describe metaphysical objects, explain complex relationships between abstract entities or objects, and deal with various metaphysical issues, the meanings that the idea-parts of the characters in the Chinese language yet reach to the metaphysical dimension, which is beyond individual things and empirical facts, as analyzed above. Besides the most influential metaphysical concepts, *yin, yang, dao, wu* 物 (Mengzi's big common name), and *li* in ancient Chinese philosophy, they became metaphysical concepts expressing metaphysical objects by the light of philosophers' endowments and interpretations and reinterpretations by later philosophers, not depending on those words or terms themselves, nor going through changing the shapes or formats of the characters. Based on the unique features of characters in the Chinese language, philosophers found their solution: analogy, exemplification, and analogies were widely employed by Chinese philosophers. It is difficult to explain why ancient Chinese philosophers used alternative methods and approaches to describe metaphysical objects, deal with metaphysical issues, and construct metaphysical systems. We may continue exploring the reasons my work here just aims to stress that ancient Chinese philosophers widely used analogical methods to deal with metaphysical objects and issues metaphorically and partially explain why the metaphysical methods and approaches differ from that of other philosophical traditions.

Positive Methods and Negative Methods

The classification of metaphysical methods is relative but not absolute because the crossing factors break down the boundaries between different methods; the same type of method could be attributed to another class when we change a criterion. The positive method belongs to direct methods, and the "negative method" proposed by Feng Youlan essentially belongs to indirect methods. The differences consist only in that we define the metaphysical methods from different angles in terms of other criteria. When philosophers describe metaphysical entities or dealing metaphysical issues directly borrowing no mediator, like individual things, empirical facts, or any physical existence, their methods can be characterized as direct methods; if those philosophers described the metaphysical objects with confirmations of the features of the objects, their methods were positive; when philosophers dealt with metaphysical objects or metaphysical issues with the help of mediators, they described the objects indirectly. Their methods are indirect; if those philosophers offered their assumptions about the objects with negative statements, like Laozi, the *dao* that can be spoken of is not the permanent *dao*, their methods are negative. Suppose philosophers described metaphysical objects by talking about the counterpart of the object, as Feng Youlan said, to paint the moon by painting the clouds outside the moon (*hongyun tuoyue* 烘雲托月). In that case, the method is also indirect and negative.

The core of drawing the moon by drawing the clouds outside the moon is to draw the moon directly instead of drawing the clouds around the moon directly. I would say Laozi successfully used this negative method. For instance, he did not directly describe what his *dao* was. Instead, he described the features of *dao*: "*Dao* is empty, yet its function is inexhaustible. Fathomless, oh, it seems ancestral to all things! Hidden in the deeps. Oh, it seems ever-present! I do not know whose child it is; it seems to have preceded every god."[1] Here, empty, inexhaustible, ancestral, deep, ever-present, child, and gods are indirectly what the features of the *dao* have. It is the same as drawing the clouds around the moon, but he did not touch upon the *dao*/moon itself. We may characterize the method Laozi describes *dao* characterized as an indirect method, but we may also characterize the method as a negative method.

In another chapter, Laozi said, "*Dao* as a thing is both elusive and evasive, oh, yet it has something formal [image] in it! Elusive and evasive, oh, yet it has something real in it! Dim and dark, oh, yet it has something essential in it! Its essence is very real, and it has truth in it."[2] According to Laozi, *dao* is elusive and mysterious; for the unfathomable *dao*, Laozi used an image (*youxiang* 有象), something (*youwu* 有物), spirit (*youjing* 有精), and trust (*youxin* 有信) to describe the *dao*, just like drawing the moon by drawing the clouds around the moon. We can see that the moon shines in the night, shows different shapes in different seasons, and appears and disappears with the changes in weather. There is an essential difference. However, both the moon and clouds are visible. When we draw the moon, we know its shape, size, and color, while for the *dao* or *li*, and other metaphysical objects, we cannot know what it looks like, how it works, and where it exists. Strictly speaking, drawing the moon by drawing the clouds surrounding the moon and describing a metaphysical object like *dao* by describing its opposites is incomparable, so we should understand Feng's famous analogy metaphorically.

Feng's Negative Method (*fude fangfa* 负的方法) is essentially indirect. For the objects that philosophers intended to describe, the harmful method avoided talking about those objects directly; instead, talking about their counterpart parts to let the objects be described. One difficulty is that philosophers practically speak about the counterparts or outsiders of the metaphysical objects that philosophers wanted to talk about, but still not the metaphysical objects themselves, which philosophers really wanted to talk about. Since philosophers did not discuss those metaphysical objects, how could they describe them accurately? In Feng Youlan's writings, we cannot find more explanations about how to use the harmful method except for the analogy of drawing a moon by drawing the clouds surrounding the moon.

Further, about the core concept of *li*, Feng did not exemplify how to use negative methods to talk about his *li* and relevant metaphysical issues. Indeed, as an analogy, Feng used the example of drawing clouds surrounding the moon to achieve the goal of explaining the negative method metaphorically. Still, we need to recognize that, as the audience, we can see the moon and clouds in the painting no matter how the artist drew the picture—drawing the moon directly or by drawing the clouds surrounding the moon. How can we see the undescribed metaphysical objects that philosophers did not talk about at all? Is the method of drawing clouds to show the moon comparable with the method that talks about metaphysical objects by talking about their counterparts or nonmetaphysical objects?

The negative method keeps unspeakable objects not described, then focuses on the opposite or counterparts of the metaphysical object. For using the negative method, philosophers must identify the metaphysical objects they intend to deal with. They must figure out the counterparts, outsiders, or relevant that they can directly describe. Once philosophers got all the information, they could talk about the objects by talking about their counterparts.

My purpose is not to minimize the significance of Feng Youlan's negative method. I would assert that Feng's negative method still cannot efficiently describe, express, and convey the essence and characteristics of metaphysical objects if we think from the angle of metaphysical objects. Considering Feng Youlan's *li*, as a metaphysical category, how can the *li* be described by describing the counterparts of *li*? Can we describe the *li* by describing what corresponds to the *li*? For instance, can we describe the *li* of the airplane by describing all particular airplanes? The problem is that no matter how many and how we describe the particular airplanes, what we did was to describe individual physical airplanes; how can we present the *li* of the airplane to other people? If we say the physical airplanes are not the counterparts of *li*, metaphorically, they are not the clouds outside of the moon. Then, what are they? Where are they? How can we show the *li* (moon) by drawing them? I assert that the metaphorical method is more functional than the negative one. In the history of Chinese philosophy, it was not popular for philosophers to use the negative method to deal with metaphysical issues, including describing metaphysical objects. Feng Youlan did not use the negative method to deal with his new *li*.

Logical and Metaphorical Methods

The logical method here is limited to the logical method in the Chinese philosophical tradition; nothing is related to the Western philosophical tradition. In the Pre-Qin philosophy, Hui Shi (About 370–310 BC), Gongsun Long (320–250 BC), Mozi, and Xunzi contributed to logic or used logic methods to deal with metaphysical issues. The latter directly relates to our topic, so I choose Gongsun Long to exemplify how ancient Chinese philosophers used logical methods to deal with metaphysical issues.

Gongsun Long distinguished between a common name and a proper name in philosophy, extension, and intension/connotation in logic. He said, "'white horse is not a horse, is this right?' 'Yes.' 'Why?' 'Horse names the shape, white names the color. To name the shape differs from naming the color, so a white horse is not a horse.'"[3] If we analyze the famous proposition from a philosophical perspective, we may say "horse" is a common name, while "white horse" is a proper name or class name. As an abstract concept, the former is the generation of all horses, and the latter is a class name referring to all horses with white color only. From a logical perspective, Gongsun Long distinguished the extension of the concept of the horse and that of the white horse. He said, "to seek horses, yellow and black horses may come. To seek white horses, yellow and black horses cannot come."[4] The extension of the concept of "horse" is wider than the extension of the "white horse." Gongsun Long employed a logical method to express abstract objects. The concept of "horse" is the conceptualization of all individual horses; this is the primary method to deal with metaphysical objects. Although "horse" is not yet a metaphysical concept, we may conceptualize all other individual things by Gongsun Long's method to create metaphysical concepts. Gongsun Long's argument about things can support my assertion.

Gongsun Long argued, "thing is only a coreference, but the coreference is not what the coreference referred to. If there was no coreference in the world, nothing could be called a thing."[5] Thing (wu 物) is the highest abstract concept of all things because it generalizes all individual things. Until today, the concept of *wu* 物 is still the highest abstract concept denoting all physical things in the world. Gongsun Long distinguished between the "thing" as a concept and the "thing" as physical existence, a primary method of dealing with metaphysical objects. All physical existences are concrete and individual when we think of the myriad things in the philosophical dimension. We must conceptualize the myriad things and use the coreference to stand for the myriad things and then be able to think of the myriad things through the coreference.

Gongsun Long's method differs from the metaphorical, indirect, and negative methods; his method is a logical analysis of concepts. The metaphorical method belongs to indirect methods, but this method differs from the negative one. Philosophers who intend to use metaphorical methods to deal with metaphysical objects need to meet the following terms: similarity, comparability, and analogizable.

The ground of analogy is the similarity between the objects that possess high abstractness or transcendental features that the philosopher intends to describe and other objects that are visible and verbally expressible. How is it possible to find similarities between the objects in the realm of metaphysics and the objects in the physical world and analogize one with another? Laozi analogized the invisible *dao* with the mother because the mother can give birth to children. Similarly, the *dao* gives birth to one, two, three, and myriad things. Zhu Xi analogized *li* with the Moon to describe the relationships between *li* and countless individual things. Ancient philosophers' practice convinced us it was possible. The similarities or resemblances of form, essence, nature, function, role, position, and feature of metaphysical objects and empirical things between the metaphysical and empirical realms are the basis for conducting analogies. From the Pre-Qin to the modern era, philosophers always carefully observed the myriad phenomena, causes, and effects and analogized them to invisible metaphysical entities. They successfully constructed their systems of metaphysics with analogical methods. The similarity is the premise of dealing with metaphysical objects and issues analogically or metaphorically.

The comparability between the metaphysical objects that philosophers intended to describe the visible and verbally expressible objects is another condition that philosophers who use the metaphorical method in dealing with metaphysical issues need to meet. One object looks like another, which does not mean the two objects are comparable in all aspects. We can compare a toy vehicle with an actual vehicle about their forms in terms of its outside shapes, but we cannot compare the functions of a toy vehicle with the functions of an actual car because there are no comparable functions in the toy car. The toy's function is for fun, while the vehicle is for practical use. There is no comparability between the two kinds of function; we cannot ask a kid which one is more enjoyable because the function of the actual vehicle is not for enjoyment. In the cases of metaphysical objects, we have more strict requirements for compatibility.

Picking up one example from ancient Chinese philosophy to explain the importance of the similarity of analogical methods, Mengzi analogized human nature with water, claiming that human nature was good inborn like the water always flows to a lower place. Evils were caused by postnatal factors like water flowing over people's heads or up to a mountain. Mengzi's analogy seems strong because water always flows to a lower place, as human nature is always good. Let's carefully analyze Mengzi's analogy of water and human nature. We will find an essential difference between human nature and water: humans can choose their behaviors autonomically, while water can only passively flow to any place lower than its current place. Water has no autonomic choices, while humans are living beings with profound knowledge and abilities that affect humans' choices. Whether Mengzi's claim that "human nature is born good" is reasonable, is not an issue we need to discuss here; his analogy is short of the similarity between human nature and water. Strictly speaking, Mengzi failed to argue for his claim that human nature is good, demonstrating the importance of similarity in employing analogical or metaphorical methods and approaches.

Comparability is necessary for us to conduct analogies of metaphysical concepts with empirical objects must meet; otherwise, our arguments will not be apparent or even lead to incorrect conclusions. When ancient Chinese philosophers analogized *Yin* and *Yang* with female and male, the high rate of compatibility made the metaphysical concepts of *yin* and *yang* understandable; when philosophers extended the distinction between female and male to physical existence, the analogies turned to be far-fetched. The generality of the concepts of *yin* and *yang* was significantly affected negatively.

The rationality of analogy is the guarantee of describing metaphysical objects and dealing with metaphysical issues metaphorically. In *Mengzi*, the great debate about rituals, food, and sex is an excellent example of explaining the rationality of analogy. One asked if there are rituals, food, and women, which one is most important? The answer is rituals. Asked again, suppose that if following the ways, you cannot get food, you cannot get married, but if you do not follow the rituals, you can get food, marry, and do you still think that the rituals are most important? Mengzi indicated the irrationality of the analogies, which is the same as putting a foot-long wood on the top of a tall building to show that the one-foot wood is taller than the building.[6] To better understand the rationality of analogy, we may consider "heaven," which was widely accepted in ancient times. A king or an emperor in a kingdom on earth was regarded as the son of heaven, and the relationship between heaven and the king was analogically transformed to the relationship between father and son. The son's duty was to govern the kingdom according to the will of heaven, the same as carrying out the will of the father, including attacking another kingdom. The analogy was believed to be accurate and rational in ancient China. Still, today, if a leader of a country tells his people to attack another country and announces it is the will of heaven, no one will believe what he said. The analogy between heaven and the leader is no longer regarded as rational, and heaven as a superpower with an entire personality is no longer considered rational. If our metaphors are reasonable, the metaphorical methods are still functional; for instance, if we analogize the sincerity of nature with humans' sincerity, we may draw correct conclusions. Nature is sincere because, after spring, summer follows, and after summer, winter follows; nature always keeps its gravity and never cheats on humans. We, as humans, should learn from nature, behave as nature does, and cheat no one. These conclusions are derived from the analogy between the personalized nature (as if it had the choice to be sincere and human). The conclusions were made by the metaphorical method, but no logical inferences were involved. I would stress that the representative methods based on analogies are still helpful, functional, and rational in dealing with metaphysical issues even today when science and technique have been highly advanced.

The classification of metaphysical methods is based on the features of a different type of method. I propose the following methodological principles according to the features of Meta-One, Multi-One, and Utter-One.

METHODOLOGICAL PRINCIPLES FROM META-ONE

As we have explained, corresponding harmony was potentially implied in Meta-One, it currently exists in the stage of Multi-One, and is completed in the stage of Utter-One. Hence, the methodological principles essentially are embodiments of the corresponding harmony at different stages in the process of Meta-One through Multi-One to Utter-One. We may draw the following metaphysical principles from the first stage of Meta-One.

Methodological Principle of Holism

When we think of the Meta-One from the methodological perspective, we need to refer to its features. The key features of the Meta-One are potentialities and possibilities; anything on the stage possesses these features. A natural thing like a seed looks like a single entity but implies all potentialities and possibilities; for an artificial event like war, in the stage of Meta-One, the war is a plan as an entity possessing different potentialities and possibilities. Based on the feature that all potentialities and possibilities are implied in one entity, we withdraw the methodological principle of holism.

Meta-One emphasizes one; analogically, the universe is one, the earth is one, human society is one, all countries on the planet are one—a global village; the world of animals comprises a unique world, and all living beings are in one. An organization, a single person, or any other single item is one, and a single cell is one . . . ; although these have comprised distinct elements, parts, or pieces, we may think of them as single entities. We may locate every aspect, position, or component within the entities. For instance, as humans, we may identify ourselves within the entity of the universe and apply the holistic view to observe the relationship between ourselves and the universe.

Ancient Chinese philosophers did so. Zhuangzi announced that the myriad things equal me because he reached the realm where he thought of himself as part of the universe. When we locate ourselves in the universe and think of ourselves as parts of the universe, we can acknowledge our infinitesimal and shape a humble personality: what we know about the universe is extremely limited, and it is far for us to see the world ultimately. When we locate ourselves in a society, a country, or a social organization, we recognize our rights and equalization with another; we also know our limitations and duties, which may affect the existence of the society, the country, or the organization in which we are members.

The principle of holism can apply to a country, a social-political organization, an economic group, and anything as a complete entity comprising multiplets. The entire human society, a country, a social-political organization, or an economic entity like a company is like a train; each part of the train has unique functions and importance. Indeed, the train's engine could say that the train could not move without my work, but the wheels also could say that the train could not move without my work; and the train could say that the train could be a useless toy without us. If we deconstruct the train, it means nothing, but if we respect each part and recognize each part's unique functions and contributions to the train transportation tool, all parts realize their values in the complete entity.

Chinese people admire collectivism but do not admire individualism and anarchism. In ancient China, people believed that a state was an extended family, and a family was a minimized country. In ancient China, Mozi claimed universal love and benefitting each other; in Modern China, Sun Zhong Shan/Sun Yixian proposed that "the world belongs to All" (*Tianxia weigong* 天下为公); in the contemporary era, China claims that shared prosperity (*gongtong fuyu* 共同富裕), a global community of shared future (*renlei mingyun gongtongti* 人类命运共同体), coexistence in harmony and mutual wining cooperation (*hexie gongchu, hezuo gongying* 和谐共处，合作共赢); all these claims are the embodiments of the holistic view of the world in dealing with state and international affairs.

The holistic view was deeply rooted in Chinese cultural tradition as a methodological principle. It has become a primary method to observe the world, including recognizing humans themselves and transforming the method as an attitude of behavior. I attributed this methodological principle to the category Meta-One because concept One is traditional, and Meta-One incorporates the core concept One. The principle of all-in-one and one in all developed from the category Meta-One and requires recognizing that the potential war is one in which all elements are implied. The potential fight is just one of all probable events in an entity—a country.

Methodological Principle of Centralism

Meta-One can metaphorically refer to any entity in which multiple things, parts, or elements were implied, as we have defined. All entities the Meta-

One referred to are conceptualized abstract entities because Meta-One, as a metaphysical category, does not directly refer to any actual entity. Still, all the abstract entities originated from the entities in the physical world, human society, and human consciousness. Thus, we talk about entities in the real world through conceptualized abstract entities.

The Meta-One is an entity in which multiple potentialities and possibilities are implied; among all potentialities and possibilities for both natural and artificial things, there must be one potentiality or possibility that plays a central role in deciding the direction of the development of the entity. Any entity must have a central point, a central element, a central part, a central role, and so forth, and all other things, parts, elements, and roles either exist as surrounds of the central point or associate with the central point geologically, or service, cooperate, or support to the central point functionally. If the entity is a physical object, there must be a geological center part; if the entity is a social-political event, there must be a central mission; if the entity is a system of ideas, there must be a central idea; if the entity is an administration of an organization, there must be a central figure; if the entity is a country, there must be a constitution law as a central principle to unify and regularize all peoples' speech and behavior, including president; if the entity is a kingdom, state, or a country, there must be king, emperor, or president and his/her administration as a central part of the country.

The Meta-One implies multiple potentialities and possibilities, and among all potentialities and possibilities, there must have one as the central element; the central element determines the direction of the development of the entity, and other elements service to achieve the goal that the central element determined. The methodological principle of centralism is developed from Meta-One.

The centralist methodological principle can apply to any entity in which multiple things, parts, or elements are implied. For natural things like the seed of an apple tree, there must be a potential plumule as the central element. All other parts of the seed support the plumules growing up. Once the plumule grows up, all leaves, roots, and branches serve for the seeding as the central element. The central element determines the direction of the entire seed until it grows up and maturates to be an apple tree with flowers and apples. When all potentialities and possibilities completed themselves and became what they are, the central element grew up to be a stem central of the tree.

For a social-political event like a war, if it is a defensive war, then defense is the primary mission of the war. The mission of defense functions as a central role, and all other activities service to achieve the central task throughout the war. During the war, a commander of the military general becomes the center of the war. Among the military generals, there must have a chief commander to lead the commander center. Mostly, from ancient till now, behind and beyond the military commander center is a political center comprised of kings, emperors, or today's presidents and their administrations. The political center determines the nature, the scale of the war, and the diplomacy with other countries. Anytime other than during war, every kingdom, state, or country has its political, military, and economic centers. Each center has its central figure, either king, emperor, or president, all the time. An ancient Chinese saying still applies to all countries today: a country cannot be without a king for one day. In the entire world today, no country can be without a king or president for one day.

There must be a central figure in a country, a family, among superiors, an organization, and even a group. Not just a country, in the *Records of Rituals*, Zengzi said, "There were no two Suns on the heaven, no two Kings on the earth, no two Masters in one family, and no two superiors in respect."[7] Except for the fact that both husband and wife can equally be the masters of a family, all others are still significant today.

It is an objective fact that there must be a central part or central element in any natural things in the physical world and a central part and central figure in human society. This objective fact effectively exemplified the characterizations of the Meta-One in which multiple potentialities and possibilities implied a central part of a central element determining the direction of the development of the entity that Meta-One metaphorically referred to.

Theoretically, the methodological principle of centralism is developed from Meta-One, and Meta-One provides the metaphysical foundation for the metaphysical principle. Still, the principle is rooted and originated from the objective facts in the physical world and human society. We may use the methodological principle of centralism to observe, analyze, and explore the physical world and human society. For instance, when we observe human society as a global village and identify each country's specialties in political systems, we need to recognize the common features of all countries: not any country gets rid of the centralist principle. The centralist phenomena widely exist in social-political reality in the world; once we grasp the principle, the methodological principle can help us recognize the world's reality, shape our ideals and attitudes toward real life, and direct our practice in the physical world and social life.

Methodological Principle of the Precognitivism

In the stage of Meta-One, everything is potential, but has not yet happened. Although a critical feature determines that a seed of an apple tree must grow up an apple tree and cannot be a pear tree, there are many other potentialities and possibilities. The seed could be picked up and taken away by a bird, could be dry without enough water, could be damaged by storms, could be cut when it grows up; a defensive war could turn into an offensive war, could win, could lose the war. The feature of the stage of Meta-One requires us to analyze different potentialities and possibilities to predict what could happen, although what we can predict is limited. The multiple potentialities and possibilities provide the opportunity to predicate the directions of development of things and the dynamical process from Meta-One via Multi-One to Utter-One allows us to predict the future of things because of the process from Meta-One via Multi-One to Utter-One is a necessary process. We may predicate a thing's development by tracking the process from potentiality through realizing to completion. The methodological method of precognitivism is derived from the dynamic process of Meta-One through Multi-One to Utter-One.

All natural and artificial things have undergone, or are experiencing, or have undergone a stage in which all potentialities and possibilities are implied. That stage can be described metaphorically by Meta-One. Since Meta-One is a stage fulfilled with potentialities and possibilities, if we analyze the potentialities and possibilities, we can partially predicate the direction of the development of things.

Natural things like a seed of an apple tree—once we identify it as a seed of an apple tree—we can know its potentialities and possibilities of growth in the future. We would know what conditions it demands to grow up and produce apples; we also could understand how we should protect it in growing and avoiding any potential damage. For an artificial event like war, there is a time when the war potentially exists in the stage of a plan, which is also what Meta-One metaphorically describes. Before the war, we need to identify the potentialities and possibilities of the results of the war. As for how we calculate the ratio of winning, we may use scientific and technical skills to calculate the ratio of results. These are not philosophical issues and will not be discussed here. As a methodological principle, it functions to observe the world and an attitude to handle all kinds of things, like political, social, personal, and all others, following the principle of prerecognition.

Humans are probably the most intelligent living beings in the universe, but one thing is hardest for humans to know: the future. As humans, the future lets us look forward but also makes us feel fear. We can investigate the things that happened in the past. We know today what is happening very well, but we do not know what will happen tomorrow. From ancient times until now, science and technology have been highly developed, but what we know about the future is still tiny and extremely limited. In the Chinese tradition, people use different ways to predict the future. They developed profound theories and methods like division, the five elements, the twelve zodiacs, and people's times, dates, and years to predicate a person's future. I would completely ignore this part of Chinese tradition because its rationality is hard to be corroborated by science and technology. The methodological principle of precognitivism does not exclude uncorroborated divination and leaves room for further investigation in the future. Ancient Chinese philosophers' discourses about the necessity and importance of predicting the future are our precious legacy.

In *Analects*, Confucius said, "if a man takes no thought about what is distant, he will find sorrow near at hand. Gentleman should think of the hidden trouble and prevent it in advance."[8] Confucius stressed the importance of prerecognizing the future. Confucius's disciple Yan Hui regarded the prerecognizing future as the core of wisdom. In the *Documents of Mean*, we are told that the future of a kingdom could be known in advance.[9] Confucius and his disciples believed that prerecognition and preparation are keys to success and thought these are applicable to all things, not just some or any particular things.

Confucius gave a series of particular examples to support this argument. He said, "if what is to be spoken is previously determined, there will be no stumbling. If affairs are previously determined, there will be no difficulty with them. If one's actions have been previously determined, there will be no sorrow in connection with them. If principles of conduct have been previously determined, their practice will be inexhaustible."[10] This practical advice tells people to prepare for things that have not yet happened but could happen in the future.

Xun Zi brilliantly explained the necessity of a precognizing future.[11] In the Western Han, Liu Xiang (77–6 BC) explained the advantages of prerecognition and the disadvantages of without prerecognition in the future.[12] Wang Fu in the Eastern Han (102–167) indicated that to govern a country, you need to investigate the truth-ness and fake-ness both far and near you, and prerecognize where the good luck and disasters come from. You can let all ministers devote themselves to protecting the country.[13] Zhu Xi defined the word 预 Yu: to know in advance when he explained the idea in the *Doctrine of Mean*. Although it was not his original idea, he accepted it and advised people to be conscious of the future to prepare for colossal disasters and good luck in the future.

Ancient philosophers' expositions of the necessity and importance of the prerecognition of the future encourage us to employ the methodological principle of prerecognition in real life. Whatever we plan to do, we always need to take attainable goals or results that the project aimed to reach into count, although the goals or results are potential and possibly not real at all. In planning, we predict what could happen and what we could get if our prerecognition is based on the analyses of the potentialities and possibilities and tracks the process from potentiality through realizing to completion.

METHODOLOGICAL PRINCIPLES FROM MULTI-ONE

Multi-One is the stage in which all potentialities and possibilities identify themselves and realize themselves; some potentialities and possibilities realize themselves gradually, while many other potentialities and possibilities might decrease or even disappear. This is a process full of changes. Among all kinds of changes, although there is a central element determining the direction of the development of that thing, other elements function simultaneously. While identifying the central element, we must recognize all other elements and analyze their natures, features, and functions. Although the central element determines the direction of the development, all other elements function positively, passively, or neither positively nor negatively. Their functions change with the changes in the interaction between various elements. To recognize the complexity of things at the stage of Multi-One, we need the methods of pluralism, interactionism, and synergism.

The Methodological Principle of Pluralism

All things, parts, or elements were potential in the entity the Meta-One metaphorically refers to. When the entity develops from Meta-One to Multi-One, all things, parts, or elements identify themselves, realize themselves, and become what they are and should be, so the entity at the stage of Multi-One is a pluralist unity in which all different things, parts, or elements coexist together. Based on this, we withdraw the methodological principle of pluralism.

In different systems of theory, pluralism has been defined differently and may have different meanings. People could apply this term to express multiple features of political, economic, social, and public opinions about public affairs. In this project, I borrow this term and accept the core meaning of the concept, multiple elements coexisted in one entity. The original potentialities and possibilities identify and realize themselves when things develop from Meta-One to Multi-One, and various elements coexist simultaneously; as we know, this is the essential feature of Multi-One.

When we use the ideas of Meta-One to characterize the universe, the universe as an entity corresponds to the stage of Multi-One and is undergoing the process of multiple things coexist. The coexistence of different things in the universe will continue until the day when the life of the universe ends if we accept the heat-death theory of the universe. In the stage where all things coexist, the universe is a plurality of living beings, nonliving beings, and all other things.

Among the world of living beings, human society is a plurality of different political, economic, social, and religious groups. Human society is a plurality; any subjective desire and effort to destruct the plurality are disobeyed to the objective reality. This reality requires us to observe the world according to the method of pluralism; the method of pluralism was developed from Multi-One theoretically but rooted in as originated from reality practically. When we use the method of pluralism to observe our human society and transform the principle as an attitude toward the real world, we must recognize the right of each person as a member of humans, the right of each racial group, each social class, and each country.

The natural world is comprised of all things, and each has its nature, characteristics, and functions; a tree in the natural world is comprised of roots, trunks, branches, leaves, flowers, and fruit. For artificial things, a piece of music corresponds to the principle of pluralism; it comprises distinct sounds, tones, and rhythms; a social-political organization consists of unique members in different ranks, at unique positions, and playing different roles. If the world had only one kind of thing, the world would not be the world today; a tree has only a trunk without branches, leaves, and roots would not be a tree; a piece of music with the same sound, tone, and rhythm, it cannot be music; an organization in which all the members are all leaders with the same authority cannot be functional. The real world is a plurality, and the methodological principle of pluralism is derived from objective reality. When we use the method to observe the world, the method and reality verified, multiply.

When we transform the methodological principle of pluralism into an attitude toward the reality of the world, for instance, international affairs, we should hold an attitude: no matter whether rich or poor, strong or weak, large or small, each country has its unique role and importance in international affairs in the global village, and their right to existence needs to be respected. The methodological principle of pluralism also requires us to appreciate different genders, races, religions, histories, cultures, different customs, styles of life, and habits in teams, in community, and in political, economic, and social organizations. It requires us to accept the plurality of human society.

In short, the methodological principle of pluralism requires people to recognize the plurality of the universe, the human society, a country, a community, an organization, and a team; it eventually leads people to live in harmony with each other.

Methodological Principle of Interactionism

According to Multi-One's characterization, Meta-One describes a stage at which multiple things, parts, or elements identify themselves and realize themselves. During the process, all of them interact with each other. The ways of interaction are various; one could benefit another, support another, or promote another; they also could cooperate with each other, be opposite against each other, or conflict or even fight with each other; more seriously, they could damage each other, or overcome each other, or destroy each other. The multiple interactions happened in the entity that the Multi-One metaphorically refers to, and the results vary accordingly. The entity could be a unity in which all things, parts, or elements coexist together harmoniously and continuously if all of those cooperate; the entity could be significantly changed and form a new entity with new features if changing or replacing the role of the central element; the entity could be destroyed and turn into another entity with another nature, characteristics, and functions if external forces wipe out the entity. These are the components of the potentialities and possibilities implied in the Meta-One and potential reality in the Multi-One, and the methodological principles are based on and derived from the components of the Multi-One.

The history of the evolution of the universe is a history of interactions of all things in the universe; the history of humankind is a history of the interactions between human beings and the natural environment, including the interaction between human beings with ferocious beasts; the history is a history of interactions between kingdoms, states, or countries. In the past, there were corporations between kingdoms, and all people lived in harmony. There were fights and wars between kingdoms, and people lived in the chaos caused by the wars. Until today, some countries and groups of countries are cooperating, supporting, and helping each other, and their people live in harmony. Some other countries and groups of countries are in conflict with each other, fighting each other, and even destroying each other, so their people live in a horrible environment or are dying in the attack of modern advanced weapons.

Again, the methodological principle of interactionism is extended from the features of the Multi-One, but is based on reality. The principle of interaction is the theoretical reflection and generalization of reality; when we use the principle to observe reality, it becomes a method.

Among the various models of interactions, we should appreciate the cooperative interaction and stay alert to the model of destroying each other. The cooperation with each other as a major progressive force and overcoming fighting against each other as an opposing force in early eras, human beings could survive and develop themselves by protecting themselves and not be destroyed by the pernicious natural environment and fierce floods and savage beasts. Human beings benefit from cooperative interaction; we should appreciate it and keep it for today and tomorrow. Otherwise, we could gradually step into the humankind self-destroying model if we choose the wrong interaction model. The methodological principle of interactionism provides us with a methodological principle to observe the world but also guides us to think of the world objectively, choose correct models of interaction, and avoid the models of destroying each other among us human beings.

The methodological principle of interactionism also applies to a country's authorities when we transform the direction of interactionism into an attitude to direct our behaviors. As an example, the leaders face very complex interactional and domestic affairs; the leaders must be able to clarify the complex relationships and locate their countries and people in the net comprising various associations and distinguish positive and negative interactions among different political, ministry, social, religious, and racial groups within the country and the interactions among this country and other countries. The authorities must consider all domestic and international interactions when taking military action against another nation or diplomatic activity, like an ally with other countries. Leaders' decisions and choice of interaction models with other countries certainly influence all sides of different governments and global society. The interactions between countries are dynamic and need to change with the interactions between all sides. Authorities must be able to associate with the progress of the interactions among various sides, respond to the changes and development of the interactions from different sides by choosing proper models of interactions with all other sides during the dynamical process, and finally achieve their goals. Suppose the authorities are unaware of the nature and the tendency of the development of the various interactions between different sides or even isolate their plan from the interactions between domestic and international society. In that case, the authorities could lead their country and people into a serious disaster.

In human society, it is normal for different kingdoms and countries to fight each other for recourse of land, for extending boundaries, and for political, ideological, economic, religious, racial, and regional reasons. Some countries could ally with others for their common interests; some people in a country, an organization, or a team could cooperate for specific shared interests or conflicts with each other. This is an unavoidable reality, but if we follow the principle of interactionism to identify the natures of various interaction models, we choose the models that benefit the entire entity. The entity could be the human society, the human beings, the global village, a country, a social-political organization, or a small team. A country for partial and temporary interests to destroy another country may be followed by destruction by another country, earlier or later; for the interests of the entire entity and long-term beneficence to choose cooperative models of interaction, we finally protect each other and ourselves. These are possible results caused by the diversity of distinct elements and their interactions in an entity. Just like a human, if his heart and brain or other parts of his biological body are not in a cooperative interaction model, he cannot usually survive. The difference is that the existence or demise of human beings and human society is a prolonged and long-time process, so the partial victories of a country or groups of countries are far from reflecting the horrible tendency.

The methodological principle can widely apply to observe, analyze, and recognize the interactions in the physical world, human society, human beings, animal world, country and between countries, social-political organizations, and personal behaviors like leaders and ordinary individuals. When we transform the principle into an attitude of behavior, it guides us to make proper choices from various interactions to promote positive models of interactions to achieve personal, organizational, country, and human beings' common goals—coexisting together in harmony.

Methodological Principle of Synergism

In the process of interaction between multiple things, parts, or elements, the positive interactions lead the entity to develop toward its natural direction, and the negative interactions prevent the entity from developing in its natural direction; the interactions, neither positive nor negative, are unharmful for the natural development of the entity. As mentioned before, the entity is fulfilled with various models of interactions between things, parts, or elements, depending on what the entity is metaphorically referred to. From a dynamic perspective, all those interactions change from time to time as the entity develops from the stage Meta-One described via the stage the Multi-One described, and then to the stage the Utter-One described. Among the various interactions, positive interactions could transform into negative ones, and neutral interactions could change into positive or negative ones. In the entire process of changes, the entity is mostly more significant than the sum of its parts; I believe this is because of the interactions, especially the cooperative interactions. Even negative interactions always exist as a general tendency. Cooperative interactions are the mainstream of all entities. The existence and continued existence of the universe, the natural world, humankind, and myriad things strongly proved the general tendency of the development of all entities. Based on this objective reality and Multi-One features, I borrow the term "synergism" to propose the methodological principle of synergism.

Whether for natural or artificial things, we need to identify all kinds of elements, figure out positive factors, avoid negative aspects, and grasp the direction of development. If it is a natural thing and human effort cannot affect the direction of development, we need to know the development trend; if it is an artificial event, we need to distinguish between positive and negative elements and promote the thing to develop toward its correction direction. The methodological principle of synergism is formed in terms of these considerations.

The methodological principle of synergism stresses the cooperation of multiple elements, members, or parts in an entity. In the world of animals dominated by the law of the jungle, bigger, stronger, and more ferocious animals take the smaller, weaker, and puny for food; humans take other animals as food. Although we stand at the top of the food chain, on this point, we are members of the world of animals, and we abide by the law of the jungle. Why is the world of animals so horrific? We need to explore the nature of animals. A horse eats grass inborn; a tiger eats animal meat inborn. We cannot let a horse eat animal meat or allow a tiger to eat grass. They were so when they were born so. We cannot find reasons to blame them; what we can do is think of them as what they are. When we think about the entire world of animals, we find that the world of animals is harmonious. In each group of animals, there is the spirit of synergism. Groups of sheep, zebra, giraffe, bison, elephant, and many other animals that are easy to take as food by other ferocious animals, always stay together and cooperate to strengthen them. For instance, some watch and are alert when discovering dangerous animals; others create a rear guard so the majority can eat, process, or run to survive. The spirit of those animals' synergism was endowed at birth but functioned well in protecting them from attacking and reducing causalities. Ferocious animals like hyena wolves, lions, and tigers also cooperate in hunting, living, and migrating; in this way, they maintain their intensity and power. The spirit of the synergism of animals was naturally born, and the harmony of the entire world of nature is also naturally reached. The speed and amount of the propagation of all kinds of small or weak animals are much higher than that of ferocious animals, so the entire world of animals keeps its balance naturally.

Indeed, suppose we observe the world of animals from the perspectives of civilized human beings. In that case, we may find that the complete picture in which the food chain of animals is the core subject looks not lovely, even ugly, because it is full of traps, ensnarement, and slaughter, although it is naturally so. As a particular class of animals, we humans have the reason, wisdom, knowledge, and ability to go beyond the law of the jungle. If we say that the synergism of animals was naturally born, I will say that the spirit of the synergism of human beings is not self-conscious. In ancient times, Chinese people expressed similar meanings of the term "synergism" expressed analogically. Old generations used to educate their children in this way: they asked children to break down ten chopsticks with their hands one by one, and kids broke them down quickly and easily; then, old generations put ten chopsticks together, asking children to break them down again. Children tried their best but could not even break any single chopstick. Children learned from the practice that a united team is more vital than a single person; a united team can achieve what a single person cannot. This is the spirit of cooperation, unification, working together, and synergism.

The reality today shows us that our civilized human society is not ideal either; the law of the jungle is still functional to a certain degree. Since human society comprises multiple political, economic, social, racial, cultural, historical, and religious groups, conflict with political, economic, and social systems and ideologies, values, and resources among different groups is unavoidable. The history of human society tells us that when conflicts went beyond the tipping point of harmony, war followed; when the war reached an ending point, a period of harmony followed. The history of human society is just a history of peace to fight, and even today, wars are still ongoing in some regions on the earth. War is one method of solving conflicts. For human beings it has been time-tested and effective, but the negative effects and costs for both sides of the war are tremendous. As ancient Chinese people said, by killing one thousand enemies, you lose eight hundred soldiers. It is hard to estimate the victory and failure of the war, but the results mostly were that neither side gained in the war. War certainly is not an ideal method to solve conflicts, but conflicts always happen, from ancient times to today. We need to find better ways to solve different disputes. In the system of Meta-One, we suggest the methodological principle of synergism as one of the methodological principles to solve conflicts. This principle requires us to acknowledge the objective fact that multiple elements coexist in an entity; here, various countries and regions coexist in today's human society; we recognize the necessity and importance of the interactions among various elements; here, different countries and regions; and admire the spirit of synergism. With synergism in mind, various authorities, countries, regions, groups, organizations, and individuals need to cooperate instead of confront each other; benefit, not damage, and develop together.

However, resources on the earth are limited; how do we cooperate without conflict and fight for the limited resources? The limitation of resources is just one reason our human society needs to cooperate. A country or region may not have enough grains but is full of oil; another country or region may abound with grains without oil. If one isolates from another, the oil cannot transform into food, and the grain cannot let cars move. Cooperation is an effective way to solve these problems.

Cooperation with each other among different countries can exploit and develop new resources like new renewable energies, including migrating to other plants. The spirit of synergism stresses that the capacity of a united team is much stronger than that of single individuals. If we disobey the methodological principle of synergism, isolate from each other, or exterminate opposites for exclusive use of the resources on the earth, the resources will be depleted, and they will be earlier or later demised. When the methodological principle applies to solve the conflicts in human society, it is one of the effective methods to lead humans to live in harmony with each other via cooperation.

METHODOLOGICAL PRINCIPLES FROM UTTER-ONE

The Utter-One describes the completed stage of the development of an entity. When we conceptualized an objective existence as an abstract entity and expressed it by the category Utter-One, the entity possessed three features: completion, infiniteness, and systematics. When an entity develops to the stage of Utter-One, that entity has completed. It has completed the process from Meta-One via Multi-One to Utter-One; the entity has completed but not yet ended. It implied new beginnings and moved into another process of development. The entity is in a system of objective existence and is just one element in a more extensive system. Based on the three features, I propose the three methodological principles: the principles of perfectionism, infinitism, and systematism.

Methodological Principle of Perfectionism

The first methodological principle developed from Utter-One is the principle of perfectionism; I borrow the term "perfectionism" but use it in a broad sense. We have different definitions of perfectionism in psychology, moral philosophy, and ethics. I define perfectionism as a wish or desire for everything to be perfect and characterize the wish as a healthy subjective ideal. The principle of perfectionism is based on the gap between the completion implied in the entity the Utter-One described and the perfection from human's subjective ideals. The gap exists because the completion is not equal to perfection, but humans always wish a completion is also perfect and even equalizes the completion to perfection. Completing an entity's development process is based on objective reality, but perfection is derived from humans' subjective desires. The principle requires the unification of the objective reality of imperfection and humans' objective desires for perfection when we recognize the world and when we transform the principle into a principle of behavior.

Completion is not equal to perfection. At the stage of Utter-One, the entity has completed the process from Meta-One via Multi-One to Utter-One, the universe cannot exemplify the stage of completion because the universe is still at its stage of Multi-One. As a complete entity, the universe is still individualizing and realizing itself. It is far from completion. The natural world is an entire entity; it is also at the stage of Multi-One and is undergoing individualizing and realizing itself. However, if we observe the universe and the natural world as entire entities, in this movement, they have been relatively completed: the universe has been formed, the natural world has been shaped, and they exist in harmony. If we suppose the universe is completed in harmony as a complete entity, the universe is not perfect. There is a potential risk if energy drives and maintains the universe. Once the energy is exhausted, the existence of the universe in its current way will be impossible; if planets colliding is possible, then the natural world being significantly damaged or even perishing will be possible. The risk and possibilities, and many other problems not mentioned here, may cause the imperfection of the universe and the natural world.

All living beings are perfectly made and shaped as part of the natural world. Still, for all living beings, there is a common attribution that determines all living beings are imperfect, all living beings have life, but all living beings have death. Why does death cause the imperfection of human beings? Human beings desire to live for a long time, so since early ancient China, people devoted themselves to seeking a way to have a long life. Longevity has become people's dreams for thousands of years. Even today, people still wish to live healthily and for as long as possible. Among living beings, birds can fly in the sky but cannot swim in water; fish can swim in water but cannot live on the ground; animals can run anywhere on the ground but cannot live in the water; humans can think, can create tools, and make many things and other living beings under control but cannot fly and swim—not as well as birds and fishes. All living beings, although they completed the process from potentialities via individualization to completion or mutuality, are not perfect.

Strictly speaking, almost no artificial thing can be characterized as perfect. Buildings, machines, airplanes, ships, weapons, transportation tools, fine art, music, literature, writings, and so on, for those artificial things themselves, once they were made, they completed the process from potentialities via individualization and realization to the construction of artificial creatures. The creatures are imperfect because they need to be changed and improved in their design, function, shape, colors, and so forth, or humans' requirements and desires are higher than the completed creatures. For the creatures themselves, they have become what they are and exist as they are objectively, neither perfect nor imperfect. There always are gaps between the creatures as objective existences and the humans' desires for perfection. I call humans' desires to pursue perfections "perfectionism" and shape it as a methodological principle.

As a methodological principle, we must distinguish between completion and perfection when we observe and recognize reality and should not equalize completion to perfection. In epistemology, we gain factual knowledge about the natural world and human society in terms of the completion of things; we form our understanding of value by identifying the perfection and imperfection of the completed things—could be natural things or artificial things. In acquiring factual knowledge, we observe, analyze, and investigate the process of the completion, the functions of the completed things, or the value of the completed things or works. According to the investigation's results, we made our judgments and got factual knowledge. Factual knowledge answers one question: what is it? Based on factual knowledge, we further ask what is meaningful for us. We construct our understanding of value by identifying the significance of things. When we say something is valuable, we acknowledge the value of that thing; if we say something is useless, we deny the value of that thing. Based on the knowledge of value, if we ask what it should be or should be like, then perfectionism is involved, and we input our subjective ideas into our judgments and increase what the objective things are short of.

Now we have or partially known the origination of the universe and the process of evolution until today, so we have gained a factual knowledge of the universe; if we further ask what the universe means to us, we may answer that it is meaningful and means a lot to us because we could not exist without the universe, and then we have shaped our knowledge of value about the universe. If we continue asking, what should the universe be or should like? Now we can land on the moon, Mars, and other planets soon after. For later generations in the far future, humans could say the Sun is too close or too far from us; we need to move it. Today, it seems nonsense, but we can imagine or take it as a philosophical hypothesis. Whether it is possible, perfectionism was involved in the epistemological process of value. We are not satisfied with the existing universe; we desire to improve the current universe. This is the conjunction between epistemology and practice. Subjective perfectionism drives us to move beyond reality and develop our imaginations and creative ability to reform the world in practice: improve the natural world like the universe and human-created things like airplanes or reform the existing and completed political, economic, or governmental system.

The analysis above shows us the methodological principle of perfectionism is a method to observe and recognize the world. It is also an attitude toward reality and a technique to direct our practice and behaviors. When we follow the principle of perfectionism to observe and recognize the world, we need to distinguish between completion and perfection and avoid bringing our desires for perfection into the factual knowledge to gain objective truth; when we follow the principle to improve reality, we need to bring our subjective initiative into practice. By doing so, we may eliminate the gap between the objective imperfection of reality and the personal desire for perfection and balance objectivity and subjectivity to reach harmony.

Methodological Principle of Infinitism

As we have explained, the entities the Utter-One metaphorically described are relatively complete, but the completion was not equal to perfection. The completed entity always implied imperfect things, parts, or elements. The imperfective things, parts, or elements are the sources of new beginnings. Based on the features of the Utter-One in which completion with imperfections and new beginnings were implied, I withdraw the methodological principle of infinitism.

The Utter-One described the stage of an entity completing its process from potentiality via multiplicity to reach completion. At the stage of Utter-One, there are continuously undergoing changes and developments. This feature of Utter-One has its objective source but is not our subjective imagination or intellectual innovation, so in ancient China, philosophers talked about the "infinite" in different ways.

In *The Classic of Changes*, the hexagram, *weiji* (未济),[14] describes the complete process but has not yet ended. The *Doctrine of Mean* described the infinite characteristics of heaven and earth, including largeness, deepness, highness, and wideness of heaven and earth. The heaven accommodates the sun, moon, and stars; the world carries high mountains, ocean, sea, and rivers; tortoises, iguanas, iguanodons, dragons, fish, and turtles live in seas; plants, grass, and trees, birds and beasts all live in the mountains. Heaven and earth are not just large, comprehensive, high, and deep, but unceasing. Zhuangzi expressed similar ideas; he said the number of things is unlimited, and time never ceases.[15] Besides repeatedly stressing that time never ceases, he further indicated that, as human beings, our ability to know the world is limited, but the world is infinite. He said, "Our life has a boundary, but there is no boundary to knowledge. To use what has a boundary to pursue what is limitless is dangerous; with this knowledge, if we still go after knowledge, we will run into trouble."[16] Zhuangzi extended the idea that heaven and earth are unceasing to the sage King Wen, saying that the virtue of King Wen (文王 1152–1056 BC) is also unceasing.

Zhu Xi indicated from another angle that the minds of sages were infinitive, even though the world had been governed very well. However, the sages were still worried about what it was, nothing that had not been achieved, and what should be down, so the sages like Yao and Shun never felt satisfied with their governances.[17] Zhu Xi noticed that the sage kings were humble and had infinite minds pursuing perfection, which belongs to the sages who required themselves to be perfect in everything, not humans' subjective recognition of reality and indicates endless characteristics of humans in exploring the world. It seems to Feng Youlan that sages were sages just in the sense of morality. Sages could not know everything,[18] but he said the world and all things in the world never cease. In Feng's words, "Existence is a flow"; he repeatedly stressed this point.[19]

We learned from ancient philosophers that heaven, earth, humans, and the myriad things are unceasing and infinite; humans' ability to know the world is limited, but we have a strong desire to pursue perfection in our behaviors and incomprehensible world. As Zhuangzi described, we push ourselves into a situation where we fully intend to know the infinite world with our limited abilities. Ancient philosophers' work laid a foundation for us to develop the methodological principle of infinitism, which corresponds to the features of the Utter-One in our system.

The universe, the natural world, and the development of human society are infinitive. These have undergone, are undergoing, and will undergo all changes. The sun, moon, and stars mentioned in *the Documents of Mean* run periodically, and the four seasons, Spring, Summer, Autumn, and Winter, come back to us by turn endlessly. All living beings, including us as human beings, appeared on the earth generation by generation; all things are running in a circle ceaselessly.

The infinitive methodological principle differs from the cyclical theory; the former claims the entire world is moving forward unceasingly, while the latter claim the myriad things run cyclically. The sun, moon, and stars are new every day, the four seasons is recent every year, and the countless things in the universe are new every minute, every day, and every year. We, as human beings, are new every day and every year. Once we leave this world, we will leave this world permanently and have no chance of returning to the world again. What does this mean for us in the sense of methodological principle? It means that the knowledge about the world we have gained through observation, experiments, and thinking reflects the world at this stage. Our knowledge and the ability to gain knowledge are limited. Everything is new, including humans ourselves, and our knowledge cannot be absolute truth; it needs to be justified, changed, and developed with the progress of new generations' further studies; later generations in the future will adjust, make changes, or overthrow some of the knowledge we gained and verified today.

Suppose we believe that metaphysical truth is just *li* and that the knowledge about the concrete things that possess the *li* is all empirical knowledge. In that case, our understanding of the world might be limited to recognizing the *li* (essentially name). The *li* of the square is true, and the truthiness of *li* does not rely on exact square things. Because we can deduce there is no XX thing from there is no XX *li*, but we cannot conclude there is no XX *li* from there is no XX thing.[20] *Li* exists before concrete things and continues living if tangible things are banished. *Li* is an empty class without confirmation of individual things and generalizes all *li* from a realm of *li*.

The logic of this claim is the same as the syllogistic reasoning of Aristotle's formal logic, the premise itself is correct, and here, the *li* itself is true. Following this logic, to gain the truth of one thing is to grasp the *li* of that thing; to get the reality of the myriad things is to learn of the *li* of the countless things. *Li* essentially is a name or a logical concept. Once know the terms of the myriad things on earth, can we announce that we have gained the truth of the countless things? How can metaphysical truth reflect the changes and development of the unceasing myriad things? Yes, empirical knowledge reflects the changes and growth of countless things. Our understanding of the never-ceasing myriad of things has been exhausted. These questions puzzle me to conduct further research. Still, I would stress here that the methodological principle of infinitism takes the infinity of the world and the limitations of humans' cognitive ability into account and leaves room for the development of human knowledge and abilities, including metaphysical truth.

When we transform the methodological principle of infinitism into an attitude and method to guide our behaviors, we also consent that humans' abilities are limited, but the unceasing world is infinite. It is easy for us to know what we can do. Still, it is hard for us to understand what we cannot do because advanced science and technics cause a hallucination that we human beings are omnipotent and there is nothing we cannot do; for instance, we can make a weapon to destroy the earth in several minutes, and we can fly into outer space to build labs. However, we are powerless to create a civilized human society. The limitation of cognitive abilities affects only the depth and width of our knowledge of the world.

The vulnerability in building a civilized society lets humans live in fear of war. Among the limitations of humans' abilities, the worst limitation is failing to solve conflict among countries peacefully. The battles among nations and the horror of attacks on innocent civilians warn us that the world is changing unceasingly. Our techniques and means of killing people and destroying humans are advancing unceasingly. Although the mainstream is still peaceful among countries and civilians, the uncountable fear behaviors of nations and individuals in history show that we live in an uncivilized era, far from a highly civilized human society. Only when the day comes that humans solve all kinds of conflicts among countries and people with peaceful talk will we be civilized. When all countries, whether large or small, strong or weak, rich or poor, with no divisions of race, culture, language, religion, or skin color live in harmony, we step into a civilized human society. With this self-awareness in mind to exercise the methodological principle of infinitism, we must rethink our limited abilities and significantly rethink our limited ability to recognize ourselves when we explore the infinite universe. The goal of the methodological principle of the infinite is to guide us to recognize limited ourselves within the endless universe and create a highly civilized human society, becoming a part of the harmonious universe.

The features of completion with new beginnings implied in the Utter-One are the theoretical foundation of the methodological principle of infinitism. The characteristics of the infiniteness of the things in the objective world are the objective grounds of the methodological principle of infinitism. The principle as a method can help us observe and recognize the infinitives of the natural world and the finite of humans. The principle can direct our behaviors and help us keep balance in pursuing the permeant truth of the infinitive world with our limited knowledge and ability.

Methodological Principle of Systematism

We may establish the methodological principle of systematism based on Meta-One, Multi-One, and Utter-One features. The methodological principle of systematism originated from the core feature of Meta-One—One-ness—and developed from the feature of Multi-One diversity, and completed based on the feature of completion in the Utter-One. The future of Oneness comprises Meta-One, Multi-One, and Utter-One, but it performs in different ways. Meta-One is a potential system with the feature of oneness. Multi-One describes an existing system as individualizing and realizing multiplicities. Utter-One denotes a completed system in which all individualized and realized multiplicities have gained their natures and accomplished their goals or destiny. One-ness is the essence and theoretical foundation of a system as a system, and different systems are embodiments of One-ness at different stages of the development of things.

I use the concept of "systematism" in a philosophical method. It means to think of the universe, human society, a government, an organization, a social event, a person, an insect, and so forth as systems and put things, parts, or elements into their systems to study systematically.

The methodological principle has its realistic bases. The universe is a system comprising unlimited things. There are uncountable subsystems like ecosystems and human society; human society is also a system with many subsystems, including countries, social-political organizations, and different groups. The methodological principle of systematism applies to all systems and subsystems when we study the things, parts, or elements of those systems.

A country is a system in which many subsystems are included. If we employ the methodological principle of systematism in a country, we need to know the subsystems, the macro-structure, and the functions of departments of the country; we need to examine further the relationships among different subsystems comprising various organizations of governance, their connections, and the functions of each organization, official, and employers, their duties, the ways of cooperating each other. Based on the basic knowledge of a state's system, we need to investigate further the invisible elements of the system, the history, culture, ideology, governing philosophy, law, policy, and regulations of the country. All those departments in the system, as political, economic, military, social, religious, and cultural organizations, functioned respectively but cooperatively. When we see a political or social event happen in the country, we need to think of that event within the system and cannot isolate that event from other aspects of the system. Suppose we disobey the methodological principle of systematism. We cannot make correct judgments about that event, aren't able to get objective knowledge about that event, and aren't able to take actions to respond to that event, no matter whether we live in or outside of that country. If we isolate one aspect from others in the county, we disobey the methodological principle of systematism and cannot know the event and the nation.

There are higher requirements for a leader or authorities of a country to exercise the methodological principle of systematism. A country is just one among many countries, no country is isolated from other countries, and a nation is just one subsystem in a parent system. In addition, to make correct judgments about the social event, get objective knowledge about it, and take action, for instance, a massive demonstration and strike, the leader and authorities need to locate their own country in the parent system to identify the nature, estimate its influence, and response from the international society. Correct judgments, objective knowledge, and actions come from accurate methods. More severe and complex, to launch a war against another country, it is essential for the leaders and authorities to apply the methodological principle of systematism to plan the war. They need to put their country as a subsystem into the international society as a parent system to consider their action; they need to know that the action as a single project is widely related to all kinds of domestic and international elements. The war in question is an open subsystem with dynamic changes and developments, and the subsystem is related to multiple domestic subsystems, including political, economic, and social systems, and the parent system of international society.

Suppose the authorities decide to start a war based on military ability only and isolate the war from other domestic factors and the concerns of international society; the war could cause serious problems for their country. It is a technical issue to analyze those systems and determine the interactions among the multiple elements in domestic systems and the parent system (a country is just a subsystem of the international society), for instance, using mathematical models, military simulation, or logical inferences. Please do not mention that the results of the war are difficult to expect; their methods of deciding are short of systematic views, which is the core of the methodological principle of systematism; their action is perfunctory and irresponsible to their country, their people, and the international society.

It is the same for us as individual people; we need to think of our speech and behaviors in a particular system, whether that be a team, an organization, a group, or a country, and consider the significance, functions, and results of our speech and behaviors to the system. Suppose we isolate discourses and behaviors from a particular system and do whatever we want according to our profits. In that case, we either cause a negative influence on other individuals and the system, or are discarded by the system. For natural things like ecology, humans need to put our actions into the system to think, plan, and design our artificial projects because the ecological environment is a system that includes human beings. If we isolate our projects from the environmental climate, we will break down the balance of ecology, and the natural disasters caused by our projects could backfire on us. In short, the methodological principle of systematism possesses high generality; it guides us to think, behave, and take actions within specific systems and live in harmony with each other, society, and the natural world.

In this chapter, we have classified methodological methods into direct and indirect, positive and negative, and logical and metaphorical methods in terms of the ways philosophers deal with metaphysical objects; we extended a series of methodological principles from the categories of Meta-One, Multi-One, and Utter-One, and analyzed the methodological significances of those principles. We have also shown the functions of the methodological principles to direct us to take action and behave properly in practice.

NOTES

1. Laozi, *Daodejing: A Literal-Critical Translation*, translated by Joseph Hsu (Lanham, MD: University of America, 2008), 10.
2. Ibid., 36.
3. Wang Guan (王琯) *Gongsun Longzi Xuan Jie*《公孙龙子悬解》*Clarifications of the Suspensions in Gongsun Longzi* (Beijing: Zhong Hua Shu Ju, 1992), 42.
4. Ibid., 43.
5. Ibid., 44.
6. Mengzi, *Mencius*, translated by Irene Bloom, edited and with an introduction by Philip J. Ivanhoe (New York: Columbia University Press, 2009), 132.
7. Sun Xidan (孙希旦撰),《礼记集解》中*Collections of Commentaries of the Records of Rituals*, vol. 2 (Beijing: Zhong Hua Shu Ju, 1998), 522.
8. *The Four Books*, translated by James Legge (Hong Kong: Hui Tung Book Store, 1969), 185.
9. Ibid., 29.
10. Ibid., 19.
11. Xunzi, *Xunzi: The Complete Text*, edited and with contributions by Eric L. Hutton (Princeton, NJ: Princeton University Press, 2014), 293–94.
12. *Shuo Yuan Jin Zhu Jin Yi*《说苑今注今译》*New Commentary and Translation of Shuoyuan*, noted and translated by Lu Yuanjun (卢元骏) (Taibei: Commercial Press, 1977).
13. 《潜夫论》[东汉] 102年–167年. 王符著, translated by Anne Behnke Kinney《实边》as "Populating the Frontier." See *The Art of the Han Essay: Wang*

Fu's Ch'ien-Fu Lun. (Tempe: Center for Asian Studies, Arizona State University, 1990), 56. [Han] Wang, Fu [汉] 王符著, *Qian Fu Lun Qian Jiao Zheng* 《潜夫论笺校正》 (Beijing: Zhong Hua Shu Ju, 2011), 278–79.

14. Geoffrey Redmond translated the hexagrams *Jiji* 既济 as Cross the River and *Weji* 未既 as River Not Yet Crossed. See *The I Ching (Books of Changes): A Critical Translation of the Ancient Text* (London: Bloomsbury Publishing, 2017), 320–323.

15. Zhuangzi, *Zhuangzi*, tanslated by Martin Palmer with Elizabeth Breuilly (London: Penguin Group, 1996), 140.

16. Confucius said talked about sages cultivate themselves, Zhuangzi, *Zhuangzi*, translated by Martin Palmer with Elizabeth Breuilly (London: Penguin Group, 1996), 22.

17. Zhuxi's comments were based on Confucius words, "He [sage] cultivate himself so as to five rest to all the people—even Yap and Shun were still solicitous about this." *The Four Books*, 130–31.

18. Feng Youlan (冯友兰), *Complete Works*, vol. 4, 183.

19. Feng Youlan (冯友兰), 存在是一流行 Existence is a flow. *Complete Works*, vol. 5, 130–31.

20. Ibid., 129.

Chapter Five

Meta-One: Metaphysical Foundation of Chinese Philosophy

The process from Meta-One via Multi-One to Utter-One reflects the vertical development of all elements in one entity. Different corresponding harmony narrates the horizontal interactions among various elements in that entity. The vertical descriptions are incorporated with the dynamical processes of Great Ultimate producing *yin* and *yang*; *dao* generating one, two, three, and the myriad things; the process from Non-Ultimate to Great Ultimate; and the process turning the Great Ultimate into *li* outlines a dynamic process of the development of all things at metaphysical dimension. The vertical processes and the horizontal interactions were all rooted in the Meta-One, the Multi-One is the multiplication of the Meta-One, and the Utter-One is the realization of the Meta-One. Thus, when we explore Chinese philosophy's metaphysical foundation, we concentrate on the core category Meta-One. I suggest the Meta-One as the foundation of Chinese philosophy, including natural, social-political, moral, and Chinese aesthetics.

METAPHYSICAL FOUNDATION OF NATURAL PHILOSOPHY

Natural philosophical thought denotes philosophers' thinking of the physical universe, the natural world, and the myriad things, including humankind, which differs from cosmology, astrology, biology, botany, or physics. Philosophers think of the natural world as a philosophical dimension, not a scientifical one. In ancient China, there was no strict distinction between science and philosophy. Philosophers were curious about the physical universe, the natural world, the myriad things, and humankind. They expressed different ideas, but their ideas were not structured as a systematic natural philosophy in a strict sense, so I call them natural philosophical thought. Since I mainly explore the metaphysical foundation of natural philosophical thought, I will not get into details about the ideas like *yin* and *yang*, *taiji* 太极, and eight hexagrams corresponding to natural phenomena heaven, earth, thunder, wind, water, mountain, and marsh. In addition, I will also not consider the concepts of *yinqi* and *yangqi*, the Five Elements, melt, wood, water, fire, and earth, which are related to natural philosophical issues. The primary task of this part is to suggest Meta-One as the metaphysical foundation of traditional Chinese natural philosophy and argue the rationality of the suggestion by selectively examining ancient philosophers' views about the universe or cosmos, heaven, earth, and myriad things, including humankind and their relationships.

I suggest Meta-One as the metaphysical foundation for natural philosophy based on the three features of Meta-One: Meta-One implies a metaphysical suggestion about the beginning of beginning as we have discussed in the previous chapter, Meta-One denotes a unity with the combination of oneness and diversity, and the dynamic process from Meta-One via Multi-One to Utter-One is incorporated with the critical concept of transformation as an invisible change in traditional Chinese natural philosophical thought.

Beginning of the Beginning

Meta-One implied the metaphysical hypothesis of the beginning of the beginning. I called the first beginning a black hole in philosophy because what exactly the beginning is still unclear to us, but we assumed there must be a beginning before the beginning. The second beginning means the beginning of current existence. The universe or cosmos now exists, and we partially know its beginning: how the physical universe started, called the second beginning. However, what is the beginning of this beginning? We do not know yet. Meta-One leaves room for later generations to continue exploring the beginning of a beginning, reflecting what we know about the universe, the natural world, the myriad things, and humankind.

The hypothesis of the beginning of the beginning in the Meta-One is not just incorporated with ancient philosophers' recognition of the origin of the universe or cosmos, including heaven, earth, the myriad things, and humankind, but also covered and developed the ideas about the beginning of the universe.

The origination of the universe or cosmos, heaven, earth, and humankind is a scientific question, but ancient Chinese philosophers provided their answers. Almost all philosophers from all academic schools talked about heaven and earth and treated heaven and earth as the core concepts in their arguments about the physical universe, the natural world, humankind, and the myriad things. This section focuses on the ideas of the origination of heaven-earth, humankind, and the relationships between heaven-earth and humans. When discussing the origination of heaven and earth, I completely ignore all mystery and legendary stories and pay attention to philosophers' observations and relevant elaborations only because I deal with this issue in the metaphysical dimension.

The hypothesis of the beginning of the beginning cooperates with traditional ideas of the universe's origination, including heaven, earth, myriad things, and humankind. In the Chinese philosophical tradition, an unnamed early ancient philosopher called the universe/cosmos *yuzhou* 宇宙 in terms of the combination of space and time, said, "upper and down plus four directions are called *yu* 宇 and before past via today to future are called *zhou* 宙."[1] According to this description, the universe comprises six directions without boundaries in space and one dimension of infinitive time. Later generations accepted this idea and used the concept widely. The concept *yuzhou* 宇宙 precisely refers to the universe or cosmos, believed to be the largest in space and unlimited in time. Ancient philosophers thought there was a beginning of the universe or cosmos, heaven, and earth were in the universe, and myriad things and humankind were between heaven and earth.

Regarding the origination of heaven and earth, different philosophers had different opinions; the philosophers of *Dao*ism believed that the heaven, earth, humankind, and myriad things originated from *dao* or appeared later than *dao*. Besides, Laozi claimed *dao* was born before the birth of heaven and earth; Zhuangzi also thought before heaven and earth, *dao* already existed, and *dao* generated heaven and earth.[2] For Laozi and Zhuangzi, heaven and earth were derived from *dao*, and *dao* existed by itself before heaven, earth, humankind, and the myriad things.

Among the Pre-Qin Confucian philosophers, Confucius did not talk about the origination of heaven and earth, but he did not deny the existence of heaven with the superpower. He regarded heaven with reverence, respect, and obedience.[3] The same as Confucius, Mengzi also was awed by heaven.[4] They felt heaven as existing, so they never talked about the origination of heaven and earth. They believed that heaven and earth harmonized, producing myriad things and humankind.[5] Obey heaven or disobey heaven and experience the results.[6] Xunzi respected heaven[7] and believed that it existed permanently.

In the *Records of Rituals* (*liji* 《礼记》), Xunzi, Dong Zhongshu, Ban Gu (AC32–AC92), Wang Chong, and many other philosophers talked about different aspects of heaven and earth, such as their sizes, eternal existence, and personalities.

Zhu Xi and Feng Youlan claimed that *li* existed before and outside of *li*. Although Zhu Xi did not use the concept of *dao*, he used *li* to replace Zhou Dunyi's great ultimate, claiming that the great ultimate is just the *li* of myriad things. In consideration of heaven and earth, there is great ultimate in the heaven and earth; regarding the myriad things, there is great ultimate in the myriad things. Before heaven and earth, there indeed was the *li*.[8] Like Laozi's *dao*, Zhu Xi's *li* is formless, with no name.[9] Feng Youlan claimed the myriad things are class names, while heaven-earth or *yu zhou* 宇宙 (universe or cosmos) are the common names (*zong ming* 总名) of the myriad things.[10] Feng's *yu zhou* (universe), great totality, or great One, cannot be spoken and is unthinkable because it is large without outsiders.[11] They are logical concepts.[12] As to the relationship between *li* and the universe, Feng stressed *li* is outside of the universe, heaven, and earth, so it is a fake question to ask which one was first between the universe and *li*.

In sum, in the Chinese philosophical tradition, ancient philosophers assumed that the beginning of the universe, heaven-earth, and myriad things were great ultimate, *dao*, or *li*. Still, they did not leave room for the beginning of the beginning as Meta-One did. The Meta-One implies the metaphysical hypothesis of the beginning of the universe or cosmos, the natural world, heaven and earth, and the myriad things, but also assumes that there is a beginning of the beginning. Meta-One acknowledges a beginning of existence but regards the beginning as the origination of existing things, such as one *yin* and one *yang*, which was called *dao*. The interaction of *yin* (*qi*) and yang (*qi*) produced myriad things. In the system of Meta-One, that beginning is still a physical explanation, not yet in the metaphysical dimension. In the metaphysical dimension, philosophers should think of the beginning of the beginning. Meta-One implied this thinking and left the question open. Meta-One can function as the metaphysical foundation, while *dao*, *yin*, and *yang*, and *li* can be attributed to the philosophical thought of the origination or beginning of the cosmos, but not yet in the metaphysical dimension because the abstractness of those concepts just reached a philosophical level.

One-Ness vs. Multiplicity

Meta-One inherited the traditional Chinese philosophical concept of One and characterized it as the core of the category "Meta-One." Meta functions to enrich the meanings of the One in the category and possess the metaphysical feature of oneness, which further qualifies Meta-One as the metaphysical foundation of Chinese natural philosophical thought. One (*yi* 一) as the highest metaphysical concept differs from many other Chinese philosophical concepts, such as *dao*, *li*, or *yin* and *yang*. One itself is abstract in terms of its literal meaning. Philosophers do not need to add modifiers to endow the One with abstract meanings. As a philosophical concept, one possesses the feature of oneness, which qualifies the category Meta-One as the metaphysical foundation of natural philosophy.

Ancient philosophers used One as a philosophical concept or even metaphysical concept. In the *Book of Change*, the sixty-four hexagrams described all kinds of changes caused by the interactions of *yin* and *yang*, while the *yin* and *yang* were derived from Great Ultimate: Great Ultimate produces two images or modes (*taiji shengliangyi*太极生两仪). If we trace back to the great ultimate, the great ultimate was a producer of *yin*, and *yang* was one and possessed the feature of Oneness. As a metaphysical concept, One does not refer to any single concrete thing. The essence of the *Book of Change* is talking about change, and all kinds of changes and movements can be traced back to One. In the commentary of *Yi Jing, Appended Remarks,* Part II, we may read, "all movements under Heaven are united into One"[13] One possesses the abstract feature of Oneness because all kinds of movements and changes can finally be attributed to One. In addition, "in the world, there are many roads, but the destination is the same. There are a hundred deliberations, but the result is one."[14] The different discourses in the *Book of Change* distinguish between phenomena and essence. All look different from one another if we observe them from their appearances, but they are essentially the same if we recognize their essence. All different things are finally united into One because of their sameness. One, as the essence, does not refer to any individual phenomenon, but no one is outside One. One possesses the highest generality because of the feature of Oneness.

Laozi said heaven becomes apparent when it reaches One, and the earth tends to be quiet when it reaches One. He said, "these of old attained one; Heaven attained one to be clear; earth attained one to be firm; spirits attained one to be mighty; valleys attained one to be full. All things attained one to be alive; lords and kings attained one to be the model of the world; all this became what they are through one."[15] Laozi's One is an abstract concept with generality. Laozi asserted that reaching One is the best situation for heaven, earth, and human societies. Indeed, when there is no snow, black clouds, or storm, we may say that the heaven or sky keeps clear, and the heaven or sky reaches One. One in this context exactly means harmony; if there is no rebellion in a kingdom, we may *say* that the kingdom reached One and is in harmony. In this sense, Laozi's One is another expression of harmony.

Zhuangzi contributed significant philosophical thought to the philosophy of nature, and he also granted One generality. Zhuangzi acknowledged the varieties of things in the world but paid more attention to the sameness and unification of the mixtures in one. Zhuangzi believed that all things in the world are all things themselves, and there are distinctions between one and another, but essentially, they are the same and exist in One. He said, "thus, it is that there are roof slats and pillars, ugliness, and beauty, the peculiar and the extraordinary. All these, by the Tao, are united and become one" (*daotong weiyi*道通為一).[16] Here, Zhuangzi generalized One from what he called "common nature." With the common nature in mind, his many other unusual discourses become understandable, such as "the universe is a finger; all things are a horse"[17] According to Zhuangzi, "there is nothing larger than the point of a hair in the world, yet Mount Tai is small." Zhuangzi said, "Heaven and Earth and I came into existence together, and all things with me are one."[18] He thinks One also cannot be spoken, but his reason differs from Laozi's. In Zhuangzi's words, "Since all things are one, what room is there for speech?" Zhuangzi asserts that once you speak of One, you create something outside One: "One plus speech makes two.[19]" In this way, Zhuangzi stresses One cannot be spoken. Laozi's *dao* and Zhuangzi's One cannot be spoken of, but they have different reasons for this. In another place, Zhuangzi borrowed Confucius' mouth, saying that "'if we see things from the point of view of their difference,' said Confucius, 'even liver and gall are as far away from each other as Chu from Yue. If we see things from the point of view of their identity, all things are one.'"[20] Zhuangzi's descriptions of One tell us that the world is One. Nothing is outside One, so One is used in daily life, but a typical metaphysical concept with the feature of One-ness. Zhuangzi's One is the metaphysical foundation of natural philosophical thought.

Meta-One, on the one hand, absorbed traditional ideas about the beginning of the universe or cosmos and merged the feature of oneness into the category; Meta-One promoted the Oneness as a typical metaphysical feature because the Oneness is no longer the Oneness of the particular entity like the great ultimate, the *dao*, or *li*, but a one with highest abstractness. The feature of Oneness in the great ultimate, *dao*, or *li* was the feature of those particular entities. The Oneness in the Meta-One is no longer limited to any specific entities. Still, it can refer to any entity, including the great ultimate, *dao*, *li*, and others. In this sense, I call the one in the Chinese philosophical tradition a philosophical concept, but the Meta-One is a metaphysical category.

Dynamic Process vs. Transforming

The third feature of the Meta-One strengthens the claim that Meta-One is the metaphysical foundation of natural philosophical thought. The Meta-One is a category implied Multi-One and Utter-One; as we have shown, the Multi-One is the realization of Meta-One, and Utter-One is the completion of Meta-One. There is no Multi-One and Utter-One outside of the Meta-One. In this sense, the three categories are essentially just one category. Since it is a dynamic process from Meta-One via Multi-One to Utter-One, change, development, and transformation were implied. I choose transformation from the three concepts of change, development, and transformation to analyze the metaphysical feature of Meta-One and explain how this feature strengthens the qualification of Meta-One to be the metaphysical foundation of Chinese natural philosophy.

The concept of transformation (化 *Hua*) was ignored in the scholarship of metaphysics in ancient Chinese philosophy because philosophers and scholars paid most of their attention to the concept of change. However, *hua* (transformation) was widely used in ancient Chinese philosophical contexts. Based on my limited search and calculation in terms of the E-version of Chinese classics on the web of Chinese Text Project, Hua (transformation) appeared 349 times in Pre-Qin documents of Daoism, appeared 870 times in Pre-Qin Confucian classics, and 5,370 times in the Song-Ming Confucian classics. The basic meaning of the term "transformation" in those documents was a change, but it was not equal to change. The transformation includes the meaning of change but does not limit to the meaning of change. It denotes three other features that the term "change" does not imply. Transformation implies an invisible process of changing, a gradual process of changing, and an irreversible process of changing. Change emphasizes results, while transformation emphasizes process; change emphasizes current time, while transformation implies the duration of changing; some changes are reversible, for instance, change of a place, position, shape, color, and so forth, while transformation is irreversible, like a person who is getting old, his aging is an irreversible process. Based on my limited search and reading of the texts I mentioned, I claim that these three metaphysical features of the concept of transformation are precisely embodied in the dynamic process from Meta-One through Multi-One to Utter-One. I focus on analyzing these metaphysical features in philosophical thought and ignore the plenty of discourses about the transformation of human affairs.

I assume that transformation includes all kinds of changes but does not refer to individual changes. When a piece of leaves turns to be yellow from green, we may say that the color of the leaf changes, but we do not use the term transformation to show that change. When we plant a tree, three trees, or ten trees, we do not call it as greening (*luhua*); and when one village turns to be a town, two, three, or ten villages turned to be towns, we use "change" to describe it, but we do not use "urbanization." Only when we plan a lot of trees, we may call it greening; and when we upgrade a lot of villages to towns, we may use the word "urbanization" (*dushihua* 都市化) to describe the changes. The term *Hua* (transformation) is more abstract than the term "change" and has higher generality than implied change. In the universe, everything is changing (*bian* 变) and transforming (*hua* 化); there are uncountable types of change and transformation. Just one kind of transformation will be enough to prove its generality, I believe. In the universe, all nonliving beings are aging, many pieces of equipment made by humans are aging, and all living beings are aging. The aging of all these existences is a process, longer or shorter; simple or complex; easy or difficult; and the process is invisible, gradual, and irreversible. As parts of the natural world, we human beings cannot see how our biological bodies are aging and cannot transform back into our younger ages. Nothing in the universe is out of the rule of this law, which convinces me to characterize the concept of transformation as a concept with metaphysical features in traditional Chinese philosophical thought of nature.

It is hard for us to select the discourses that imply the concept of transformation due to too much to choose from. Here, I exemplify the metaphysical features of the concept from the perspective of natural philosophy by referring to several philosophers' discourses.

In one commentary of *Yi Jing*, *Tuan Zhuan* 《彖传》, we may read, "The Heaven and Earth interact with each other and the myriad things were induced and transformed; the sage affected people's hearts, and the world under Heaven reached a peace. Observing what they have affected, the situations of the myriad things become visible."[21] In this context, transformation and inducement of the myriad things were caused by the interaction of heaven and earth; the peace of human society was achieved because of the affection of the sage for ordinary people. We may still feel it is hard to understand what the word "transformation" means; we may analogically say that the process from a zygote grows to a fetus can be understood as a process of transformation (*hua* 化), and when the mother gives birth to the infant, this is what we call *Sheng* (produce/induce). This analogy may not be so accurate, but it explains the two kinds of processes based on the literal meanings of the two words. It makes it easy for us to identify the differences: as we mentioned, transformation is an invisible process, a gradual process, and an irreversible process, which can be proved by the process from zygote to fetus; *Sheng*/produce, here I use the word "induce," as a process with the characteristics of sudden change, it is current, and the results are visible. This is an example of humans' transformation and inducements; it is the same in the natural world. A tree seed needs a long, gradual, and invisible process to mutilate before germinating. This is a transformation process; when germinating, the process moves to a new process, *Sheng* (producing or giving birth or inducing). I have repeatedly mentioned that Chinese philosophers always expressed their abstract concepts. All kinds of artificial physical products not do not undergo the same process: once a wood table is made (*Sheng*), it undergoes a current, sudden change and produces a visible result; once it is made, it moves into an invisible, gradual, irreversible process of aging. Transformation functions to describe changes in natural, human, and physical things. It possesses high generality and should be characterized as a concept with metaphysical features. Transformation, as an essential and most important thought of natural philosophy, the same as other philosophical concepts, heaven and Earth transformed and produced myriad things, was also metaphorically expressed and should be understood metaphorically.

According to *Analects*, "The Master said, I wish to give up speech. Zigong said, if you, our Master, were not to speak, what would we, your disciples, transmit? The Master said, does heaven speak? The four seasons take their course; a hundred things receive life from it. Does heaven speak?"[22]

Meta-One is rooted in tradition and is a continuation of our tradition. As we examine the components and features of the concept of heaven, Oneness, and transformation, we are digging into the components and features of the category Meta-One. The Meta-One incorporates the features of heaven, which were regarded as the originator of all things, covered everything, and nothing was not under its cover; incorporates the features of high abstractness and unification of One-Ness; and incorporates the features of the invisible, gradual, irreversible process of the concept of transformation implied, but we use the dynamical process to conclude these features.

Meta-One includes the feature that heaven possessed as sources of all things because Meta- (*yuan* [元]) implies the feature of initiation; as a stage fulfilled with all potentialities, Meta-One includes the process and features of the transformation; Meta-One implies the features of One-Ness throughout the process, from Meta-One via Multi-One to Utter-One. The high generality, abstractness, full metaphysical features, metaphorical functions, and the competitive dynamical process of the category Meta-One qualify it to be a metaphysical foundation of natural philosophy. All philosophical thinking of nature, or natural philosophical thought, takes the Meta-One as the premise, base, or starting point. The universe, no matter how large it is, how many subuniverses or similar universes it comprises, is closed or open; it exists in three-dimension space or four-dimension space; it began at a particular time or no beginning at all; it is endless or will be vanished in a specific time; it is ceaseless or never ceases; it is static or dynamic. We may take it as Meta-One to think or use Meta-One to describe it, develop our ideas, and construct our natural philosophy of nature. The movements and developments of everything in the universe, including the evolution of the universe itself, no matter as long to be counted by light-years or as short to be measured by light microseconds, no matter whether the process is simple or complex, fast, or slow, all can be described metaphorically with the process from Meta-One via Multi-One to Utter-One. This is what I mean by asserting that the Meta-One is the metaphysical foundation of natural philosophy.

Beginning of the beginning, heaven is a vague concept. It could refer to the physical sky, not a metaphysical *dao* of heaven. The way of a physical heaven run, personalized superpower. Thus, Meta-One; Meta-One emphasizes the dynamic process of transformation from Meta-One, Multi-One to Utter-One. When we think of the universe, cosmos, the natural world, heaven and earth, and the myriad things from a philosophical perspective, we can find that change and transformation are core characteristics of the universe and all things. Since changing is visible transforming, and transforming is invisible change, the changing and transforming are in the same dynamic process and essentially are one. The visible changing and invisible transforming make up a dynamic process, which is just the essential feature of the process from Meta-One through Multi-One to Utter-One. The features of the dynamic process in which changing and transforming were implied strongly support the claim that Meta-One is the metaphysical foundation of Chinese natural philosophy.

METAPHYSICAL FOUNDATION OF SOCIAL-POLITICAL THOUGHT

In the Chinese philosophical tradition, there was no systematic social-political philosophy. Still, there were profound ideas about how a society should be structured, how people should live together, how the rulers should govern a kingdom, the ranks of people in an organization, the structure of governing administration, and relevant issues. Instead of using social-political philosophy, I call ancient Chinese philosophers' ideas about those issues "social-political thought." This part of the chapter does not examine the history of social-political thought, but explores the metaphysical foundation of ancient Chinese political-social thought. I suggest Meta-One as the metaphysical foundation for social and political thought based on the three features of Meta-One: headiness, diversity, and wholeness.

Headiness vs. Kingship

The feature of the headiness of Meta-One provides the grounds for social-political philosophy. The feature of headiness is derived from the meta- in the category Meta-One. Meta- denotes first, head, and chief. These general features do not refer to anything with those characteristics, but all things with these characteristics can be applied. In social and political areas, the head has particular meanings. First, the head could denote people's social ranks and political positions. For convenience, I choose headiness from the three features to analyze the rationality to suggest Meta-One as a metaphysical category for Chinese social and political thoughts. Headiness is a metaphysical feature. It does not refer to any leader, but when we apply it to social and political areas, it can describe the social ranks, positions, and roles in a particular society and political system.

In any society and political system, people play a particular social role, occupy a specific political position, and stay in certain social and political ranks. The feature headiness in the Meta-One is associated with those who are on top levels, occupy leading positions, or play governing roles. In ancient China, most kings, lords, or emperors in later dynasties belonged to this category. In ancient Chinese social and political thought, people regarded the kings, lords, or emperors in a society and political system as the core roles.

All people should obey and be subject to them, in which different philosophers used different languages and ways to express their ideas. So I choose the feature of headiness from all other features of the Meta-One to show Meta-One qualities as the metaphysical foundation of ancient Chinese social-political thought.

Ancient Chinese philosophers endowed kings, lords, or emperors with critical positions in Chinese philosophy. They regarded them as the center of people's social and political life.

Different philosophical schools contributed to social and political thought in the Pre-Qin philosophy. Confucian philosophers claimed to rule a country in terms of virtue and governing or administrate by benevolence. Confucius said to rule a kingdom like the North Star, leading with virtue like all stars running around the North-port star. His benevolent administration requires lords to love people like their own children. The philosophers who admired Daoism claimed that to rule a kingdom should do nothing or no action. If no action is taken, nothing cannot be done, and people will transform themselves into good people. Legalism claimed to rule by law. Mohism offered many valuable strategies for ruling a kingdom, mostly at the technical level, including saving costs, strengthening the foundation, and encouraging and hiring talented people.

When we examine the theoretical foundations on which the social and political thought was built, Heavenly Mandate or destiny (*tianming* 天命) is a critical category. As we have seen that heaven gave birth to myriad things, including humans as animals in the philosophical thought of nature; in social and political thought, heaven oversaw all humans' destinies and all affairs; humans' destinies and affairs were predetermined by heaven, which was Heavenly Mandate.

For some philosophers, heaven was another name for nature; for most philosophers, heaven was regarded as a superpower with personality. Since King Wen (文王) Wen Wang in the Zhou Dynasty (about 1100–771 BC) was praised as the Son of Heaven and received the Heavenly Mandate to rule the entire country, the Son of Heaven and Heavenly Mandate were widely used and repeatedly mentioned in the philosophical texts of different schools from Pre-Qin to Qing Dynasty. Some philosophers who delineated heaven as an impersonal, unconscious, and natural existence—Xunzi's heaven was another name for nature, much like Spinoza's god. Humans' destinies, affairs, and everything happen naturally. The sun, the moon, the four seasons, human birth, and death, everything moves, and all occur naturally happens, and no one controls them.

Those philosophers who believed in personalized heaven admired heaven as a superpower and even worshiped heaven as a god with personality. Mostly, for them, heaven is another name for God. The god or heaven-controlled heaven where the god lived and oversaw all areas and all things under heaven, including assigning sons to rule kingdoms and managing human affairs. As the sons of heaven, the missions of lords, kings, or emperors (different titles in different eras) were to carry out the will of heaven. In the *Rituals of Zhou* (*Zhou Li*《周礼》), the king set up hundreds of official positions in terms of heaven to help the king to manage the kingdom. This official political system influenced China for thousands of years. Although the number of departments in the court was different, the basic framework of the political officials was similar. Heaven was superior, Earth was inferior, the Son of Heaven was superior, and ministers were inferior; all officials in different political positions were ranked, and their political treatments and duties were classified into different ranks. As for humans, affairs like social equalization, social justice, and social changes were determined by heaven. Heaven was believed to be the ultimate authority in maintaining equalization among ordinary people and social justice.

Both the philosophers who equalized heaven to nature, and those who worshiped heaven as a personalized god, indirectly recognized a necessity. For the latter, heaven determined everything in human society. The necessity was rooted in nature. A human's birth and death naturally happen and naturally must be so, with no superpower beyond nature to control. A man became a son of heaven and was granted the power to rule a kingdom, or a bad person was hired as the son of heaven. Unfortunately, his kingdom, kingship, and he must vanish at a particular time. He could not change his fate and end. This was his destiny and was determined by heaven. These philosophers also indirectly recognized the necessity, originating from the personalized heaven. The category Meta-One in our system incorporates the necessity implied in traditional social and political thought and merges the necessity into the process from Meta-One via Multi-One to Utter-One.

Multiplication vs. Social-Political Differentiation

The process from Meta-One via Multi-One to Utter-One is necessary from potentialities via mutualization to the realization of potentialities. It is also a process in which all individuals individualize themselves. The development of human societies, the improvement of political systems, and the advancement of political ecology follow the necessity. Let's ignore the anthropological issue about the origination of human beings and begin directly with the fact that human beings exist and will exist at a specific time. In earlier times, before the formation of tribes, suppose some humans lived separately and individually. As individuals, they could be attacked by other animals. For instance, they could be killed by natural disasters like flooding. They needed to untie together to strengthen their ability to survive. There was a necessity from the demand of reality, not from the personalized heaven or *dao*. When the individuals appeared, the necessity to be united existed potentially, which is what the category Meta-One covered. When they unite, they must grant authority and power to someone and let him lead them to find the water source, hunt for food, and locate themselves for a living. In this way, the positions, the ranks, and even classes with political features were built up from individuals to an organized group, and necessity exited throughout the process. The necessity again came from the demands of reality. If they refused to give up partial rights and did not grant certain members with authority and power to decide, they would go back to being individuals, and it would be hard to survive. Members in a group identified themselves. The leader heads the entire group, keeps food, and leads hunting, farming, and so forth. Establishing the organization or group with political features signifies that Meta-One moved to the stage of Multi-One, in which all possibilities and potentialities are undergoing the processes of realizing themselves. Not all potentialities and possibilities can be realized; only those that correspond to necessity derive from reality's demands. In the stage of Meta-One, all members could possibly become the leader of the group, but only those who met the requirements of being a leader could become a leader. No one received Heavenly Mandate, nor was a leader inborn. A member could become a leader of the group, and it was also because that member met the requirements of being a leader. Once the group or organization was built, it implied all kinds of potentialities and possibilities to be stronger and stronger day by day, and even could be a leader of all allies, could be weaker and weaker day by day and finally vanish; and could be separated from each other and could be annexed by another group. These potentialities and possibilities signify the group moved into a new stage, which falls again into the Meta-One category—after undergoing the stage of Multi-One in which only the possibilities corresponding to the necessity could be realized, then moved to the state of Utter-One. In the stage of the Utter-One, the group existed in a stably and peacefully, and all members lived in harmony with each other. All new potentialities and possibilities were implied and will move forward to a new stage. As a necessary process, the principle from Meta-One via Multi-One to Utter-One can interpret the developments of different countries, political organizations, and social groups.

Once a group was built, let's change our terminology, saying that once a country or a political organization was made, all members' lives no longer are individual but social; all potential issues about members' social lives were gestated at the same time. The issues about equalization, fairness, social justice, social security, social distribution, medical education, and so on. Since we all live in a global village, small countries must get along with big countries. The geological, economical, political, ideological, military, and cultural differences will undoubtedly influence their people's social life. When things are in a potential stage, we may use Meta-One to describe them. Still, the most important thing is to identify the issues in the stage of Meta-One and investigate the necessity that drives the possibilities to realize themselves, and accordingly make strategies in advance to rise to all challenges. When social distribution reaches a seriously unfair situation, and the foundation of government or country is strongly shacked, until this time, the leader recognizes or even not yet acknowledges the order of the magnitude that the leader failed to identify the necessity of the development of that affair from different potentialities and possibilities. When a small country allies with another, the leader should be able to identify the necessity from all possibilities and planes to rise to all potential challenges when he moves forward. To identify the necessary means to figure out if his country did what something happened. If they cannot do so, they could lead their country into danger or even be involved in a horrible war and let their personal experience sufferings. If this happens, claiming social equalization, social fairness, and social justice could be meaningless because their people could lose their normal ways of living, their homelands, and even their lives. A stringent principle is that what is rational may not be realizable; only what is accorded with necessity is realizable.

Necessity is before experience. It existed invisibly in the stage of Meta-One as the potentiality and possibilities developed and realized themselves in the stage of Multi-One, and reached the competitive stage Utter-One. The necessity drove things to build from Meta-One via Multi-One to Utter-One, but it was before experience and invisible. There is an essential difference between the necessity of natural things and social and political affairs. In natural things, like a peach seed, the necessity existed in the seed. Analogically, the Meta-One stage is prior to experience and invisible. The necessity drives it to grow as a peach tree and it cannot be any other tree. In contrast, the necessity that existed at the beginning of the social organization or a political group was built to drive the organization or group to develop to its complete stage via the stage of multiplication. In both natural things and social and political groups, their processes could be disturbed; for the former, natural disasters like storms, and the latter, fighting among members, the government's new legislation could become the force to disturb the processes of their developments even if both followed their necessities. Natural and artificial efforts could disrupt the process but not change the necessities in the seed and the just-created social organizations or political groups. The necessities are prior to experience. This feature qualified the concept of the Heavenly Mandate's function as a metaphysical foundation from which all relevant theories and thoughts were developed. The category Meta-One incorporated the idea of necessity implied in the concept of the Heavenly Mandate and avoided the disadvantages the concept Heavenly Mandate has, which was suggested to be the metaphysical foundation of Chinese social and political thought.

Wholeness and Unification

Meta-One implied the feature of wholeness, which provided a metaphysical foundation for the unification of state/nation in Chinese social-political thought. In ancient China, during the dynasties, and until now, the idea of the unification of state/nation is deeply rooted in people's minds. We may say that the concept of unification in social-political thought was derived from wholeness, so we say the feature of Meta-One functioned as a metaphysical foundation.

In the process from Meta-One via Multi-One to Utter-One, wholeness as a primary feature was implied in the category Meta-One. The One in the Meta-One denotes wholeness, and the wholeness is a typical metaphysical concept because of its high abstractness; One itself implies the meaning of whole literally, and the wholeness is the essential feature of the whole is precisely One. Meta-One does not refer to any concrete thing but can metaphorically refer to any single thing or entity. A single thing or entity is a complete unit with the feature of wholeness.

In social and political thought, the Meta-One could refer to any country, kingdom, state, nation, or social-political organization. For convenience, let's say any single unity. As a single unity, the unification of that unity is a visible characteristic embodied in that unity. It can be reflected by many phenomena, like everyone living together in harmony, working hard for common interests, and so on. When we conceptualize these phenomena, we form the concept of "unification." The concept of unification was derived from the perceptible phenomena embodied in a certain entity. What is the relationship between the concept of unification and the wholeness of Meta-One?

All social-political unities like states or organizations possess the feature of wholeness because all of those are respectively organized systematically, and all those unities are self-based, self-supported, and exist distinctly from others. At the stage of Meta-One, they were respectively whole unities potentially, for instance, an in-planning social or political organization or a to-be-established country; at the stage of Multi-One, various state institutes, governing teams, social or political organizations individualize themselves in their unities. Those unities, either a country or an organization, existed as a unity. At the stage of Utter-One, an established government or a constructed social or political organization, they respectively existed as a whole unity. In the entire process from Meta-One via Multi-One to Utter-One, the feature of wholeness existed throughout. Suppose we observe a country, a society, a state, a nation, or a social or political organization from the Meta-One perspective. In that case, we may find the relationship between the feature of the wholeness of unity, like a country or an organization, and the unification of that unity.

When we further explore the relationship between the feature of wholeness and the unification of a unity-either country, or an organization, we may find that the observable "unification" is just a phenomenon reflected by many perceptible occurrences, not the essence. The essence behind the phenomena is wholeness because "wholeness" is the fundamental feature of a country or an organization as an organization. Suppose a country or an organization loses its essential feature of wholeness. In that case, that country will no longer be a country or an organization because it lost its base to be a country or an organization. No matter how many people gather, they cannot be regarded as a country, an organization, or the people of a country or an organization. They are just massive masses, even if they work together for common interests and goals, which is just a phenomenon. The feature of wholeness implied in Meta-One is the base of the unification of a social-political entity like a country or an organization. The wholeness feature qualifies Meta-One as the metaphysical foundation of social-political philosophy.

One may concern at the stage of Multi-One, all peoples identify themselves by locating themselves in particular social ranks, political positions, and roles in the society and political system. In identifying themselves and locating them into specific social and political classes, the process may be filled with competitions, conflicts, and even fights, so the society and political system are active and growing up with changes and transformations still in the whole unities they belonged to. However, when competitions, conflicts, or wars exceed certain degrees, unification could be broken, and no longer a complete entity could exist. An old organization was broken, and a new entity was established. Before an old entity is broken, all conflicts, fights, or wars must happen in the old entity; once it is damaged, the corresponding relationships between state institutes in a country, between organizations in a society, or between peoples in an organization will be established in the new unity. All this still happened in the entity with the feature of new wholeness. Meta-One will not lose its feature of wholeness, and the new entity will possess a new feature of wholeness.

In the warring states period (475–221 BC), for instance, many kingdoms fought with each other, and one followed another; the country had disintegrated because lords or princes fought for hegemony. If we observe the relationships between kingdoms during that time, it was hard to use the concept of unification to describe. We could see the phenomena but not the essence because kingdoms still fought each other under the umbrella of the kings of Zhou. As long as the kingships of the Zhou remained, it was still a country or a whole unity. It's like a couple who, although they have lived separately for many years, are still married if they did not legally complete the divorce procedure. Their separation is just a phenomenon. Marriage is the essence. In this sense, the process of individualization still happens as a complete entity. During the warring-states period, unification seemed no longer to exist, but the wholeness as the essence of the country was still there. Based on the wholeness, the kings of the Zhou could call for reunification if willing or able, and any lords or princes could fight for unification based on the belief of wholeness. Meta-One implied the feature of wholeness because of its high-degree generality; it does not limit to a country like the Zhou. It can also refer to the wholeness of any country, government, or social-political organization.

Metaphysical Foundation of Moral Philosophy

This part of the chapter explores the metaphysical foundation of Chinese moral philosophy but does not examine the moral philosophy and ethical theories themselves. We may find a common point from all schools in the history of Chinese philosophy that almost all philosophers took heavenly *dao* (*tiandao* 天道) as the basis from which they issued different opinions, created various concepts, offered their arguments, and delivered discourses about all kinds of moral and ethical issues verbally or in writing. I suggest Meta-One as the metaphysical foundation of Chinese moral philosophy instead of the heavenly *dao,* which was treated as the theoretical basis of ancient Chinese moral philosophy.

Good and Evil vs. Goodness and Evilness

In this section, my discussion concentrates on two aspects: based on the analyses of the potentiality of Meta-One, I explore the features of goodness and evilness implied in Meta-One; based on a brief examination of ancient philosophers' work in seeking the source of good and evil from human nature and seeking a criterion of good and bad from heaven, I support the suggestion of characterizing Meta-One as the metaphysical foundation of Chinese moral philosophy.

One essential feature of Meta-One is potentiality, as we have characterized; the potentiality includes multiple factors, such as supportive factors that contribute to a thing's normal development, harmful elements that may prohibit a thing's normal development, neutral factors that are neither helpful nor harmful to a thing's development, passive factors that may slow down a thing's development, and destructive factors that may destroy a thing's existence, and so forth. I classify the multiple potential factors into positive and negative tendencies. The two tendencies are incorporated with the traditional concepts of *yin* and *yang* in terms of similarity between the negative tendency and *yin* and the positive tendency and *yang*. Still, they are different in terms of their components. *Yin* and *yang* were regarded as two opposite elements in the great ultimate, in *dao*, or *li*; negative and positive tendencies are opposite dynamic tendencies. The two tendencies are associated with the process from Meta-One via Multi-One to Utter-One and undergo a process from potentiality through reality to completion. I characterize the positive tendency as good and the negative tendency as bad. When applying the negative tendency to interpret moral and ethical characteristics of human behaviors, I call it evil, and keep calling the positive tendency good.

When human behavior is good, it is regarded as a behavior with the feature of goodness; when it is evil, it is viewed as a behavior with evilness. Those behaviors of good and evil are directly related to people's particular activities they have done. Goodness and evilness are abstract features and can be possessed by any behavior, including the behaviors in question, but do not belong to any behavior. Goodness and evilness are abstract features and are qualified to be metaphysical concepts, but good and evil are just moral philosophical concepts, not yet at the metaphysical dimension. Meta-One, as a metaphysical category, implied the positive and negative tendencies that possessed the features of goodness and evilness. Goodness and evilness could be the features of good and evil behaviors but are not limited to any behavior. Meta-One, which implied the features of goodness and evilness could refer to any behavior, the generalities of the goodness and evilness implied in the Meta-One guaranteed its role as the metaphysical foundation of entire social-political philosophy, not just a basis of any good and evil behaviors, events, or human affairs.

In the Chinese philosophical tradition, ancient philosophers acknowledged the distinction between good and evil in human behaviors. Still, they focused more on exploring the source of good and evil from human nature and finding the criterion of good and evil from heaven.

In the *Analects*, Confucius talked about good (*shan* 善) many times but did not directly claim that human nature is good. In the *Mengzi*, Gaozi, Mengzi himself, and Gongdu Zi delivered different points of view about human nature, including being good inborn, being neither good nor bad, and human nature can be good and can be evil.[23] What they did was to seek the source of good and evil from human nature or examine whether human nature itself was good or evil. Xunzi believed that the bad things made by humans in the world showed that human nature was evil, and ancient sages created rituals, rules, and laws to prohibit people from doing bad things showed human nature was evil. So-called good was not inborn but nurtured by people. Mengzi talked about good and evil in social, political, moral, and ethical areas.[24]

In the Han Dynasty, according to Dong Zhongshu, humans were endowed with admiration for good and hatred of evil from heaven.[25] Dong Zhongshu deleted the troubles under heaven, then reached the good of nature.[26] In addition, some other philosophers believed that humans' good and evil are mixed, and Wang Chong (27 BC–97 AD) claimed that good and evil were derived from parents or inborn,[27] potentially with good and evil, and depend on training/yang.[28]

As the great representative of the Song-Ming doctrine of *li*, Zhu Xi claimed that humans' nature was good inborn. Even if they make mistakes or do immoral things, they can still return to being good.[29]

Feng Youlan took the good and evil of all things into consideration and did not limit itself to discussing the good and evil of human nature.[30] It seemed to Feng that there is no distinction between good and evil because the *li* of everything has no such features of good and evil. As to human nature, human nature has no difference between good and evil in terms of the *li* of humankind, but there are distinctions between good, neither good and nor bad, in terms of material (*qizhi zhixing* 气质之性).[31] Considering the material aspects differences, the materials have good and evil, neither good nor evil. They can be good and evil, so the *things made* of different materials have the distinction between good, not good and not bad, and evil.[32]

The brief examination shows us that ancient philosophers were not satisfied with being able to judge what was good and what was evil; they devoted themselves to finding the source of good and evil: where did the good and evil come from and why there were so many good and evil things that happened, so different opinions of view served for the common purposes. Human nature, as good or evil, became the primary question of ancient moral philosophy. All other moral ideas were determined or related to how to answer this question. Based on the belief that human nature was born good, the primary way to let people be good was moral education, teaching them benevolence, justice, rituals, wisdom, sincerity, loyalty, and filial piety. Based on the belief that human nature was evil, the primary way to make people be good and punish evil was to make strict laws, rules, regulations, moral principles, including rituals based on the belief that human nature was neither good nor evil, and can be good and can be evil, then strict punishments and moral education should keep balance. Ancient philosophers formed different moral philosophical schools based on different answers to the primary question of human nature. In this sense, the theories of human nature functioned as the theoretical foundation of ancient moral philosophy.

Feng Youlan made significant progress in exploring the metaphysical foundation of moral philosophy. Feng's *li* is a *li* of myriad things, including moral and ethical behaviors, and the *li* itself has no such features of good and evil. When applying the *li* to human nature, good and evil comprise humans' material *qi*. As mentioned above, human material *qi* has three classes, so good, evil, and neither good nor evil were formatted. Feng's *li* can be interpreted as a metaphysical foundation, including the metaphysical foundation of moral philosophy. *Li* is a class name belonging to the realm of truth-ness. Understandably, *li* has no features of good or evil. However, if good or evil only comprises or is determined in the material *qi*, *li* is separated or isolated from good and evil. Indeed, we may say that good has the *li* of good, and evil has the *li* of evil; therefore, *li* and good and evil are not separated or isolated. If we keep logical consistency, we still need to say that the *li* of good and evil itself has no features of good and evil; then where does the good and evil derive from, and how can a *li* which has no feature of good and evil be a foundation of good and evil?

The Meta-One potentially implied the features of goodness and evilness derived from positive and negative tendencies. The two directions apply to myriad things, including human moral behaviors. During the process from Meta-One via Multi-One to Utter-One, the goodness and evilness were reflected by being realized or individualized by particular good and evil behaviors and accomplished by completing good and evil behaviors. In the entire process, the features of goodness and evilness either existed potentially, existed actually, or existed in the ending, and a new beginning started.

I highly admire Feng's effort and progress in searching for the metaphysical foundation of moral philosophy, but I do not recommend *li* as the metaphysical foundation of Chinese moral philosophy. Goodness and evilness, good and evil, and good and evil behaviors or things never be separated or isolated from one another. In addition, Meta-One itself is a metaphysical category with high abstractness and generality. It doesn't have the burden in language as *li* had. One of the literal meanings of *li* is the vein on marble.

We must examine the concept of heaven (*tian* 天) when we discuss ancient Chinese moral and philosophical thought. Ancient Chinese philosophers tried to discover the source of good and evil from human nature, as we just discussed, and they set up the criteria of good and evil in terms of heaven. However, the concept of heaven was so popular that almost no talking took place without the word "heaven." I can focus only on the personalized and moralized heaven from the perspective of social-political philosophy and ignore heaven with all other attributions.

Ancient Chinese philosophers endowed heaven with full personalities, justice, and moral senses. In the *Book of Poems* (*shijing*), we may read sometime that heaven was called Emperor heaven (*Huang tian* 皇天), mostly called heaven (*tian* 天). Heaven was regarded as the emperor of heaven and ruled all human affairs. Like King Wen, the emperor on earth received his destiny from heaven and was appointed by heaven.[33] As we know, King Wen was called the son of heaven. Heaven felt angry, so people should be in awe of heaven. Heaven established ranked ethical relationships, classes between superiority and inferiority, and principles of punishments for criminals. We should follow these and carry them out.[34] Heaven caused disaster to warn the people.[35] Heaven was selfless because heaven had no relatives (partiality).[36] In addition, Laozi claimed to follow heaven, for humans, including kings, lords, or emperors, must follow and behave like heaven.

We may find from the abovementioned ideas about heaven that ancient Chinese philosophers personalized heaven and endowed it with all characteristics of human beings. Heaven possessed a superpower and a kind heart, claimed justice, punished criminals, and promoted love among people. Heaven was an image of ancient Chinese people's ideal king or ruler. Seen from a philosophical perspective, heaven functioned as a premise from which philosophers extended to ethical and moral theories. Science and technology have changed our views about heaven, or sky, and the universe and told us the heaven ancient Chinese people created is no longer personalized existence. Although it was functional in ancient times, it is not good for today to be a theoretical foundation of social-political, moral philosophy, and other branches of philosophy.

Zhu Xi developed two Cheng brothers' *li* of heaven and promoted maintaining the *li* of heaven and deleting humans' desires. Although Zhu Xi's *li* of heaven was essentially a natural *li* or a *li* was derived from human nature, he still used the concept of heaven to maintain the authority of the *li*. For him, loyalty to the lord, respect for sages, and love for relatives belonged to the *li* of heaven, and nature is the *li* of heaven. Song-Ming philosophers replaced nature with *li*, stressed the *li* of heaven, and recharacterized the heavenly *li* as a natural *li*. If something is naturally so, it is a sort of the *li* of heaven. When someone asked, "Who is the master?" Zhu Xi answered, "Heaven itself. Heaven is an absolutely strong thing, *yang*, and therefore rotates without stopping."[37] Zhu Xi's answer shows the significant changes in the components of the concept of heaven; it is no longer a personalized superpower with perfect characteristics. It has been regarded as a natural existence in rotating ceaselessly. The philosophers continued using the traditional concept of "heaven" but alternated its meanings. We may find this change anywhere if we carefully read and think of Song-Ming philosophers' writings.

Theoretically, I characterize heaven as a philosophical hypothesis in ancient Chinese philosophy. It laid a theoretical foundation for ancient Chines natural philosophical thought, social-political-philosophical thought, and moral philosophy. We should not judge the rationality of the hypothesis by scientific and technical views. The concept of heaven was created in early ancient China, but it functioned as a primary source from which philosophers developed all kinds of ideas. Ancient Chinese believed in heaven, relied on heaven, were awed by heaven, and drew moral criteria and principles from heaven. Like Western logicians or philosophers deduced results from a reliable and correct logical premise, ancient Chinese philosophers found the belief for all kinds of arguments or conclusions from heaven metaphysically by analogizing heaven with all human behaviors and things. Ancient Chinese philosophers concluded metaphorically by analogizing the personalized attributions of heaven with human behaviors, while Western logicians or philosophers deduced conclusions by logical inference. This is one difference between ancient Chinese and Western philosophy in the method. Still, logical premise functions only for deductive reasoning, while heaven is the foundation for the entire Chinese philosophical tradition. We cannot skip out the core concept of heaven if we want to understand Chinese civilization.

Practically, the hypothesis of heaven functioned very well. We need to recognize that ancient Chinese philosophers used the concept of heaven metaphorically, not literally, and endowed heaven with all kinds of human emotions, like happiness, anger, and love. It has supper power to punish evils and promote good. The personalized heaven functioned well as a theoretical basis for ancient moral philosophy. Early ancient Chinese, including kings, lords, emperors, and ordinary people, worshiped, and were awed by the personalized heaven. Even today, some Chinese people are still awed by the personalized heaven. They admired heaven as the incarnation of the perfect personality and the ideal moral role model. From kings and emperors to ordinary people, they admired the personalized heaven's "behaviors" (the attributions of nature in today's language) as the standards. Considering the practical functions of the personalized heaven, it partially played religious functions. Like all other religions, the ancient Chinese moral philosophy established the hypothesis of heaven educating people to be good. It is unfair to assert that the Chinese have no religious beliefs because they do not have a god in mind. The personalized heaven was a god without the name of "God" because it practically functioned as a god. The personalized heaven created many things and humankind and made ethical relationships and moral principles for humans.

The personalized heaven exerted its theoretical and practical functions, so I highly admire ancient philosophers' creation and the unique role and functions of the personalized heaven in ancient Chinese moral philosophical thought and real life. Still, I believe that the concept of heaven is neither an ideal metaphysical category nor a metaphysical foundation of Chinese moral philosophy.

The concept of heaven is vague. Ancient Chinese philosophers shaped heaven with full personalities by transforming humans' ideal personalities to heaven, not because they had seen or knew there was a personalized heaven above their heads or in outer space. The levels of science and technology could not provide them with accurate knowledge of the out space or the universe. They did not and also could not verify what the heaven in their minds and imagination was, so the heaven was square, largest without outsiders, was fulfilled with all feelings that humans possessed, and were the standards of ethical and moral principles. As mentioned earlier, the concept of heaven was vague: heaven seemed to be a physical space in terms of its shape and size, heaven was a personal or human-like existence according to its multiple personal feelings and consciousness, heaven was superpower as a god produced heaven, earth, myriad things, and humankind and governed all of those existences. In addition, some ancient philosophers regarded heaven as nature, like Xun Zi and Wang Chong. The vagueness of the concept of heaven disqualified it as a metaphysical concept in a strict sense and the metaphysical foundation of the Chinese moral philosophy.

Heavenly *Dao* vs. Meta-One

In the Chinese philosophical tradition, heaven was a general concept. It was the primary source for natural, social-political, and moral philosophical thoughts, as we have respectively analyzed. When ancient philosophers pursued social justice, political balance, ethical relationships, and moral principles, they specified heaven by transforming the ideal personalities of humans into heaven and created the concept of the *dao* of heaven. *Dao* of heaven was the specification the personalized heaven philosophers used *dao* to specify all ideal personalities of heaven, so the ideal characters were the components of *dao*, which differed from the *dao* of heaven in natural philosophical thought, so I used heavenly *dao* to express *Tiandao* 天道, which appeared in ancient moral philosophy. So-called heavenly *dao* meant the principles of heaven handling everything and setting up for humans to follow. There was heavenly *dao*; there were also earthly *dao* and human *dao*. As the *Appended Remarks II* of *Yi Jing* stated, "there are Heavenly *dao*, Earthly *dao*, and Humanly *dao*."[38] In this part of the chapter, I first examine heavenly *dao* and analyze its components, functions, advantages, and disadvantages. Then, I argue for Meta-One as the metaphysical foundation of Chinese moral philosophy.

Since heavenly *dao* meant how heaven handled everything, then how did heaven handle everything? Laozi's analogy answered this question. He said, "the way [*dao*] of Heaven—how much like a stretched bow it is! It lowers the high and raises the low."[39] Laozi analogized heaven to a person shooting an arrow and making adjustments to target the bullseye. The way or *dao* of heaven was to keep balance and avoid being off target. However, this was not what Laozi wanted to say, so he continued, "[the Heaven] takes from those who have too much and makes up for those who have too little. The way of Heaven reduces the excessive and supplements the insufficient."[40] This is the way (*dao*) that heaven handled everything, keeping a balance between rich and poor, maintaining equalization between strong and weak, and protecting weak groups. These are ideal personal characteristics for humans, so humans should follow the heavenly *dao* because the way (*dao*) of humans is opposite to the heavenly *dao*.

Laozi's explanation of the heavenly *dao* is clear and representative; he has exemplified what the heavenly *dao* is. Laozi criticized, "the way of man, however, is not like that; it reduces the insufficient to serve the excessive. Who can use the excess to serve the world? Only [the] one who has *dao*."[41] Laozi clearly distinguished between the will of heaven and human desires. Opposite to the intention of heaven, human desires caused unfairness, injustice, and disparities between rich and poor people because humans disobeyed the wills of heaven and did not follow the heavenly *dao*. Zhuangzi distinguished between heavenly *dao* and human *dao*. He said, "what is this Tao? There is the Tao of Heaven; there is the Tao of humanity. Non-action brings respect: this is Heaven's Tao. To be active is the Tao of humanity. Heaven's Tao is the ruler; the Tao of humanity is the servant. The Tao of Heaven and the Tao of Humanity are proles spart. Do cannot reflect upon this."[42] Heavenly *dao* was widely used and popular in ancient China. There were too many elaborations about heavenly *dao* to get into details individually. I outline the main ideas as the followings based on my limited research.

Heavenly *dao* reduces excess, and heavenly *dao* benefits from humility. Heavenly *dao* hates complacency (*Tiandao wuying* 天道恶盈), heavenly *dao* augments humble man (*Tiandao yiqian* 天道益谦);[43] 功遂身退天之道, heavenly *dao* has no intimacy (*tiandao wuqin* 天道无亲);[44] heaven is the ultimate education 天道至教;[45] heavenly *dao* was trustable without words (*wuyan erxin* 无言而信),[46] heavenly *dao* does not flat anyone (*tiandao buchan* 天道不谄) and never changes its destiny (*tiandao buer* 天道不二),[47] heavenly *dao* is just one (*tiandao wuer* 天道无二),[48] Wang Chong: heavenly *dao* knows what is right and wrong (*tiandao you zhenwei* 天道有真伪),[49] heavenly *dao* supports justice (*tiandao fuzheng*天道辅正), Zhu Xi: and loyalty is heavenly *dao* (*zhongzhe tianda, shuzhe rendao*忠者天道)，恕者人道.[50] heavenly *dao* favors good and hates evil, heavenly *dao* has no bias (*tiandao wusi*天道无私), heavenly *dao* is most sincerity (*tiandao zhicheng* 天道至诚), heavenly *dao* is most brilliant (*tiandao zhiming*)天道至明, heavenly *dao* is permanently righteous (*tiandao hengzheng*天道恒正), and so on. Even today, Chinese people still use some idioms with *tiandao*天道 (heavenly *dao*), like heavenly *dao* rewards hard work (*tiandao chouqin*天道酬勤), which still encourages Chinese people to devote themselves to realize their ideals. The words *tiandao* 天道, however, no longer have the meanings of the traditional heavenly *dao*.

We may see from the abovementioned heavenly *dao* that although ancient philosophers endowed the heavenly *dao* with different personal characteristics, for instance, Daoist philosophers endowed the heavenly *dao* with pursuing balance, no action, and not striving for beneficence; heavenly *dao* has no intimacy. Confucian philosophers endowed the heavenly *dao* with sincerity, loyalty, and love. Legalist endowed the heavenly *dao* with justice, rightness, selfless, and so forth. There was a common point among all different philosophers: all of them attributed their ideal personal characteristics to the name of heaven and entitled it heavenly *dao*. The heavenly *dao* was regarded as the incarnation of an idealist personality and functioned as the ultimate criterion and role model of humans' ethical and moral behaviors. All the moral characteristics are components of the heavenly *dao* as a concept, but all those moral characteristics are practical, visible, and verifiable. For instance, heavenly *dao* with ultimate sincerity (*tiandao zhicheng*天道至诚): after the Winter follows Spring, and after the Autumn follows Winter, heaven never lies in humans. Ancient philosophers attributed the sincerity to heavenly *dao*, the way heaven handles everything. Today, we recognize sincerity as a natural phenomenon, but ancient philosophers discovered an ideal moral characteristic of sincerity from the natural phenomenon. Ancient Chinese philosophers set up the heavenly *dao* as the highest moral hypothesis, transformed humans' ideal personalities to the heavenly *dao* as its characteristics, and shaped those characteristics as general ethical principles and criteria of human behaviors. Heavenly *dao* was the source of humanly *dao* and the standard of humanly *dao*. Heavenly *dao* functioned as a practical moral standard and role model for humans in terms of its practical, visible, and verifiable characteristics. However, the theoretical foundation of ancient moral philosophical thought is not yet reached. The ideas of the heavenly *dao* were just parts of the ancient Chinese moral philosophy, so we need to find a metaphysical foundation of Chinese moral philosophy in reconstructing the metaphorical metaphysics of traditional Chinese philosophy.

Meta-One differs from the heavenly *Dao*, fulfilled with practical, visible, and verifiable personalized moral characteristics. Meta-One implies the metaphysical features of goodness and evilness. We have characterized the positive tendency implied in Meta-One with goodness and the negative tendency as bad for all things or myriad things; when we applied this division to moral philosophy, we characterized the positive tendency as good with the feature of goodness and the negative tendency as evil with the feature of evilness. The Meta-One is a metaphysical category; it does not refer to any concrete thing, an actual event, or moral behavior, so Meta-One does not refer to any good and evil behaviors. It only implies the abstract features of goodness and evilness.

Meta-One differs from the heavenly *dao*, endowed only with positive, personalized moral characteristics; Meta-One potentially implied positive and negative tendencies. The two tendencies will be associated with human behavior from a potential desire or plan. The individualized or realized stage, for instance, the positive tendency, determines the direction of behavior, but the negative tendency reduces its influence, so the behavior moves to be good and then completes the desire or plan of one's behavior, and vice versa. Associated with the two tendencies, *goodness* and evilness were potentially implied in Meta-One, realized in Multi-One, and completed in Utter-One.

Meta-One is a metaphysical category. It does not specify any ethical relationships nor offer any moral principles. Meta-One differs from the heavenly *dao*, which was believed prior to human *dao* and was the primary source of humans' moral principles. As we examined above, the personalized characteristics of the heavenly *dao* were essentially believed to have existed before humans but were derived from humans' observation of the natural world. All those characteristics of the heavenly *dao* were idealized human characteristics. Some of those humans possessed practices, and some of those humans did not, and later became ideal. Ancient philosophers collected humans' best personal characteristics and added on ideal characteristics, shaping the heavenly *dao* with a perfect personality in morality. Ancient philosophers developed profound moral philosophical thought based on the heavenly *dao*, but not yet in the metaphysical dimension. All the moral and ethical ideas, ethical relationships, and moral principles are components of moral philosophy, and the heavenly *dao* was the highest moral criterion and role model. Still, it did not function as the metaphysical foundation of ancient moral philosophy.

The heavenly *dao* fulfilled practical moral characteristics associated with good, not goodness, provided only one-side positive moral criterion and role model for humans, and played as the incarnation of the ideal human personality could not function as the metaphysical foundation of ancient Chinese moral philosophy. I argue for Meta-One as the metaphysical foundation of ancient Chinese moral philosophy because it possesses the metaphysical features of goodness and evilness; it leaves room for both good and evil to trace back to their metaphysical features of goodness and evilness, and itself is a typical metaphysical category with high abstractness and does not refer to any good or evil behaviors. Still, good and evil behaviors can find their metaphysical foundation from the potential positive and negative tendencies.

Metaphysical Foundation of Aesthetics

Similar to moral and ethical thought, there was no systematic theory of aesthetics. Still, there were abundant ideas about beauty and the meanings of beauty, the essence of beauty, the criterion of beauty, and the significance of beauty in different philosophers' writings. In this part of the chapter, I suggest Meta-One as the metaphysical foundation of aesthetics to promote the reconstruction of metaphorical metaphysics in the Chinese philosophical tradition, then examine ancient philosophers' ideas about beauty and the criteria of beauty, and finally analyze some examples of natural things, political-social affairs, and individual behaviors that ancient philosophers endowed the characteristic of beauty to exemplify the rationality of my suggestion about Meta-One as the metaphysical foundation.

Meta-One vs. Harmoniousness

As a metaphysical category, Meta-One can metaphorically refer to any entity in which multiple potentialities are implied. I have classified the multiple potential factors into positive and negative tendencies—meanwhile, the dynamic process from Meta-One via Multi-One to Utter-One was fulfilled with various types of harmony. When we analyze the trends and harmonies from the aesthetical perspective, we find that the positive tendency essentially is a power to harmonize all things, parts, or elements (elements for convenience). In the stage of Meta-One, all aspects coexisted potentially in harmony; at the stage of Multi-One, all elements individualize and realize themselves—the potential harmony was broken and moved into a new harmony. In the new harmonious entity, the multiple elements differ from one another, contest each other, and even fight each other, but this happens in the entity. At the stage of Utter-One, the interaction among the multiple elements resulted in another new harmony; in the new harmonious entity, all elements completed their nature and destiny, to borrow ancient Chinese philosophers' terms.

In the entire process, the positive factors functioned to harmonize the entity based on its feature of harmoniousness. I characterize the elements with the feature of harmoniousness as the things with the beauty feature. The negative factors affect the realization of the new harmony because of inharmoniousness. I call the elements with the feature of inharmoniousness things with the feature of ugly. We judge an aesthetical object as beautiful or ugly in terms of an entity's features. If an aesthetical object looks to be in harmony, we may think it is beautiful; if the beauty corresponds to the feature of harmoniousness, it does not just looks beautiful and is regarded as beauty; it is a genuine beauty. If an aesthetical object looks to be in harmony, but the beauty does not correspond to the feature of harmoniousness, the beauty has no ground and is not genuine beauty. Harmony is the criterion of beauty, and harmoniousness is the ground of harmony. Harmony is a phenomenon, so it has various models, as we have classified. Seen from a dynamic perspective, there are potential and factual, temporary and permanent, partial and complete, and static and dynamic harmonies; seen from a static perspective, we have unitary, binary, ternary, and multiple corresponding harmonies. These types of harmonies are based on a common ground: harmoniousness is the essence of beauty. Harmony and inharmony are external criteria we judge an aesthetical object, beautiful or ugly, while the features of harmoniousness and inharmoniousness are the grounds of beauty and ugly.

To explore the metaphysical foundation of aesthetics, instead of asking what beauty is, we need to further ask based on what a philosopher regarded something as beauty or possessed the feature of beauty. The distinction between what is beautiful and what is the ground of beauty as beauty is the distinction between the criterion of beauty and the metaphysical foundation of aesthetics. The criterion of beauty means the standard for something to be regarded as beauty must be met. If that thing meets the standard, it may be considered a thing with the feature of beauty; the ground of beauty as beauty is the ground of the criterion. An aesthetical object presents itself in harmony. That thing is beautiful; if an aesthetical object possesses the feature of inharmoniousness and is displayed as inharmony, that thing is ugly.

In aesthetics, when Meta-One refers to an aesthetical object, the aesthetical object may present as a harmonious or inharmonious entity. The harmony is derived from and corresponds to the metaphysical features of harmoniousness and inharmoniousness potentially implied in the Meta-One. I just focus on two aspects.

First, harmony and inharmony as the criteria of beauty and ugly are individual, while harmoniousness and inharmoniousness are grounds for beauty and ugly. When an aesthetical object had attributed the feature of beauty mostly when the object was treated as static, while all things in the world are changing, moving, and transforming, nothing is static. We, as aesthetical subjects, make our judgments about something as beautiful or ugly always at a certain time and place, which limits our judgments to temporary, partial, and individual.

The beauty of a famous mountain comprises the movements when we observe the mountains, rivers, lakes, trees, flowers, and other plants. Before and after the time we celebrate the landscape, the scenery could be significantly different because the landscape's scenery changes from time to time, day to day, and season to season. We, as aesthetic subjects, make our judgments about the landscape in terms of our observations of this movement. Someone could say the landscape was ugly after viewing it in the winter, but another could say it was beautiful when he watched it in the spring. Our judgments are ours and different from any other's judgments.

Similarly, for artificial creations like a painting, an artist's sculpture, a building, a poem, or a portion of writing, when we make aesthetical judgments about the features of beauty and ugliness, we always make our judgments at a specific movement in a certain time, and in a particular place. It will not be the entire process, from the painter's plan via drawing practically to completing the painting, the same as an artist's status, a building, or any artist's work. It is a dynamic process, from planning to working to shape an aesthetical object. In contrast, aesthetical judgments about the object are always made at a particular movement or time. For instance, when we treat Ancient Rome City, the Pisa tower, a Beethoven symphony, Shakespeare's sonnets, the *Book of Poems*, the Great Wall, and the Forbidden City as aesthetical objects, we make our judgments in terms of our observations and understanding at this movement in this specific time. Our judgments can only reflect what we have seen now, so we cannot take our judgments as accurate and complete recognitions of those aesthetical objects. Shakespeare's contemporaries appreciated the beauty of his sonnets, but today, we may not make the same aesthetical judgments about the sonnets as Shakespeare's contemporaries made.

Different philosophers have different points of view about the beauty and ugliness of the same event, history, and behavior, especially for the most complex aesthetical objects, like an historical event. Different viewers, as the aesthetic subjects, have their judgments. If we treat political-social events, a period of history, a person's behavior, or a piece of speech as aesthetical objects, our judgments are limited to what we have seen, what we have known, and what we have comprehended.

The harmoniousness and inharmoniousness as the common grounds of harmony and inharmony will not change with the changes of the aesthetical subjects and harmony, which are various, but harmoniousness and inharmoniousness are the same.

Second, harmony as the criterion of beauty and inharmony as the criterion of ugly is relative, but harmoniousness and inharmoniousness as grounds of harmony and inharmony are permanent. Any natural things, social-political events, individual behaviors, and other things become aesthetical objects only when aesthetical subjects are involved in the aesthetical process; otherwise, all those things are just potential aesthetical objects. No matter how beautiful a thing is, it is not yet an aesthetical object if isolated from aesthetical subjects. Aesthetical objects are objective, and they are what they are. However, are they beautiful or ugly? Their beauty or ugliness depend on aesthetical subjects' subjective judgments. For the same aesthetical object, different people as the aesthetical subjects may have different judgments simultaneously because of their emotions, personal favorites, educational backgrounds, social-political attitudes (if the object is a political event), and different aesthetical criteria. Even the same person as the aesthetical subject could regard the same object as beautiful and view it as ugly at another time because of his emotion, aesthetical attitude, or other reasons.

When beauty and ugliness are assigned to aesthetical objects, all particular beauty and ugliness is endowed with subjectivity. Subjectivity originated from the aesthetical subjects, not from the aesthetical objects. Thus, beauty or ugliness is relative. An aesthetical object is an objective existence; it will not change with people's aesthetical judgments. Beauty or ugliness is only an external sign or symbol that aesthetical subjects added to it, further showing that beauty and ugliness are subjective and relative. Aesthetical subjects make their aesthetical judgments about beauty and ugliness in terms of harmony and inharmony. In contrast, harmony and inharmony are various, dynamic, and changing. Still, the harmoniousness and inharmoniousness as the generalizations of all kinds of harmony and inharmony will not change with the changes of particular harmonies and in-harmonies.

Traditional Ideas: Harmony and *Li*

In the Chinese philosophical tradition, there were many discourses related to the issues of beauty and harmony separately. To concentrate on the theme of the metaphysical foundation of aesthetics, I briefly examine ancient Chinese philosophers' ideas of the relationship between beauty and harmony, followed by my critical analyses of Feng Youlan's ideas of *li* and beauty.

In *Analects*, Confucius regarded the music Shao as the utmost beauty and utmost good (*jinshan jinmei*尽善尽美). We know that the essential feature of music is harmony. When Guan Zi made comments about Yellow Emperor, he believed Yellow Emperor created five sounds and built up five elements. The five senses confirm humans' positions. Humans are in harmony with heaven, and then the beauty of heaven and earth is produced. For these philosophers, harmony was the ground, the beauty of different things. Instead of examining ancient philosophers' relevant ideas one by one, I would take Xunzi as an individual case to see how ancient philosophers elaborated the beauty (*mei* 美) and harmony (和).

Xunzi discussed the significance of the balance and harmony between fine customs (*meisu* 美俗) and bad customs for a state. He stated, "every state has fine customs [美俗]. Every state also has bad customs [恶俗]. When both types are present in equal measure, the state will continue existing."[51] Equalization is a type of balance and harmony; it seems to Xunzi that balance just meets the basic condition of the existence of a state. The ideal situation is that the fine customs become "the one and only one," which means harmonizing the customs of the state. If the bad customs become the one and only one, the state will perish.

Further, Xunzi claimed that the function of music is to reach harmony. He said, "music is something in which the sages delighted, for it has the power to make good in hearts of the people, to influence men deeply, and so reform their manners and customs with the facility. Therefore, the former kings guided the people with ritual and music, and the people became harmonious and congenial."[52] In Xunzi's time, the rituals functioned to regularize people's behaviors, including kings' behaviors. Music, it seemed to Xunzi, functioned to harmonize people's hearts, which was more essential and important. He claimed to keep both functioning well.

Furthermore, Xunzi valued the functions of the rituals and music in a wider and deeper sense. He said, "when music is played, intentions gain purity. When rites are studied, conduct turns out perfectly. They make one's ears acute, and they make one's eyes sharp. They give one's blood and *qi* balance and harmony; they change customs and alter habits, so all the people in the world live peacefully."[53] In the previous elaboration, Xunzi talked about the significance of the rituals and music to a state, but here, he extended it to all states and the people in the entire world.

Last but not least, Xunzi indicated the essence of music. He said, "music, moreover, is unchanging harmony, and ritual is unalterable order. Music unities that which I do the same, and ritual distinguishes that which is different. Together, the combination of ritual and music governs the human heart."[54] The unchanging harmony is the essence of music, but also, in my understanding, is the beauty of music if we think of it from the perspective of aesthetics.

After Laozi, based on my limited research, I outline how different philosophers talked about beauty from different angles, such as the beauty of speech and Good (Confucius). Zhuangzi focused on spiritual freedom and beauty, and Xunzi emphasized harmony and balance when he discussed the beauty of customs, music, and rituals. However, ancient philosophers talked about the relationship between beauty and harmony. Still, we do not have efficient sources to support the assumption that ancient philosophers took harmony as a criterion of beauty.

Feng proposed *li* as the ground of beauty at the metaphysical level; this is significant progress compared to Zhu's goodness as the ground of beauty. Feng Youlan promoted *li* of beauty to a metaphysical category. Still, regarding his *li*, if we follow Feng's logic and maintain consistency in the understanding of *li*, we will face the same question as we met when we discussed Feng's *li* in chapter 2. Particularly, *li* is essentially a name. A red thing is red when it corresponds to the name red, and a square thing is square if it matches the name of the square. *Li* exists even without concrete things, like a round thing, but the *li* of round still exists. In this dimension, Feng's *li* is powerful in explaining individual things and their names. With the same principle of logical thinking, Feng Youlan claimed that there is the *li* of beauty[55] even if there is no real red thing, the *li* of beauty still exists. If we strictly follow Feng's logic, we find that the abstractness and the generality of concept *li* are limited and cannot function as a metaphysical foundation of aesthetics.

When we grant a bunch of roses with the feature of beauty, or when we say that the bunch of roses are beautiful, are we basing this on the *li* of the rose or the *li* of the beauty of the rose? If we say that the *li* of the rose is ground with which we assert that the bunch of roses is beautiful, then what is the difference between saying that it is a bunch of roses in terms of the *li* of the rose? If we assert that a bunch of roses is beautiful in terms of the *li* of the beauty of a rose, what we need to do is first check the bunch of flowers with the *li* of the rose and confirm it is a bunch of roses. Then we need to check the bunch of roses with the *li* of the beauty of the rose and make an aesthetical judgment saying that the bunch of roses is beautiful or with the feature of beauty because it corresponds to the *li* of the beauty of the rose.

The beauty of the rose is just one of the multiple features of the rose; it has many other features like red color, freshness, shape, and so on. In making that aesthetical judgment, we equalized the *li* of rose and the *li* of beauty, putting the two *li* on the same level. The *li* of rose determines something is a rose, nothing else, and the *li* of beauty characterized the bunch of roses as beauty, not ugly. If we take harmony as the criterion of beauty, we will say this bunch of roses is beautiful because of the shapes of each branch, the pure red color, and the green leaves; all these features are in harmony. If we take *li* as the criterion of beauty, we can say that this branch of roses is beautiful because it corresponds to the *li* of beauty. How about all other aesthetical objects? A mountain is beautiful because it corresponds to the *li* of beauty. A lady is beautiful because the lady corresponds to the *li* of beauty. A piece of music is beautiful because it corresponds to the *li* of beauty.

According to the suggestion of Meta-One, however, there is a rose, the beauty of the rose, the criterion of beauty—harmony, and harmoniousness as the metaphysical ground of harmony. According to Feng's logic, there is a rose, the *li* of the rose, and the *li* of beauty. *Li* functioned as the ground of the rose to be called a rose and the beauty of the rose to be regarded as beauty, so there is a logical gap between the criterion of beauty and the metaphysical ground of beauty. The two are mixed two into one—*li*. When I said that Feng made significant progress in searching metaphysical foundation of aesthetics, I interpreted his *li* as a metaphysical ground of beauty; if we interpret his *li* as a criterion of beauty in terms of his principle that something is called beauty because it corresponds to the *li* of beauty, then *li* functioned as the criterion of beauty and his theory of beauty is short of metaphysical ground of beauty. I intend to interpret his *li* as the former and assume that the concept of *li* is vague.

Further, the abstractness and generality of the *li* of a rose are higher than the *li* of beauty because a rose has multiple features; it could be beauty, could be neither beautiful nor ugly, or ugly, while the essential feature is that it is a rose. If we follow Feng's logic, saying that there is a totality of *li* of beauty, including the *li* of the beauty of a rose, the *li* of the beauty of speech, and the *li* of the beauty of human behavior, and so forth. Feng's *li*, which generated all beauties of things, is just a *li* of a single feature among all kinds of features that the aesthetical objects possessed. The *li* of beauty is just a general term for that single feature. *Li*, as a metaphysical ground of beauty, just like a logical black hole, is short of components. In comparison, the harmoniousness in the theory of Meta-One has both high abstractnesses of metaphysical features and profound components, as we have discussed. I do not think Feng's *li* is the metaphysical foundation of Chinese aesthetics.

Harmony as Criterion: Exemplification

In the ancient Chinese philosophical tradition, philosophers talked about beauty and harmony and elaborated on the relationship between beauty and harmony. This section examines ancient philosophers' ideas of beauty, harmony, and the relationship between beauty and harmony.

Ancient philosophers used *mei* 美 to describe natural things, social-political events, people's behaviors and speeches, and artificial things. Here are just some examples, a beautiful woman (*meiren* 美人),[56] beautiful eyes (*meimu* 美目), beautiful as jade (*meiyu* 美玉), generous profit (*meili*) 美利, excellent governance (*meizheng* 美政), beautiful face (*meirong* 美容), beautiful stone (*meishi*美石), beautiful shells (*meibei* 美贝), beautiful grass (*meicao* 美草), beautiful words (*meiyu* 美语), beautiful face (*maomei* 貌美), perfect virtue and justice (*deyi mei* 德义美), and good behavior (*meixing*美行), exquisite taste (*meiwei*美味), tasty wine (*meijiu*美酒), good customs (*meisu* 美俗), good reputation (*meiming* 美名), notable virtue (*meide*美德), perfect materials (*meicai* 美材), glorious behavior (*meixing* 美行), and so on.

These kinds of beautiful things or things with the characteristics of beauty (*mei* 美) show us that ancient philosophers almost believed that everything in the world has its beauty if something was good enough seen from the philosophers' point of view. When we examine the contexts in which the concept of beauty was used, we cannot find what they based their decision to regard those things as beautiful on; it is because they were not conducting a theoretical discussion about what was beautiful and what was the criterion of beauty. They just described those things as beautiful for their arguments, so I applied the criterion I suggested, "harmony," to analyze those they regarded as beautiful to verify my suggestion was reasonable.

I believe that harmony as a criterion of beauty applies to all kinds of beauty listed above. Still, I chose some representative examples to discuss because of the limited space. Let's begin with the *meiren* beautiful lady mentioned in the *Book of Poems*. A lady can be regarded as a beautiful woman. Her body shape, hands, legs, and five facial features must be in harmony. Suppose one leg or hand is longer than another, or her five facial features are not in harmony according to traditional criteria. In that case, she cannot be regarded as a beautiful woman. The excellent governance or beautified governance (*mei zheng* 美政) mentioned in Chu Ci was expressed with the word *mei* 美 (beauty); the governance or administration must be as good as to keep the entire country or an organization as a harmonious unity. In unity, the authorities or administrators exercise control effectively, all departments of the entity cooperate reasonably, and all people or members fulfill their duties for common goals; if any parts if any parts cause the breakdown of the unification and the harmony, the governance cannot be regarded as *meizheng* 美政. As we mentioned in the warring-state period, although the Zhou was still a country, the governance of the Zhou kings could not be regarded as *meizheng* 美政. This is because, although the Zhou still possessed the feature of Oneness and wholeness, it still was a country; it was short of the feature of harmoniousness.

The perfect virtue (*meide* 美德) mentioned by Zhu Xi was called *mei* 美; all aspects of the virtue or personal characteristics must be in harmony. If a person does many things morally, except for one immoral behavior, this causes the breakdown of the harmony of his entire personality. For instance, if a person who displayed his perfect virtue at home but behaved immorally in society, his personality or moral characteristics could not be regarded as virtue or perfect virtue because his societal behaviors have broken down the harmony of his entire personality. These interpretations are based on several representative examples. Still, we may apply the same principle of harmony to analyze other things regarded as beauty or with the feature of beauty.

One more example from today's most famous phrase in the worldwide Chinese cultural circles 美食 (exquisite food) is that for food to be called *mei* 美 it must meet an essential criterion: all kinds of sauces must keep balance and the balance must be in harmony. If everything was perfect but there is too much salt, the harmony is broken, and that food cannot be described with the concept of *mei* (美).

Balance is a typical model of harmony, as mentioned in the previous chapter. Not just some ancient philosophers take harmony as the ground of beauty, but purely theoretical analyses can also support this point. The beauty of a landscape comprises all-natural mountains, rivers, and plants that coexist in harmony with each other; if we construct an artificial object, but do not consider the harmony between the building and the environment surrounding the building, we could break the harmony and negatively affect the beauty of that landscape. For music, harmony is the key element. In a piece of music, if all parts conflict with each other inharmoniously, that could be noise rather than music; otherwise, there would be no difference between music and noise. Similarly, a speech, a poem, an artist's status, a building, a person's personality, and so forth can be designated the feature of beauty if the inner elements are in harmony; if the internal aspects of these aesthetical objects coexist inharmoniously, or an artist's statue exists with its surroundings and environment inharmoniously, its beauty will be significantly affected, and even turn to ugliness.

In addition, as another model of harmony, symmetry was a widely accepted ground for the beauty of buildings. In Chinese architecture, the symmetric principle was widely employed, while symmetry is one model of corresponding harmony. The Forbidden City in Beijing is a prime example: the buildings from Meridian Gate to the Gate of Divine Might (South to North) constitute a center axis, and the buildings on the West and East sides of the center axis are symmetric and correspond to each other; the center axis is surrounded by the East side and West side, which emphasizes the respective position of the center axis. Symmetry is a typical model of the corresponding harmony, as we have analyzed in the previous chapter. The designation of the Forbidden City embodied the claim that harmony was treated as the ground of beauty in architecture. The idea of a round heaven and square earth deeply influenced the aesthetics of Chinese architecture. The buildings in history up to the contemporary era in China had two types: round and square. The round structures are mostly related to heaven, like religious towers; the *tiantan* 天坛 in Beijing was a place to communicate with heaven. People's houses are mostly square. Round and square as the fixed styles of buildings reflected the idea of Round-Heaven and Square-Earth. This is precisely the embodiment of the views of the harmony of heaven and earth.

When applying the suggestion of Meta-One, notable harmony as the criterion of beauty, to explain the aesthetical objects above, the exemplification further convinced me of the rationality of the suggestion of Meta-One as the metaphysical foundation of Chinese aesthetics.

NOTES

1. "上下四方曰宇，古往今来曰宙。" It was said Shizi (Shi Jiao 尸佼 390–330 BC) in the Eastern Zhou made this definition, but it was uncertain, so I use an unnamed philosopher.

2. Zhuangzi, *The Book of Chuang Tzu*, translated by Martin Palmer with Elizabeth Breuilly (London: Penguin Group, 1996), 50.

3. Confucius said, superior man is awed of three things: he stands in awe of the ordinances of heaven, great man, and sages' words. In *The Four Books*, translated by James Legge (Hong Kong: Hui Tung Book Store, 1969), 148. Confucius also said, "He who offends against Heaven has none to whom he can pray." Ibid., 18. 《泰伯》：子曰："It is only Heaven that is grand, and only Yao corresponded to it." Ibid., 62.

4. Mengzi said, "He who delights in Heaven, will affect with his love and protection the whole empire. He who stands in awe of Heaven, will affect his love and protection his own kingdom." Ibid., 31.

5. *Records of Rituals*《礼记》："天地合配，则万物生焉。"《礼记集解》中【清】孙希旦撰，北京：中华书局，1989年，第608页。*The Collection of the Explanations of the Records of Rituals*, vol. 2 (Beijing: Zhong Hua Shu Ju, 1989), 707.

6. Mengzi said, 孟子曰："顺天者存，逆天者亡。" "They who accord with Heaven are preserved and they who rebel against Heaven perish." *The Four Books*, trans. Legge, 161.

7. Xunzi said, "The gentleman is opposite of the perry man. If the gentleman is great-hearted then he reverses Heaven and follows the Way [*Dao*]." Xunzi, *Xunzi: The Complete Text*, with contributions and edited by Eric L. Hutton (Princeton, NJ: Princeton University Press, 2014), 18.

8. Zhu Xi, *Zhu Zi Yu Lei*, vol. 1., edited by Jingde Li (Jingdu: Chinese Press, 1979), 147. 朱熹 《朱子语类》上卷（京都：中文出版社），1979 年第 147页.

9. Zhu Xi, (朱熹), *Zhuzi Yulei*《朱子语类》上卷*Citations of Zhu Xi*, vol. 1, edited by Jingde Li (黎靖德) (Jingdu: Chinese Press, 1979), 147.

10. Feng Youlan, "此说天地或宇宙，是从全之观点以观万物，天地或宇宙是其总名。" Feng Youlan (冯友兰) *Xin Lixue*《新理学》*New Doctrine of Li*, *Sansongtang qujie*《三松堂全集》*Complete Collections of San Song Tang*, vol. 4 (Zheng Zhou: He Nan People's Press, 2000），26.

11. Feng Youlan, *New Doctrine of Li*, vol. 4 (Zheng Zhou: He Nan People's Press, 2000), 27.

12. Ibid., 28.

13. 【唐】等注疏。沈阳：万卷出版公司，2009年第318页。[Tang] Kong, Yingda (孔颖达) etc. noted; 李英健编审 *mingjia pizhu zhouyi*《名家批注周易》*Famous Scholars' Commentaries on Zhou Yi* (Shen Yang: Wan Juan Publishing, 2009), 318.

14. *A Source Book of Chinese Philosophy*, edited by Wing-Tsit Chan (Princeton, NJ: Princeton University Press, 1969), 268.

15. Laozi, *Daodejing: A Literal-Critical Translation*, translated by Joseph Hsu (Lanham, MD: University Press of America, 2008), 65.
16. *Zhuang-Tzu*, translated by Feng Youlan (Beijing: Foreign Language Press, 1989), 45–46.
17. Ibid.
18. Ibid.
19. Ibid, 49.
20. Ibid, 81.
21. "天地感而万物化生，圣人感人心而天下和平，观其所感，而天地万物之情可见矣。" *Yi Jing*, Tuan Zhuan 《象传》。274.
22. *The Four Books*, translated by Daniel K. Gardner (Indianapolis: Hackett Publishing Company, 2007), 46.
23　*The Four Books*, trans. Legge, 251–58.
24. Xunzi, *Xunzi: The Complete Text*, trans. Hutton, 248.
25　Dong Zhongshu, *Dong Zhongshu: Chun Qiu Fan Lu* (Luxuriant Dew of the Spring and Autumn Annals," vol. 6, chap. 19, edited by Wang Yun Wu (Tai Bei: Wen Yuan Ge: 1975), 9. 董仲舒《春秋繁露《玉杯》第二　第9页》。
26. Dong Zhongshu, *Chun Qiu Fan Lu*, 5. 董仲舒《春秋繁露》《盟会要》第十，卷5第5页。
27. Huang Hui（黄晖）*Proof Readings of Lun Heng*, vol. 1《论衡校释》第一卷 (Beijing: Zhong Huan Shu Ju, 1990), 51.
28. Ibid., 132–33.
29. Zhu Xi, *Si Shu Ji Zhu*《四书章句集注》*Collections of Contemporaries of the Four Books* (Taibei: Shift Jie Shu Ju, 1969), 112.
30. Feng Youlan, *The Complete Works of Feng Youlan* (Zhengzhou: Henan Renmin Chu Ban She, 2000), 85, 87.
31. Ibid., 87.
32. Ibid., 90–96.
33. Huang Kan（黄侃），《黄侃手批白文十三经》*Thirteen Classics: Huang Kan Manually apostilled punctuations* (Shanghai: Shanghai Ancient Books Publishing House, 1983), 108.
34. "天命有德，五服五章哉！天讨有罪，五刑五用哉！" Ibid., 7.
35. "皇天降灾"《尚书》《伊训》Huang Kan（黄侃），《黄侃手批白文十三经》Ibid., 17.
36. "惟天无亲"《尚书》《太甲下》《黄侃手批白文十三经》Ibid., 19.
37. Zhu Xi (朱熹), *Reflections on Things at Hand*, the neo-Confucian anthology compiled by Chu His and Lu Tsu-Chien, translated with notes by Wing-Tsit Chan (New York: Columbia University Press, 1967), 9.
38. Huang Kan *Thirteen Classics*, 49.
39. Laozi, *Daodejing, A Literal-Critical Translation*, trans. Hsu, 128.
40. Ibid.
41. Ibid.
42. Zhuangzi, *The Book of Chuang Tzu*, trans. Palmer and Breuilly, 90.
43. *The Classic of Changes*, a new translation of the I Ching as interpreted by Wang Bi, translated by Richard John Lynn (New York: Columbia University Press, 1994), 229–30.

44. Laozi, *Daodejing, A Literal-Critical Translation*, trans. Hsu, 131.

45. 《礼记集解》中 《礼器》："天道至教,圣人至德。"【清】孙希旦撰,北京:中华书局,1989年,第659页. *The Collection of the Explanations of the Records of Rituals* (Beijing: Zhong Hua Shu Ju, 1989), 659.

46. 《礼记集解》下《乐记》"天则不言而信。"【清】孙希旦撰,北京:中华书局,1989年,第1029页. *The Collection of the Explanations of the Records of Rituals*, vol. 3 (Beijing: Zhong Hua Shu Ju, 1989), 1029.

47. Huang Kan, *Thirteen Classics*, 409. 《黄侃手批白文十三经》,《春秋左传》《昭公二十六年》。"天道不谄,不贰其命。"上海:上海古籍出版社,1983,第409页。

48. Dong Zhongshu (董仲舒), *Chun Qiu Fan Lu*《春秋繁露》*Luxuriant Dew of the Spring and Autumn Annals*, vol. v, chap. 51 《天道无二》:"一而不二者,天之行也。" 王云五主编,台北:文渊阁1975 年, 卷五第五十一章第5页。

49. Huang Hui (黄晖),《论衡校释》卷一 第75页:"天道有真伪。"*Proofreading of Lun Heng*, vol. I (Beijing: Zhong Hua Shu Ju, 1990), 75.

50. Zhu Xi (朱熹), 《四书集注》" 第二卷第四章 "忠者天道,恕者人道" *Collections of Commentaries of the Four Books*, vol. 2, chap. 4 (Taibei: Shi Jie Shu Ju, 1969), 23.

51. Xunzi, *Xunzi: The Complete Text*, trans. Hutton, 109.

52. Ibid., 220.

53. Ibid., 221.

54. Ibid.

55. Feng Youlan, *Complete Works*, vol. 4, 150.

56. Huang Kan, *Thirteen Classics*, 18. /黄侃,《黄侃手批白文十三经》。上海:上海古籍出版社,1983,《诗经》《国风》第18页。

Conclusion

Chinese philosophy and metaphysics in Chinese philosophy have been widely recognized and have achieved the status they deserve on the stage of world philosophy. Scholarship in the study of Chinese philosophy in the 1980s to the 1990s and the significant progress in the study of metaphysics in traditional Chinese philosophy in recent years have successively rectified their names. The progress laid a solid foundation for us to study the specific topics of metaphorical metaphysics further. This project specifically proposed an initial scheme to reconstruct metaphorical metaphysics from a methodological perspective.

In this project, I first clarified the metaphysical object, method, and essence of metaphysics in Chinese philosophical tradition. I characterized the metaphysical object as an all-in-one entity, the primary method as metaphorical reasoning, and the essence of metaphysics as pursuing harmony and human happiness. These features shaped the metaphysics of Chinese philosophical tradition as a unique one different from all other systems of metaphysics in other philosophical traditions. The way ancient philosophers described metaphysical objects analogically argued for their metaphysical ideas primarily through analogical reasoning. The metaphysics aimed not to pursue pure knowledge but for better human life. All these specialties shaped the metaphysics in Chinese philosophical tradition as metaphorical metaphysics. These clarifications of the specialties of the metaphysical object, primary method, and purpose laid a foundation for us to reconstruct the metaphorical metaphysics in Chinese philosophical tradition.

Based on the clarification of the object, method, and essence of the metaphysics in traditional Chinese metaphysics and the examination of the advantages and disadvantages of most influential traditional concepts, I then proposed three new metaphysical categories: Meta-One, Multi-One, and

Utter-One. The three categories are conceptualizations of the myriad things, so they can metaphorically refer to any metaphysical objects and describe a dynamical process from the origination in a potential stage through the individualization and realization to the completion of things' development. The features, components, and functions of each category and the process from the Meta-One as potentiality through the Multi-One as an intermediate stage to the Utter-One as the completion of development properly reflected the process of things' objective development.

As a dynamic process from Meta-One through Multi-One to Utter-One, each stage was fulfilled with profound components and associated with various models of harmony. Based on the brief examination of traditional ideas of harmony, I clarified the core concept of corresponding harmony and then classified harmony into potential versus factual, temporary versus permanent, partial versus complete, and dynamic versus static models of harmony from a dynamic perspective; and then classified harmony into unitary, binary, ternary, and multivariate models of harmony from a static perspective. The combination of static analyses of the three categories and the dynamic analyses of the process of the Meta-One via Multi-One to Utter-One released the essence and content of the Meta-One, because the Multi-One and Utter-One are unfolded of the Meta-One, and there is no Multi-One and Utter-One outside of the concept of the Meta-One. The Meta-One is the core of the system of metaphorical metaphysics. It is incorporated with traditional metaphysical concepts like *dao* and *li* but is beyond those concepts because of its clarity, generality, and profound components.

In chapter 4, we systematized the methodological principles of metaphorical metaphysics. We classified metaphysical methods into three types: direct versus indirect, positive versus negative, and logical versus metaphorical methods, considering how philosophers deal with metaphysical objects. We specifically extended three methodological principles from the Meta-One: holism, centralism, and precognitivism; three principles from the Multi-One: pluralism, interactionism, and synergism; and three principles from the Utter-One: perfectionism, infinitism, and systematism. All these efforts aim to systematize the theory of the metaphysical method in the metaphysics of Chinese philosophical tradition.

After we clarified the metaphysical object based on a brief historical examination and components, analyzed the various harmonies as the core content, and established a series of methodological principles, we finally explored the position and functions of metaphorical metaphysics in traditional Chinese philosophy. The features of the beginning of the beginning, one-ness, and the dynamical development of the Meta-One qualified the metaphorical metaphysics as the metaphysical foundation of natural philosophy, the features of headiness, multiplication, and wholeness provided the theoretical grounds for the kingship, differentials of social classes, and the unification of a country or organization; therefore the Meta-One functioned as the metaphysical foundation for social-political philosophy. Because of the disadvantages of the personalized heaven and the heavenly *dao*, the Meta-One replaced the traditional concepts of heaven and heavenly *dao* to be the metaphysical foundation of ethical and moral philosophy; the feature of one-ness and harmoniousness implied in the Meta-One and the feature of harmoniousness functions as a theoretical ground for the criterion of beauty. Metaphorically, the Meta-One can metaphorically refer to a potential harmonious entity, the Multi-One can refer to an individualized harmonious entity, and the Utter-One can refer to a completed entity. Hence, harmony existed in all stages and the entire process. Harmony is a visible phenomenon, and invisible harmoniousness is the essence and ground of harmony. Naturally, the Meta-One is the metaphysical foundation of traditional Chinese aesthetics.

The entire project aims to reconstruct metaphysics in Chinese philosophical tradition by initiating a system of the Meta-One, so this book can be entitled 《元一论》 in Chinese. In this book, we have recharacterized the metaphysical objects and conceptualized the development of things as a process from Meta-One via Multi-One to Utter-One, collated and extended the models of harmony as the core of the components of the Meta-One, relocated the metaphysics as the metaphysical foundation of traditional Chinese natural, social-political, ethical, and moral philosophy, aesthetics, and systematized the methodological principles. This is just an initial step and an immature endeavor. It is far from establishing a complete system of metaphysics. Chinese philosophical tradition is extremely complex. From different angles, there are many ways to reconstruct metaphysics in the Chinese philosophical tradition. This project is limited to defining the metaphysics and thinking of reconstruction of the metaphysics from a methodological perspective. This project is limited to referring to the school of *yin* and *yang* based on the Classic of Change, Daoism, Confucianism, and Mohism, but did not touch on other schools of the Pre-Qin philosophy. After the Pre-Qin philosophy, I did not refer to the Two-Cheng brothers' work; I primarily referred to Zhu Xi's work but ignored his contemporaries, like Lu Jiu Yuan and Wang Yang Ming, and their doctrine of mind, although they have profound metaphysical thought. For the contemporary philosophers, I focused on Feng Yon Lan and his doctrine of new *li* but skipped all his contemporaries.

The abovementioned limitations are based on the following reasons. We traced back to the source per the theme, but not in terms of the chronicles, consciously avoiding debates between different schools and philosophers. Otherwise, we will be off the topic. Further, we traced back to the traditional source to seek the roots of our new categories but not to conduct a complete historical study; this project intended to continue *Li*'s tradition and speak after Feng You Lan. These limitations narrowed the historical examination and concentrated on metaphorical but not general metaphysics. Although strictly limited to a narrow topic, reconstructing metaphorical metaphysics is still a vast project requiring continuous work for generations of scholars. Suppose this project can call for more scholars to join in promoting and developing traditional Chinese philosophy in different areas from different perspectives. In that case, the goal of the project will be achieved.

Bibliography

Aristotle. *Aristotle's Metaphysics*. Translated and with commentaries and glossary by Hippocrates G. Apostle. Grinnell: The Peripatetic Press/Indiana University Press, 1966.

———. *Aristotle's Metaphysics: Books M and N*, translated by with introduction and notes by Julia Annes. Oxford: Clarendon Press, 1976), 91 (1076a 10).

Armes, Roger T. *Returning to Zhu Xi*. Edited by David Jones and Jinli He. Albany: State University of New York Press, 2015.

Beebee, Helen, Nikk Effingham, and Philip Goff. *Metaphysics: The Key Concepts*. London and New York: Routledge, 2011.

Chan, Wing-Tsit. *A Source Book of Chinese Philosophy*. Princeton, NJ: Princeton University Press, 1969.

Chen, Derong, *Metaphorical Metaphysics in Chinese Philosophy: Illustrated with Feng Youlan's New Metaphysics*. Lanham, MD: Lexington Books, 2011.

———. "Di 帝 and Tian 天 in Ancient Chinese Thought: A Critical Analysis of Hegel's Views" (English). *Dao: A Journal of Comparative Philosophy* 8, no. 1 (March 2009):13–27. Springer.

———.（陈德荣）. "Three Meta-Questions in Epistemology: Rethinking Some Metaphors in Zhuangzi." *Journal of Chinese Philosophy* 32, no. 3 (September 2005).

The Classic of Changes, a new translation of the I Ching as interpreted by Wang Bi. Translated by Richard John Lynn. New York: Columbia University Press, 1994.

The Complete I Ching, the definitive translation by the Taoist Master Alfred Huang. Rochester, VT: Inner Traditions International, 2004.

Confucius. *Analects*. Translated and with an introduction and notes by Raymond Dawson. Oxford: Oxford University Press, 1993.

———. *The Analects*. Translated by Simon Leys. Edited by Michael Nylan. Berkeley: University of California, 2014.

Dong, Zhong Shu（董仲舒）. *Chun Qiu Fan Lu*《春秋繁露》*Luxuriant Dew of the Spring and Autumn Annals*. Edited by Wang Yun Wu. Tai Bei: Wen Yuan Ge, 1975.

Duan, Yu Cai（段玉裁）, noted; edited by Xu, Shen（许慎）; collated by Xu, Weixian（许惟贤）. *Shuowen Jiezi*《说文解字》*Explain the Graphs and Unravel the Written Words*. Nan Jing: Feng Huan Press, 2007.

Feng, Youlan（冯友兰）. *San Song Tang Quanji*（《三松堂全集》*Complete Works of Feng Youlan*. Edited by Cai Zhongde（蔡仲德）, vol. 4. Zheng Zhou: Henan Remin Chubanshe, 2000.

The Four Books. Translated by Daniel K. Gardner. Indianapolis: Hackett Publishing Company, 1990.

The Four Books. Translated with introduction and commentary by Daniel K. Gardner. Indianapolis: Hackett Publishing Company, 2007.

The Four Books. Translated by James Legge. Hong Kang: Wei Tung Book Co., 1969.

Getting to Know Master Zhu Xi: English Translations of Selections from Zhu Zi Yu Lei. Translated by Wang Xiaonong and Zhao Zengtao. Beijing: China Social Science Press, 2018.

Gorbunov, Dmitry S., and Valery A. Rubakov. *Introduction to the Theory of the Early Universe: Hot Big Bang Theory*. Singapore: World Science Publishing Co., 2011.

Han, Fei Zi. *The Complete Works of Han Fei Tzu*, vol. 1. Translated with introduction and notes by W. K. Liao. London: Percy Lund, Humphries & Co., 1961.

Huang, Kan（黄侃）. *Huan Kan Shoushu Baiwen Shisanjing*《黄侃手批白文十三经》*Thirteen Classics: Huang Kan Manually apostilled punctuations*. Shanghai: Shanghai Ancient Books Publishing House, 1983.

I Ching: The Book of Changes. Translated by David Hinton. New York: Farrar, Straus and Giroux, 2015.

The I Ching. Translated by James Legge. First published by the Clarendon Press in 1899. Second edition: New York, Dover Publication, 1963.

The I Ching (Book of Changes): A Critical Translation of the Ancient Text. Translated by Geoffrey Redmond. London: Bloomsbury Academic Publishing, 2017.

Kong, Yingda et al.（孔颖达）. *Mingjia Pizhu Zhouyi*《名家批注周易》*Famous Scholars' Commentaries of Zhouyi*. Shenyang: Wanjuan Chuban Gongisi, 2009.

Laozi. *Daodejing: A Literal-Critical Translation*. Translated by Joseph Hsu. Lanham, MD: University Press of America, 2008.

———. *Tao Te Ching*, translated by D. C. Lau. Hong Kong: The Chinese University Press, 2001.

Li, Chenyang and Franklin Perlins. *Chinese Metaphysics and Its Problems*. Cambridge: Cambridge University Press, 2016.

Lu, Simian（吕思勉）. *General History of Chinese*. Edited by Zhonguo Tongshi《中国通史》. Chang Chun：Jilin Publishing Group, 2013.

Lu, Yuanjun（卢元骏）. *New Commentary and Translation of Shuo Yuan*. Noted and translated by Shuo Yuan Jin Zhu Jin Yi《说苑今注今译》. Taibei: Commercial Press, 1977.

Mengzi（孟子）. *Mencius*. Translated by Irene Bloom. Edited and with an introduction by Philip J. Ivanhoe. New York: Columbia University Press, 2009.

———. *Mencius*. Translated with an introduction by D.C. Lau. London: Penguin Books, 1970.

Mou, Bo (牟博). "Becoming-Being Complementarity: An Account of the *Yin-Yang* Metaphysical Vision of the *Yi-Jing*." In *Comparative Approaches to Chinese Philosophy*. Edited by Bo Mou. Aldershot: Routledge, 2003.

———. *Chinese Philosophy A–Z*. Edinburgh: Edinburgh University Press 2022.

Mozi. *The Mozi: A Complete Translation*. Translated by Ian Johnston. New York: Columbia University Press, 2010.

Sun, Xidan (孙希旦). *Liji Jijie*《礼记集解》中册*Collections of Commentaries of the Records of Rituals*, vol. 2. Beijing: Zhong Hua Shu Ju, 1998.

The Texts of Taoism, vols. 1 and 2. Translated by James Legge. Singapore: Tynron Press & Graham Brash, 1989.

Wagner, Rudolf G. *A Chinese Reading of Daodejing: Wang Bi's Commentary on the Laozi with Critical Text and Translation*. Albany: State University of New York Press, 2003.

Wang, Fu (王符). *Qian Fu Lun*《潜夫论》*The Art of the Han Essay: Wang Fu's Ch'ien-Fu Lun*. Tempe: Center for Asian Studies, Arizona State University, 1990.

Wang, Guan (王琯). *Gongsun Longzi Xuanjie*《公孙龙子悬解》*Clarifications of the Suspensions in Gongsun Longzi*. Beijing: Zhong Hua Shu Ju, 1992.

Wang, Jipei (汪继培) and Peng Duo (彭铎). *Qianfulun Qian Jiaozheng*《潜夫论笺校正》*Endowments and Contextual Checking of* Qianfulun. 汪继培笺，彭铎校. Beijing: Zhong Hua Shu Ju, 2011.

Xunzi. *Xunzi: The Complete Text*. Translated and edited by Eric L. Hutton. Princeton, NJ: Princeton University Press, 2014.

Zhou, Dunyi (周敦颐). *Zhou Dun Yi Ji*《周敦颐集》Checked and noted by Chen Keming (陈克明). *The Collections of Zhou Dunyi*. Beijing: Zhong Hua Shu Ju, 1990.

Zhu Xi (朱熹). *Chu His: Learning to Be a Sage: Selected from the Conversations of Master Chu, Arranged Topically*. Translated by Daniel K. Gardner. Berkeley: University of California Press, 1990.

———. *Further Reflections on Things at Hand*. Translated by Allen Wittenborn. Lanham, MD: University Press of America, 1991.

———. *Reflections on Things at Hand: The Neo-Confucian Anthology*. Compiled by Chu Hsi and Lu Tsu-Chien. Translated with notes by Wing-Tsit Chan. New York: Columbia University Press, 1967.

———. *Zhu Xi: Selected Writings*. Edited and translated by Philip J. Ivanhoe. Oxford: Oxford University Press, 2019.

———. *Zhuzi Yulei*《朱子语类》上卷*Citations of Zhu Xi*, vol. 1. Edited by Jingde Li. Jingdu: Chinese Press, 1979.

Zhuangzi. *The Book of Chuang Tzu*. Translated by Martin Palmer and Elizabeth Breuilly. London: Penguin Group, 1996.

Index

abstract, 10, 11, 14, 19, 20, 24, 25, 26, 27, 28, 42, 45, 56, 57, 58, 61, 65, 67, 68, 71, 72, 78, 79, 85, 101, 104, 125, 126, 127, 128, 131, 136, 146, 161, 164, 165, 175, 183, *See also* abstractness

abstractness, 19, 23, 24, 25, 45, 55, 56, 59, 61, 65, 66, 67, 68, 71, 72, 78, 112, 125, 131, 161, 163, 166, 172, 177, 184, 189, 190

actual things, 17, 19, 21

actuality, 16, 61

aesthetical object, 185, 187

aesthetical attitude, 187

aesthetical judgments, 186, 187

aesthetical subject, *187*

aesthetics, 13, 158, 184, 185, 187, 188, 189, 190, 192, 198

all-in-one, 14, 15, 16, 27, 28, 48, 56, 57, 59, 72, 98, 99, 135, 196

Analects, 30, 31, 37, 49, 72, 74, 86, 139, 166, 175, 187, 200

analogical reasoning, 10, 14, 28, 29, 30, 31, 33, 34, 35, 38, 39, 40, 42, 43, 44, 47, 48, 52, 82, 83

analogies. *See* analogical reasoning

analogy, 25, 31, 32, 34, 36, 38, 42, 55, 57, 72, 83, 84, 98, 100, 128, 129, 130, 131, 132, 133, 165, 181, *See* metaphor

Andrew Lambert, *87*

Aristotle, 15, 16, 17, 18, 19, 20, 21, 24, 48, 49, 125, 126, 151, 200

beauty, 33, 37, 61, 116, 117, 118, 162, 184, 185, 186, 187, 188, 189, 190, 191, 192, 198

beginning, 11, 14, 23, 49, 53, 54, 55, 57, 58, 59, 75, 79, 80, 91, 95, 96, 98, 99, 100, 101, 103, 104, 105, 108, 110, 114, 116, 159, 160, 161, 166, 167, 171, 177, 197

being, 16, 21, 23, 24, 30, 33, 51, 63, 64, 69, 75, 91, 92, 93, 95, 98, 100, 103, 112, 113, 114, 115, 116, 122, 126, 147, 170, 176, 177, 181

category, 11, 12, 16, 17, 19, 44, 52, 53, 54, 55, 56, 57, 58, 59, 60, 61, 62, 64, 65, 66, 67, 68, 69, 70, 71, 72, 73, 74, 75, 76, 77, 78, 79, 80, 81, 82, 83, 84, 91, 93, 96, 99, 104, 112, 116, 125, 130, 135, 136, 147, 158, 161, 163, 166, 167, 168, 169, 170, 172, 175, 177, 180, 183, 184, 189, 197

centralism, *136, 137, 197*

characteristics, 10, 20, 22, 26, 27, 36, 47, 61, 62, 69, 70, 71, 83, 84, 94, 101, 105, 120, 125, 130, 142, 152, 165, 167, 175, 178, 181, 182, 183, 190, 191

195

Cheng Yi, 37
ChunQiu Fan Lu《春秋繁露》, 34
class name, 19, 20, 39, 66, 80, 177
Classic of Changes. See I Ching
common names, 161
Comparability, 133, analogy
completeness, 75, 76, 78, 79, 80, 82, 84, 85, 90, 104, *See* fulfillment
components, 11, 12, 13, 19, 26, 27, 28, 29, 40, 41, 46, 52, 55, 56, 57, 59, 62, 64, 65, 66, 68, 69, 70, 73, 76, 78, 79, 80, 81, 82, 84, 85, 88, 90, 92, 93, 110, 124, 142, 166, 175, 180, 181, 182, 183, 190, 197, 198
concepts, 11, 12, 14, 15, 16, 17, 18, 19, 20, 21, 22, 26, 27, 28, 36, 41, 48, 52, 53, 55, 58, 59, 67, 68, 76, 77, 78, 79, 80, 85, 91, 92, 93, 94, 95, 103, 115, 125, 127, 128, 131, 133, 159, 161, 163, 165, 166, 174, 175, 196, 197, 198
conceptualization, 18, 19, 28, 56, 131
Confucianism, *22, 54, 91, 198*
Confucius, 22, 29, 30, 49, 62, 63, 64, 72, 108, 139, 156, 163, 168, 175, 187, 188, 193, 200
corresponding harmony, *192*, See harmony
corresponding relationship, 93, 104, 114, 115, 116, 117, 118, 119, 120, 121, *See* corresponding harmony
criterion of beauty, 184, 189, See harmony

dao,
Daodejing, 24, 49, 51, 60, 72, 86, 88, 123, 155, 194, 201, 202
Daoism, 53, 91, 160, 164, 168, 198
daoji 道纪, 54
daoti zhiquan 道体之全, 76
daoxue 道学, 43
daquan 大全, 43, 53, 74, 78, 79
David Hinton, *86*
de, 23, 29, 35, 41, 42, 43, 46, 70, 78, 80, 83, 97, 127, 146, 148, 149, 171, *See* virtue, *See* virtue, *See* virtue

dequan 德全, 75
Derong Chen. *See* 陈德荣
diversities, 59, 60, 61, 62, 64, 68, 69, 70, 79, 82, 90, 95, 96, 97, 98, 104, 110, 114
Dong Zhongshu, 29, 34, 195
Duck Huan of Qi (齐桓公), 108
dynamic perspective, 12, 75, 90, 108, 111, 116, *See* static perspective
dynamic process, 85, 90, 91, 92, 96, 99, 101, 102, 103, 105, 106, 107, 108, 111, 112, 113, 114, 121, 138, 158, 164, 167, 197
dynamical harmony, 110, *See* harmony

ecology, 155, 170
elements. *See* parts
empirical factors, 18, 28
entities. *See* entity
epistemology, 11, 13, 200, *See* knowledge
Erya《尔雅》, 53
essence, 12, 13, 16, 17, 18, 19, 20, 24, 27, 30, 39, 40, 46, 48, 52, 66, 69, 70, 76, 111, 124, 126, 129, 130, 153, 162, 173, 174, 184, 185, 188, 196, 197
eternality, 16, 45, 61, 68, 71, 72, 73
existence, 15, 17, 19, 21, 22, 30, 36, 38, 42, 49, 55, 56, 58, 60, 61, 66, 67, 72, 73, 80, 84, 100, 106, 116, 120, 121, 128, 131, 133, 135, 141, 143, 144, 146, 147, 159, 161, 163, 169, 178, 180, 187, 188
extension, 18, 24, 26, 125, 126, 131

features, 11, 12, 13, 16, 22, 23, 26, 27, 28, 29, 30, 32, 39, 41, 42, 45, 46, 47, 53, 54, 57, 58, 59, 60, 61, 62, 69, 70, 71, 73, 75, 79, 84, 85, 94, 101, 102, 106, 113, 118, 124, 125, 127, 128, 129, 131, 134, 137, 140, 141, 142, 144, 147, 149, 151, 152, 153, 159, 164, 165, 166, 167, 168, 170, 174, 175, 176, 177, 183, 184, 185, 186, 189, 190, 191, 196, 197

Feng Youlan, 10, 11, 13, 21, 22, 25, 28, 29, 38, 40, 43, 44, 51, 52, 65, 66, 67, 74, 78, 85, 87, 88, 125, 127, 128, 130, 156, 161, 187, 189, 193, 194, 195, 200
Five Elements. *See* 五行
form, 4, 16, 17, 18, 20, 21, 22, 24, 25, 98, 114, 117, 118, 132, 141, 148, 172
fude fangfa 负的方法, 129
function, 13, 16, 20, 41, 42, 57, 59, 73, 82, 83, 84, 103, 124, 129, 132, 140, 148, 161, 172, 183, 188, 189

generality, 23, 24, 45, 61, 69, 71, 72, 73, 83, 95, 104, 112, 133, 155, 162, 164, 166, 174, 177, 189, 190, 197
God, 27, 169, 179
Gongsun Long, 130, 131
gongtong fuyu 共同富裕, 135
goodness, 32, 34, 35, 54, 117, 174, 175, 177, 183, 184, 189
Goodness, 34, 83, 174, 175, 177
Great Ultimate, 53, 62, 63, 111, 112, 113, 114, 158, 162
gua ci, 22

Han Fei Zi, 29, 33, 34
Han-Wu Emperor, 120
harmoniousness, 184, 185, 186, 187, 189, 190, 191, 198, *See* harmony
harmony, 11, 12, 41, 58, 90, 91, 92, 93, 102, 103, 104, 105, 106, 107, 108, 109, 110, 112, 114, 115, 116, 117, 118, 119, 120, 121, 134, 135, 141, 142, 144, 145, 146, 147, 149, 152, 155, 158, 162, 171, 172, 184, 185, 186, 187, 188, 189, 190, 191, 192, 196, 197, 198
heavenly *dao*, 10, 32, 174, 180, 181, 182, 183, 198
Hegel, 87, 126, 200
Heidegger, 21, 126
Helen Beebee, 17
hexie gongchu, hezuo gongying 和谐共处，合作共赢, 135
holism, 134, 135, 197

hongyun tuoyue (烘云托月), 128
Huang Kan (黄侃), *49*
Huang Hui (黄晖), *194*
human beings, 32, 33, 39, 77, 142, 144, 178
human beings, 142, 148, *See* humankind
human behavior, 45, 73, 175, 190
human behaviors, 10, 38, 43, 44, 47, 175, 179, 182
human society, 30, 43, 68, 69, 73, 103, 107, 109, 116, 117, 118, 134, 135, 137, 140, 141, 143, 145, 146, 152, 153, 165, 169

individual things, 17, 19, 26, 27, 38, 39, 80, 81, 117, 120, 125, 128, 132
individual things, 80
individualization, 80, 95, 96, 97, 148, 174, *See* individuality, *See* individuality
infinitism, 149, 151, 152, *See* infinity
Interactionism, 141
interactions, 92, 103, 104, 117, 118, 119, 141, 142, 143, 144, 146, 154, 158, 162

jian ai tianxia 兼爱天下, 87
Jiujia yi《九家易》, 53
justice, 30, 31, 61, 94, 119, 120, 169, 171, 176, 178, 180, 182, 190

King Jie, 32

Laozi, 21, 22, 23, 24, 25, 30, 41, 42, 43, 49, 51, 52, 53, 54, 55, 56, 60, 61, 65, 72, 74, 83, 86, 87, 88, 92, 101, 103, 112, 113, 114, 115, 116, 123, 125, 127, 128, 129, 132, 155, 160, 161, 162, 163, 178, 181, 188, 194, 201, 202, *See* 老子
li, 10, 11, 12, 22, 25, 26, 27, 28, 36, 37, 38, 39, 40, 42, 43, 44, 52, 57, 59, 61, 63, 64, 65, 66, 67, 68, 69, 70, 71, 77, 78, 80, 87, 98, 101, 111, 112, 115, 116, 127, 128, 129, 130, 132, 151, 158, 161, 163, 175, 176, 177, 178, 187, 189, 190, 197, 198, *See* 理

Liji Jijie《礼记集解》, 86, 123, 202
living beings, 33, 53, 95, 107, 134, 148, 165
lixue 理学, 43
liyi fenshu 理一分殊, 86
logical pragmatism, 20
logical reasoning, 10, 34, 82
Lu Siman, 123
Lu Yuanjun (卢元骏), 155
Luheng jiaoshi《论衡校释》, 195

matter, 11, 16, 17, 20, 21, 28, 67, 68, 70, 72, 78, 82, 84, 106, 130, 141, 154, 166, 173, 187
meanings, 11, 23, 24, 29, 34, 36, 41, 53, 54, 55, 56, 60, 64, 68, 71, 72, 77, 87, 101, 102, 127, 128, 140, 145, 161, 165, 167, 177, 179, 182, 184
Mengzi, 29, 31, 49, 61, 128, 132, 133, 155, 175, 176, 193, 201
Meta-One, 3, 5, 11, 12, 13, 52, 53, 54, 55, 56, 57, 58, 59, 60, 61, 62, 71, 72, 73, 82, 85, 90, 91, 92, 93, 95, 96, 97, 98, 99, 100, 101, 102, 104, 106, 109, 110, 111, 112, 113, 114, 115, 121, 124, 134, 135, 136, 137, 138, 140, 141, 142, 144, 146, 147, 153, 155, 158, 159, 160, 161, 162, 163, 164, 166, 167, 168, 169, 170, 171, 172, 173, 174, 175, 176, 177, 178, 180, 181, 182, 183, 184, 185, 186, 188, 189, 190, 192, 194, 196, 197, 198, 214
metaphor. *See* analogy
metaphorical metaphysics, 10, 11, 13, 14, 15, 47, 84, 124, 196
metaphorical functions, 57, 73, 85, 90, 95, 97
metaphysical dimension, 19, 57, 75, 124, 125, 158, 161
metaphysical metaphysics, 10
metaphysical foundation, 13, 29, 47, 137, 159, 161, 163, 164, 166, 167, 168, 172, 173, 174, 175, 177, 180, 181, 182, 183, 184, 185, 187, 189, 190, 192, 197

metaphysical objects, 10, 14, 15, 16, 17, 18, 20, 22, 23, 25, 27, 28, 48, 52, 124, 125, 126, 127, 128, 129, 130, 131, 132, 155, 197
method. *See* methodology
methodological principles, 13, 124
methodological principle, 134, 135, 136, 137, 138, 139, 140, 141, 142, 144, 146, 147, 148, 149, 151, 152, 154
ming 命, 38
moral philosophy, 174, 177, 178, 179, 183, 198
moral behavior, *83, 183*, *See* morality
morality, 40, 41, 42, 43, 46, 47, 48, 52, 75, 76, 77, 83, 183, *See* 道
Mother, 23
Mozi, 29, 32, 33, 49, 50, 87, 130, 135, 201
Multi-One, 5, 11, 12, 13, 52, 59, 60, 61, 62, 64, 65, 66, 67, 68, 69, 70, 71, 72, 73, 74, 81, 82, 85, 90, 91, 92, 93, 95, 96, 97, 98, 99, 100, 101, 102, 104, 106, 109, 110, 112, 114, 115, 121, 124, 134, 138, 139, 140, 141, 142, 144, 147, 153, 158, 159, 163, 164, 166, 167, 169, 170, 171, 172, 173, 175, 177, 183, 184, 196, 197, 198
mutuality, 71, 75, 148
myriad things, 20, 23, 25, 30, 34, 44, 49, 53, 54, 60, 61, 63, 65, 67, 69, 71, 75, 77, 78, 92, 93, 94, 100, 101, 103, 112, 113, 120, 122, 131, 150, 151, 159, 160, 161, 166, 168, 177, 180, 183, 197

nature, 16, 17, 18, 19, 20, 25, 29, 30, 31, 32, 33, 34, 35, 36, 37, 38, 39, 41, 42, 43, 46, 48, 54, 61, 62, 63, 64, 65, 66, 69, 70, 75, 76, 77, 80, 82, 83, 87, 94, 98, 105, 109, 111, 115, 122, 132, 133, 137, 141, 142, 143, 144, 145, 154, 162, 163, 165, 166, 168, 169, 174, 175, 176, 177, 178, 179, 180, 184
necessity, 22, 85, 93, 106, 139, 146, 169, 170, 171, 172
Nikk Effingham, 17
non-being, 113, 114, 115, 116, 126

non-ultimate, 91, 92, 93, 112, 115, *See wuji* 无极

one. *See* Oneness
originality, 23, 55, *See* origination
origination, 11, 57, 59, 93, 94, 96, 99, 108, 112, 113, 149, 159, 160, 161, 170, 197

perfectionism, 147, 148, 149
Philip Goff, 17
Plato, 126
pluralism, 140, 141, 197, *See* multiplicity
Pluralism, 140, *See* multiplicity
possibilities, 58, 104, 105, 106, 134, 136, 137, 138, 139, 140, 142, 147, 170, 171
potentiality, 11, 16, 55, 58, 59, 60, 90, 91, 93, 98, 99, 101, 104, 113, 115, 136, 138, 150, 171, 174, 175, 197
Precognitivism, 137
principles, 10, 13, 29, 31, 32, 40, 44, 45, 46, 47, 60, 73, 76, 83, 84, 87, 111, 124, 126, 134, 139, 142, 146, 147, 155, 176, 178, 179, 180, 182, 183, 197, 198
propositions, 10, 11, 12, 40, 45, 46, 67, 91, 92, 93, 95, 113, 125

qi, 21, 31, 36, 53, 77, 87, 88, 161, 177, 188, *See* 气
Qian Fu Lun《潜夫论》, 155
qiandao bianhua, gezheng xingming "乾道变化，各正性命", 98

R. Rorty, 127
reality, 18, 21, 28, 38, 41, 43, 45, 57, 58, 59, 60, 65, 66, 67, 68, 70, 79, 98, 99, 100, 109, 115, 118, 121, 137, 140, 141, 142, 143, 144, 145, 147, 148, 149, 151, 170, 175
realization, 58, 60, 75, 79, 80, 96, 97, 105, 108, 148, 158, 163, 170, 184, 197
re-construction. *See* reconstructing
relationships. *See* relations

renlei ming yun gongtongti 人类命运共同体, *135*
renli 人理, 39
Richard Rorty, 11
Richard John Lynn, 48, 86, 122, 19*4*, *200*
righteousness, 30, 31, 32, 43

sameness, 29, 61, 162, *See* similarity
sangang wuchang 三纲五常, 47
shangshan ruoshui 上善若水, 83
Shi Jiao 尸佼, 193
Shi Yi《十翼》, 22
Shijing《诗经》, 195
shu (殊), 59, 61
Shuo Yuan Jin Zhu Jin Yi《说苑今注今译》, 155
Shuwen Jiezi《说文解字》, 53
similarities, 29, 38, 73, 79, 82, 83, 94, 132
Sishu Jizhu《四书集注》, 195
Socrates, 126
static harmonies, *110*
substance, 16, 17, 19, 20, 21, 41, 76, 125, 126
Sun Xidan (孙希旦), 86, 123
Synergism, 144

Taiji sheng yinyang 太极生阴阳, 92
taiji 太极, 63
tiandao 天道, 174, *See* Heavenly Dao
tiandi 天地, 71
tianli 天理, 43
tianming 天命, 168
tianxia wanwu shengyu you, you shengyu wu 天下万物生于有，有生于无, *24*
tradition, 10, 13, 14, 15, 16, 20, 21, 22, 25, 28, 29, 32, 40, 41, 44, 46, 47, 48, 52, 55, 59, 71, 72, 74, 77, 83, 84, 85, 91, 92, 93, 95, 98, 101, 107, 114, 117, 118, 119, 120, 124, 125, 126, 127, 130, 135, 138, 160, 161, 163, 166, 167, 175, 179, 180, 184, 187, 190, 196, 197, 198, 199
transcendental knowledge. *See* transcendence

transformations, 99, 100, 108, 110, 173, *See* changes
truth, 10, 11, 14, 41, 43, 44, 83, 85, 117, 129, 149, 151, 152, 153, 177

unification, 20, 53, 58, 69, 75, 104, 107, 108, 119, 145, 147, 162, 166, 172, 173, 174, 198
universe, 36, 43, 55, 57, 68, 69, 70, 71, 72, 73, 78, 79, 80, 82, 92, 95, 96, 99, 100, 105, 106, 107, 108, 109, 110, 111, 118, 120, 121, 134, 135, 138, 140, 141, 142, 144, 147, 148, 149, 151, 152, 153, 158, 159, 160, 161, 163, 164, 165, 166, 167, 178, See cosmos, See cosmos, See cosmos
Utter-One, 5, 11, 12, 13, 52, 62, 73, 74, 75, 76, 77, 78, 79, 80, 81, 82, 83, 84, 85, 90, 92, 95, 96, 97, 99, 100, 101, 102, 104, 106, 110, 112, 114, 121, 124, 134, 138, 144, 146, 147, 149, 150, 151, 152, 153, 155, 158, 159, 163, 164, 166, 167, 169, 170, 171, 172, 173, 175, 177, 183, 184, 197, 198

value, 10, 14, 40, 41, 42, 44, 45, 46, 70, 77, 83, 84, 125, 148, 149
virtue, 25, 31, 34, 41, 42, 75, 77, 92, 168, 190, 191, *See* 德

Wang Fu (王符), 155
Wang Guan (王琯), 155
Wittgenstein, 126
wu geyi qixing 物各一其性, 62
wu 物, 128
wuji er taiji 无极而太极, 92
wuji 无极, 91
wuxing 五行, 75
wu 无, 58

xian tiandi zhisheng er sheng 先天地之生而生, 92
Xiang Zhuan 《象传》, 51
xing, ji li ye 性，即理也, 63
Xu Shen (许慎), 85
Xunzi, 29, 31, 32, 49, 51, 130, 155, 160, 169, 176, 187, 188, 193, 194, 195, 202

yang, 21, 22, 25, 26, 27, 28, 36, 48, 52, 53, 54, 63, 65, 75, 76, 91, 92, 93, 94, 95, 98, 101, 103, 104, 110, 111, 112, 113, 115, 116, 122, 125, 126, 128, 133, 158, 159, 161, 162, 175, 176, 178, 198, *See* 阳
yao ci 爻辞, 22
Yi Zhuan 《易传》, 22
yin, 21, 22, 25, 26, 27, 28, 36, 48, 52, 53, 54, 63, 65, 75, 76, 91, 92, 93, 94, 95, 98, 101, 103, 104, 110, 111, 112, 113, 115, 116, 122, 125, 126, 128, 133, 158, 159, 161, 162, 175, 198, *See* 阴
Yin Zhouwang (殷纣王), 32
Yizhao 依照, 39
*yuan, heng, li zhe*n, 元, 亨, 利, 贞, 122
Yuanyi 元一, 60
yue ying wan chuan 月映万川, 87

zhenji 真际, 78
Zhong Yong 《中庸》, 51
Zhou Dunyi, 62, 63, 64, 65, 75, 76, 77, 78, 88, 112, 115, 202, *See* 周敦颐
Zhou You Wang 周幽王, 32
Zhu Xi, 22, 25, 28, 29, 36, 37, 38, 42, 43, 50, 62, 63, 64, 65, 66, 67, 71, 74, 75, 76, 77, 78, 86, 87, 88, 92, 98, 110, 111, 112, 116, 121, 123, 125, 127, 139, 150, 161, 176, 178, 191, 193, 194, 200, 201, 202, *See* 朱熹
Zhuangzi. *See* 庄子

About the Author

Derong Chen received his first PhD in Western philosophy from Wuhan University in 1990 and a second PhD in Chinese philosophy from the University of Toronto in 2005. As a visiting scholar, he completed nondegree advanced study at Columbia University in New York from 1994 to 1996. He taught philosophy at Sichuan College of Education in Chengdu from 1981–1987 and at Sichuan University as an associate professor. Simultaneously, he served as supervisor and coordinator for MA graduate students in the philosophy department from 1990–1994. In 1996, as a new immigrant, he landed in Canada. From the following year to 2005, he studied Chinese philosophy in the Department of East Asian Studies at the University of Toronto. After graduating from the University of Toronto, he was appointed as a full professor and served as the director of the center of comparative studies in the college of philosophy at Wuhan University from 2006 to 2008. In 2008 he returned to Toronto and started teaching Chinese language and culture in the Department of Language Studies at the University of Toronto Mississauga until now.

Derong Chen has published two books: *A Study of Locke's Theory of Meaning* (Chinese, China, 1992) and *Metaphorical Metaphysics in Chinese Philosophy: Illustrated with Feng Youlan's New Metaphysics* (English, United States, 2011), and a new book is in progress, *Reconstructing Metaphorical Metaphysics in Ancient Chinese Philosophy: Meta-One vs. Harmony* (English). All these books deal with philosophical issues from the perspective of language. He translated A.J. Ayer's book, *Hume*, from English to Chinese and published it serially in the *Journal of Sichuan College of Education* in 1987.